CONFRONTING OMNICIDE

CONFRONTING OMNICIDE

Jewish Reflections on Weapons of Mass Destruction

A Simon Wiesenthal Center Project

edited by

Daniel Landes

Jason Aronson Inc.
Northvale, New Jersey
London

Library of Congress Cataloging-in-Publication Data

Landes, Daniel.
    Confronting omnicide : Jewish reflections on weapons of mass destruction / edited by Daniel Landes.
        p. cm.
    Includes bibliographical references and index.
    ISBN 0-87668-851-2
    1. Nuclear warfare—Religious aspects—Judaism.   2. Nuclear warfare—Moral and ethical aspects.   3. War—Biblical teaching.
    4. War (Jewish law)   5. Holocaust, Jewish (1939–1945)—Influence.
    I. Title.
    BM538.A8L36   1991
    296.3′878732—dc 20

                                                                        90-48358

Manufactured in the United States of America. Jason Aronson Inc. offers books and cassettes. For information and catalog write to Jason Aronson Inc., 230 Livingston Street, Northvale, New Jersey 07647.

To Simon Wiesenthal
for his warning of the inferno created
when hatred combines with modern technology

CONTENTS

PREFACE

The enormity of the nuclear threat is indicated by our almost schizophrenic attitude toward it. When the idea of this book was initiated it was greeted by many with skepticism. The inevitability of a nuclear conflagration seemed assured. The "progress" of the twentieth century after all has been constant along its journey of horrors—from the massacre of the Armenians, to the genocides of European populations, and finally the Holocaust—the nearly successful elimination of an entire people from the face of the earth. Add to this litany the infamy of Stalin's Gulag and the unique suffering of the killing fields of Cambodia, and Omnicide— the destruction of everyone—becomes a dreaded but expected end to the road.

With the sudden breakup of the Communist empire in Central and Eastern Europe and the change within the U.S.S.R. itself, this fatalism has perhaps blown away. A perfumed scent of freedom, liberation, and goodwill now fills the air. While certainly welcome, this new atmosphere is also dangerous in its intoxicating power. The prevailing attitude is that the cold war is over and we have won. Many now blithely reject any sober discussion of Omnicide as a recourse on an old, and therefore useless, thinking.

These two attitudes of despair and bliss are actually mirror images of each other. They both seek to deny reality by avoiding any responsibility for the need to transform it. Our first obligation is to face the current situation. While promising steps have been taken to reduce the nuclear threat, we are far from the build-down needed to end it. Major decisions involving ethics and values, apart from issues of politics and power, will have to be considered. In the meantime, as the U.S.S.R. breaks apart into smaller ethnic groups, the resulting instability is ushering in a new period of danger. Simply put—are the people we are negotiating with now the same who will control nuclear arms in the near future?

Finally, tensions between East and West have hidden two dangerous new developments: the spread of nuclear weapons throughout the Third World, and the increased use of highly potent chemical weapons by these countries. A number of these countries—themselves highly unstable—have made provocative threats against neighboring and other states. Additionally, some are active participants in worldwide terrorist actions. As this book is being published, a dictator in Iraq threatens the region with nuclear, chemical, and biologic devastation. The mega-threat of United States-U.S.S.R. war has been reduced, but has been replaced by the threat of (initial) local use of other awesome weaponry from other sources.

The purpose of this volume is not to advocate specific strategic or political positions. It rather attempts to create a vocabulary and language for confronting the difficult decisions that will need to be made by both policy makers and an informed citizenry. The resources employed are diverse and rich. They include the Bible, rabbinic literature, Jewish law and thought, as well as the Jewish historical experience, with special attention to the Holocaust.

The writers for this volume represent a wide variety of backgrounds, expertise, and viewpoints. They are reflective of the Jewish community as a whole and no methodological or theological agreement can be assumed. The writers are united only in that they are Jews who consciously confront a danger that is in fact common to all humanity.

ACKNOWLEDGMENT

This collection of specially solicited articles was the idea of Marvin Hier, dean and founder of the Simon Wiesenthal Center. It was inspired by the vision of Simon Wiesenthal, who has always advocated the broadest application of the lessons of the Holocaust. This volume is part of the larger agenda of the Center as articulated by Samuel Belzberg, chairman of the Board of Trustees. The project was supported and urged on its way by Abraham Cooper, associate dean. It has been my good fortune to be associated with these four men of sterling worth since the day the Center opened its doors. I am thankful for the counsel of Gerald Margolis, director of the Center and for the good efforts of Meyer May, Susan Burden, Avra Shapiro, and Rich Trank—the senior staff of the Simon Wiesenthal Center. I have been aided by Adaire Klein and the Center's library staff: Margo Gutstein, Carole Perl, Bella Sitnyakovsky, and Susie Bernstein, along with Aaron Breitbart, senior researcher at the center.

I am indebted to Elisa Vandernoot for her excellent editorial assistance in all areas of completing this work; I appreciate the expert advice of Jack Kolb, associate professor of English at UCLA; I thank Gloria Jordan, production editor at Jason Aronson, for her careful and caring work. Finally I wish to express my gratitude to Sheryl Robbin for her insights and for her forbearance, and to our children, Hannah Lauren and Isaac Jerome, for being never-ending sources of delight and hope.

Can the World Survive It Again?

Reuven Kimelman

According to ancient lore the prosperity of the antedeluvians afforded a carefree and happy existence. Technological sophistication formed the backbone of their affluence. Agronomy allowed a single harvest to suffice for forty years. The sun and moon were harnessed through advances in astrophysics. Obstetrics enabled pregnancies to reach term in several days while pediatrics nurtured a walking–talking babe shortly thereafter. The days of infant mortality were fading from memory.

Success was not long in sowing the seeds of moral breakdown. The same technological breakthroughs that provided for space and leisure also increased opportunities for vice and iniquity. High on the list of infamies were rapacity, unchastity, and other depredations. Business fraud, sexual anarchy, and violent sprees were the order of the day.

Even that generation's prodigious power was outstripped by their overweening arrogance. Noah's warnings of an impending flood were met with derision. Their technology led them to believe that no window of vulnerability had been left open.

1

Having taken initiatives in all areas of strategic defense, they felt all contingencies to be covered. Placing their trust in an advanced extinguishing weapon system, they jeered at any threat of a flood of fire. As regards a flood of water, they relied on a newly discovered mechanism to cover the earth with sheet metal to contain any water bubbling up from the surface. As far as being deluged by flood waters from above, they believed themselves to be shielded by their new aqua-absorbers, shooting across the skies to counter any such threat.

With such conceits prevailing, doom crouched at the door. Before long, that once life-giving fluid was found engulfing them from above and seeping up from below. The structures of order collapsed and the process of creation was reversed as water resurged everywhere to cover the face of the deep.

That Omnicide had a survivor—to tell us the story.

Based on *Sanhedrin* 108b
and midrashic literature

OUR SITUATION

1

A Vow of Death

Daniel Landes

The fundamental problem of our generation is how to avoid self-destruction. The perception of that seeming inevitability renders us immobile. The flip-side to fatalistic apathy during time of tension is a fantastical conviction, when political tensions are reduced, that crisis has been decisively averted. Both are unresponsive and irresponsible reactions to the challenge of survival. We need to enter the human structures of (self-) destruction in order to explore two questions: what is it that brings us to the brink of tragedy, and what prevents us, at that moment, from finding a way of stepping back from disaster?

Crucial tools for our exploration of the human propensity for mass suicide are the biblical narrative and rabbinic commentary. Taken together they create stories that incorporate but move beyond the recounting of history and the explication of law and ethics. Compellingly, these many-layered accounts reproduce our situation as embedded within the perennial human condition. This allows not only for an acceptance of the reality of crisis, but simultaneously gives rise to the need to confront and contain it even if a once and final resolution is not realistic. Our focus is the problematic story of Jephthah and his daughter, in which tragedy seems the inevitable result of military victory.

Jephthah was the son of a prostitute and Gilead, who also had legitimate children. The brothers, after Gilead's death, threw out their half-brother Jephthah and denied him any status as their father's heir. Jephthah was a first class warrior and fled to the land of Tob, accompanied by a band of mercenaries. When the invading Ammonites declared war on Israel, Jephthah was recalled with an agreement that, in exchange for leading the Gileadites victoriously in battle, he would become their ruler. Jephthah attempts to forestall war through negotiation, historical argument, and even an appeal to theology which tacitly acknowledges Ammon's god: "Do you not hold what Chemosh your god gives you to possess? So we will hold on to everything that the Lord our God has given us to possess" (Judges 11:24).

Nonetheless, anticipating Ammon's failure to come to terms, he sets the condition for battle:

> I have not sinned against you; yet you do me evil by waging war on me. May the Lord, the Judge, decide sentence today between the Israelites and the Ammonites. [Judges 11:2]

Jephthah the warrior reveals himself as a strict believer, consigning the war to God's hands. God as the ultimate judge will decide the relative merit of the two sides. Evidently this means not only the merits of the two positions—as in any lawsuit—but the merits of the two plaintiffs themselves. And, as the first person usage of this verse reveals, Jephthah, as the leader of Gilead, identifies himself as embodying the people of Israel. These three notions of judgment, merit, and personalization help explain the strange vow of Jephthah—now imbued with the Lord's spirit—upon mobilizing his troops:

> And Jephthah vowed a vow unto the Lord, he said: "if you shall indeed give the Ammonites into my hand; then that departee who departs from the door of my house to greet me upon my return in peace from the Ammonites shall be the Lord's—I shall offer up as a [burnt] offering. [Judges 11:30-31]

Jephthah endeavors to secure his own proper merit and thereby victory for Israel through a promise of sacrifice of that unknown personage which he would certainly hold dear and identify with—for who else would be the first to greet a returned warrior? Through this offering Jephthah would also at the moment of triumph increase his personal glory in dramatic and public submission to God's will.

The reader, impressed with Jephthah's willingness to give his all, is nonetheless disturbed by the recklessness of this open-ended commitment. As the Talmud (*Ta'anit* 4a) points out, an expectation could be that an unclean animal (Rashi: a dog or a pig) would be the first out of the door. While such a pet is certainly dear, it is not a suitable sacrifice. Our disturbance is increased by the very sanctity of a vow, for it must be fulfilled. Indeed, while ostensibly only an utterance, a vow within the biblical-rabbinic continuum is the creation of a reality even before its fulfillment in practice.

Such forebodings prove not to be dark enough. After a decisive victory:

When Jephthah returned to his home in Mizpah, there was his daughter going out to meet him, with music and dancing! She was his one and only child; except for her he had no other son or daughter. On seeing her, he rent his clothes and said: "Ah, my daughter! You have brought me low; you have become my troubler. For I have opened my mouth to the Lord, and I cannot retract." [Judges 11:35]

His daughter, accepting the judgment, requests and is granted two months to privately bewail her virginity. She returns home and her father fulfills his vow.

Reading this account we are aghast. We protest that while the result is perhaps poetic justice for Jephthah "opening his mouth," nonetheless neither he nor certainly his innocent daughter deserves this absurd conclusion. Surely a way could be found out of this unnecessary ugliness during the two months' leeway created by the daughter's self-mourning.

Rabbinic texts, sharing our outrage, explore possible alternatives. The simplest resolution is the annulment of the vow by the High Priest. Why was that route not taken?

And was not Phinehas there [in that generation]? and [nonetheless Jephthah] said: I cannot retract! But Phinehas said: I am the High Priest, son of the High Priest. Shall I lower myself and seek out an ignoramus! And Jephthah said: I am the head of the tribes of Israel, chief of the Captains. Shall I lower myself and seek out a commoner! Between the two of them the wretched maiden was lost. The two were held guilty of her death. . . . [*Midrash Tanhuma*: end of Leviticus]

Pride, power, and position lead to disaster and moral corruption.

Another rabbinic exegesis takes the position that there was no need even to annul the vow. This is understood in two ways in Genesis *Rabbah* (60:3). Rabbi Jochanan affirms that Jephthah's vow could simply be fulfilled through the substitution of monetary worth dedicated to sacred purpose: "If a man makes a singular vow, to give to the Lord the estimated value of persons, then the estimation shall be. . ." (Leviticus 27:2–8). The last part of Leviticus provides detailed instruction regarding such a procedure. This was a normative religious move—to "as if" offer oneself up to God by the vicarious donation of worth valued in money. One could perhaps counter that Jephthah's vow as stated would exclude substitution. The response, then, would be to follow Resh Lakish's view that such a vow was in any event defective. Its flaw is the application to a creature definitionally unfit for an offering. The vow is ridiculous and retroactively void, for a human being is not meant for ritual sacrifice.

In the midrashic account, Jephthah's daughter offers that argument in a broader form that gets to the heart of our own protest:

His daughter said: My Father, is it written in the Torah that one should offer up children on the altar? Is it not written: "When any of you presents an offering to the Lord—you shall choose your offering from the herd or from the flock . . . " [Leviticus 1:2]: "From the herd" and not "from the human!" He replied: My daughter, I made a vow: "that the departee who departs. . . . " She said, Jacob our father vowed: "all that you shall give me I will set aside a tithe for you" [Genesis 28:22]: The Holy One Blessed be He gave him twelve tribes, perhaps he sacrificed one of them? Furthermore when she [Hannah] vowed, saying: " . . . if you shall grant your maidservant a male child, I shall give,him to the Lord all the days of his life" [1 Samuel 1:11]; did she perhaps sacrifice her son to the Holy One Blessed be He? All these things she said to him and he did not listen to her. She said to him: permit me to go to Court, perhaps one of them [the judges] will find a loophole out of your words [vow] . . . she went and they did not find the loophole.

Jephthah's daughter has convincingly demonstrated that the weight of Torah is against death and in favor of life. Indeed, she does not even need to mention that the "passing through the fire" (2 Kings 16:3) of children is considered the height of impurity and profanes God's holy name (Leviticus 18:21; 20:2-5). The rabbis cannot bear to defend Jephthah and his barbarous action—they consider it indefensible.

Nonetheless, Jephthah's career is generally distinguished and he appears as a person who would prefer to avoid extreme actions. Why, then, his refusal here to turn around the situation?

Nahmanides' understanding of Jephthah's initial stumbling block is crucial. Nahmanides believed that Jephthah misunderstood a difficult verse in Leviticus that offers an exception to the laws of monetary substitution for personal dedication: "None doomed [cherem] of men, can be ransomed; he shall be put to death" (Leviticus 27:29). Nahmanides interprets this verse literally and applies it to a time of war. Enemies who are in the category of doom-herem, or literally, "dedicated," are not to be taken prisoner. If, as Rabbi David Zvi Hoffmann explains, they are so categorized by a recognized authority—king, court or leadership—they must be killed. A classic example of such "doom" is found later in Judges when the citizens of Jabesh-gilead disregard the oath taken by Israel to come to Mizpeah: "So the assemblage dispatched 12,000 of the warriors, instructing them as follows: 'go and put the inhabitants of Jabesh-gilead to the sword, women and children included" (Judges 21:10).

Nahmanides concludes that Jephthah mistakenly believed that this verse should also apply to a private situation—therefore his daughter's fate was sealed. No argument to the contrary would avail; no revocation was possible.

This explanation, if deepened, goes to the heart of our discussion and its relevance to our current situation. The Book of Judges clearly presents the fact that during war there are occasions when destruction of the enemy is mandated and must be total. Quarter can neither be sought nor can it be given. This severity stems both from the nature of war and also from the nature of its perpetrators. The anachronistic evocation by the Midrash of Phinehas as High Priest during the time of the Judges is appropriate. Phinehas is the very exemplar of ruthless zealotry in defense of faith:

> When Phinehas, son of Aaron the Priest, saw this, he left the assembly and taking a spear in his hand, he followed the Israelite into the Chamber and stabbed both of them, the Israelite and the woman, through the belly. . . . The Lord spoke to Moses, saying: Phinehas, son of Eleazer, son of Aaron the Priest, has turned back my wrath from the Israelites by displaying among them his passion for me. . . . [Numbers 25:7–8, 10]

Jephthah's vow, taken within this context of both doom and passion, becomes more understandable. He believed that offering and fulfilling a sacred resolve was crucial for attaining victory. Indeed, when one departs from Midrash, one notes in the scriptural text the daughter's insistence that her father's vow be kept: "My Father" she said, "you have opened your mouth to the Lord; do to me what has proceeded out of your mouth; for the Lord has taken vengeance for thee of thy enemies, the Ammonites" (Judges 11:36).

If they do not keep the vow, she, following her father, believes that victory would be imperiled. Retraction of the vow would mean retraction of salvation. Positively stated, Jephthah and his daughter are certainly devastated by the result of the vow, but they believe it to be the very cost of ensuring victory.

In the structure of destruction of one's enemies there is a necessary consequence of self-destruction. A high price is to be paid for victory and that is the loss of one's very self—here, through one's only child. The point of this simple story is that within the structure of destruction there is no escape for exacting that price. The myth of a painless or easy or even clear victory is revealed to be a chimera. You will lose—by your own willingness to go to the brink in order to ensure victory—the most dear part of yourself that goes out to greet you, with music and dancing, in that victory.

The biblical account taken with rabbinic explication provides us with a tale of foreboding of the consequences of ruthless war. Such a war is fought in order to win, and winning means the readiness to sacrifice the very thing one is fighting for: the lives of one's children. This story warns us of the utter folly that lies in articulated, planned for, and played at mutually assured destruction. Such a system, once put into motion seems impossible to stop. The story of Jephthah's daughter is a cry to break out of the straitjacketed rigidity of these structures of destruction. It urges us to revoke such vows, to assume the risk of losing by restraint in the very process of struggle, and never to place this mechanism in motion: "He [Jephthah] rose and slaughtered her before the Holy One, Blessed be He. The Holy Spirit cried out: "They have put their children to fire. . . . which I never commanded, never decreed, and which never came to My mind" (*Midrash Tanhuma*, Jeremiah 19:5).

2

The Dialectics of Power: Reflections in the Light of the Holocaust

Irving Greenberg

The right to human survival is unconditional; it needs no validation in terms of the Holocaust. Humans are called upon—in biblical language—to choose life. Still, people do consistently tend to link Hiroshima and Holocaust when reflecting on this issue. The obvious reason is that the Holocaust and the atomic destruction of Hiroshima occurred, chronologically, so closely to each other that, as the historian Yehuda Bauer has suggested, there might be some relationship between them. The Holocaust broke taboos against mass killing, thereby rendering further mass death more conceivable and "plausible." The less obvious reason is that as people have considered the tremendous scope of destruction possible with nuclear weaponry, they turn to the record of the Holocaust because it represents a kind of ultimate confrontation with death, naked and unmediated. People ask for the "lessons of the Holocaust" as some possible source of guidance or insight in dealing with the ultimacy of weapons of mass destruction.

HOLOCAUST AND OMNICIDE:
ANALOGY OR BLASPHEMY?

The analogy has been drawn from the very beginning. This was the case in the pioneering work by psychiatrist Robert Jay Lifton who, in his book *Death in Life: Survivors of Hiroshima*, explored the impact of the bomb and the experience of those who survived that destruction. Lifton drew heavily upon the documentation of the concentration camps and of the Holocaust in general for insights into the psychic processes of survivors as well as other questions generated by the event. For other thinkers as well, there has been a natural, almost automatic, turning to the Holocaust for guidance in facing the present reality.

On the other hand, from the beginning—and that includes the reactions to Lifton's book—survivors and others have objected that the very analogy of Auschwitz and Hiroshima and its use represent the denial of the uniqueness of the Holocaust. At the least it is a "too easy" use of a connection. The past decade has witnessed a tremendous growth of interest in the Holocaust. Side by side with that interest has come an increasing attack on what is perceived as the trivialization of the Holocaust by excessive invocation. Words once said with awe and fear are now spoken too quickly and easily, say these critics. In the very process itself of remembering and memorializing, there is the danger of domesticating and diluting. Even attempts by people of goodwill to wrestle with the Holocaust and its meaning, precisely *because* they believe that a confrontation with ultimate death is needed in our generation, frequently run afoul of this criticism. They are charged with improper use of an analogy; they are pronounced guilty of treading roughshod upon holy ground.

This essay will offer little consolation to those who hope for a complete or easy reconciliation of these conflicting claims. The Holocaust is no magic talisman or magic bullet that protects us from dangerous policies or from loss of moral distinctions. That is why I affirm that the right to oppose or be concerned about weapons of mass destruction is independent of the Holocaust and has a right to stand on its own. There is no necessity to invoke the

Holocaust to justify the sense of terror evoked by weapons of mass destruction.

On the other hand, the attempt to learn lessons from the Holocaust and to draw firm political, religious, or philosophical conclusions from it is in itself an inherently flawed act. The event itself is so radical that it overthrows existing norms much more than it supplies meanings. The more one studies the Holocaust, the more its implications are profoundly paradoxical, unfailingly dialectical rather than unequivocal. Most attempts to give clear answers from or about the Holocaust either speak from lack of knowledge of what actually happened or, worse, seek to make propaganda; in other words, they seek to use the victims for selfish advantage. There is a great shock effect in invoking the Holocaust; and sometimes—even for good causes—one is tempted to do so. This is morally objectionable. The ultimate indignity the Nazis inflicted upon the Jews was to not let the dead lie in peace, but to convert their bones and ashes into soap and fertilizer. There is a risk that in confronting the Holocaust, one will turn the dead not from the abyss of forgetfulness into life, but into propaganda for one side or the other.

Of equal importance is that there was no category of thought, whether religious, political, philosophical, or intellectual, that unfailingly produced in its adherents or its opponents the proper response or even adequate resistance to the Holocaust. Therefore, the Holocaust should never be invoked to prove the univocal validity of one position or category. None has earned that kind of validation.

For example, a fundamental lesson one might learn from the Holocaust is the danger of dictatorship and the central importance of democracy. As one studies the record, the obvious question is how such a decision to commit mass murder was taken and how could it be carried out. At the very least, we can note the fact that the absence of counterforces or institutions to resist a governmental process in the fascist dictatorship was clearly central to the success of the genocidal program. Conversely, it appears that no democracy could have upheld such a total human destruction process. Silencing the independent centers of moral judgments and objections made possible the unprecedented decision to kill every last human being in the category of

Jew. It took the *Gleichschaltung* (Nazi term: bringing or forcing citizens into line)—the removal of the potential sources of resistance possible only in a totalitarian system—to carry forward the destruction of the Jews with such concentrated force.

Yet, before one glorifies democracy as the answer to the Holocaust, one must come to grips with the fact that the democracies showed general apathy at the process of destruction; they ignored countless opportunities to resist or stop the ongoing Holocaust. In many ways, the ideology of universal democracy— for example, the argument that the overall purpose of World War II was to liberate Europe, and win the war for democracy—was used as an excuse *not* to bomb the death factories and *not* to take special steps to save Jews. In the democratic ideology that existed then, asking for particular help for Jews was a "violation" of universal principle. This democratic rationale was fundamental to the ability to resist the demand for special efforts to save Jews. Take a war to save humanity and turn it to the "self-interest" (survival) of the Jews and one had lost the moral superiority of the Allied side! Thus, the very ideology of democracy served as a moral cover for those who were apathetic to the Holocaust.

Another example: The preservation of Communism was seen by the left as essential to human liberation. But the preservation of the sole Communist society in the world and its self-exemplary role as an agent of human liberation and of social justice was the rationalization of the Stalin government for hiding the facts of the ongoing annihilation of the Jews of Poland from Soviet Jews. The government argument was that it must avoid offending Germany. If the Stalin government became too visible, by calling attention to what was happening, there was a risk that the one existing (Communist) hope of the world (as it saw itself) would endanger its own existence. Therefore, the Soviet government felt morally justified to hide what was going on from its Jewish population. This lack of knowledge rendered hundreds of thousands of Jewish victims unaware and defenseless when the Nazis entered Russia.

Many good Christians were inspired by Christianity to resist the ongoing destruction—to hide Jews, to protest, to risk their lives, and to oppose murder. But countless more were indifferent or even participated in the persecution—in some cases because of

their very belief itself. The Vatican and a number of national
Catholic churches were inspired by their commitment to the
humanity of those who shared their faith in Christ and protested
against the treatment of converted Jews, that is, Jews who had
converted to Christianity. At the same time they remained silent
about the treatment of other Jews. The rationale for silence is
parallel to the previous example: By speaking out, one endangered oneself as well as the position of the church. During the
postwar period, that was the fundamental defense of Pope Pius
XII's policies. Yet, Catholics took risks under those circumstances
for those who shared their faith in Christ as the redeemer. So the
very religious commitment that was able to inspire selfless sacrifice and a capacity to risk life to save some Jews was simultaneously capable of inspiring indifference to the collective Jewish fate.
Indeed, the Christian contempt for Jews can be credited with
encouraging the aggressors by placing the Jews outside the circle
of societal solidarity.

It would be easy to label the left as the opponents of Hitler and
the right as those who were generally more receptive to National
Socialism. In Germany this was true. Yet, in some cases, as for
instance Franco Spain, it was the right wing—even Fascist—tendencies of Franco that led him to shelter Jews. Part of Franco's
motives apparently stemmed from a sense of Jewish "ancestry";
part of his motivation was his sense of national corporate solidarity
which led him to enable some Jews to come into the country and to
resist their destruction—if not by active resistance then by blocking
Nazi attempts to deport them and by refusing to hand over Jews.

This critique of the moral effectiveness and integrity of ideological systems does not apply only to external philosophies.
Inside the Jewish Holocaust universe, the Zionist and revolutionary movements were a major source of armed resistance. Zionist
and revolutionary youth groups had a strong sense of ideology.
Therefore, as a peer group of young people less influenced by past
quietistic Jewish behavior, and out of their opposition to the
establishment, the revolutionary and Zionist groups had the
strength to organize armed resistance at a time when the Jewish
establishment (an involuntary establishment imposed by the
Nazis) was against such an undertaking. Yet, initially, Jewish revolu-

tionary groups opposed armed resistance on the grounds that Jews should not revolt until the revolution was prepared, that is to say, until the proletariat truly understood the need. They waited for their counterparts in the PPR (Polish Communist Party) in the Communist and Socialist elements on the Polish side, to express their willingness to revolt before they were prepared to support armed resistance. Several months later, after several hundred thousand Jews had been deported, it became clear to them that they were going to die as Jews, and not as members of the proletariat. Only then did they realize that it was more important for them to coordinate with those who were prepared to fight—other Jews—than to worry about those who they thought were the agents of international solidarity. And the Zionist groups were equally guilty of ideological purism which finally led to two separate fighting forces: the Jewish Fighting Organization with the left and center together; and the Z.Z.W. (Polish Jewish Resistance), the Revisionist (right wing) group. The latter was dismissed by the others as "Fascist" in its tendencies. Thus, in both cases, the very ideology that yielded insight also blinded people to their common destiny and cause.

One is reminded of existentialist novelist Albert Camus' speech to a group of monks in southern France after the war.[1] When he started his career in the underground in France, Camus testified, he did not trust Catholics. As an atheist and Communist he knew that Catholics were servants of the bourgeois and the exploiting classes, and the church was the very incarnation of the old regime. As the Nazi process continued and as Camus saw its full horror, he began to realize that whether a person was Communist or Catholic did not predict how he would respond to Nazi behavior. On the contrary. Some of his "best friends" who shared Communist values sold out to save their necks or for some other reason. Yet some people who were "guilty" of reactionary religious views gave their lives to fight the evil. Camus decided finally that the only true inclusion criterion was whether you were for or against what was going on. Those who were for it were on the other side and those against it were on his side—the issue of belief in God or social philosophy was irrelevant.

Camus added that he who was no Christian, repeatedly turned to Rome longing for a word that could galvanize everyone—including himself—in the ongoing struggle. The word never came (in distinguishable form). In short, Camus argued that being Christian in no way predicted whether a person was more or less likely to assist Hitler. Camus' sad conclusion was that the term Christian had been emptied of all significant content by that failure. Were the term Christian a significant prediction of behavior, then even atheists would have embraced it. Now that it proved not to be significant on the greatest questions, it could only continue to be used as a guide to behavior on trivial issues.

In sum, no one philosophy or religious world view in its reactions during and toward the Holocaust earned the credibility of being adequate to the task of grasping and opposing that enormity. This should make one all the more skeptical of univocal claims made in the name of some ideology claiming to be validated by the Holocaust or of a policy decision purporting to be the lesson of the Holocaust. Let us stipulate: there is no magic formula under which the Holocaust shows the moral way. There is no single philosophy to be derived from it; no consistent code that unfailingly created a field of moral force to contain the risks of megadeath. The Holocaust offers, at best, dialectical moves and elliptical understandings, lessons that stretch the capacity to learn, applications that torment and draw forth conflicted behavior.

This stipulation, paradoxically, allows us to draw some lessons from the Holocaust. One recognizes instinctively that a willingness to be torn by one's moral responses is right; perhaps that is the only way one should live after the Holocaust. The answers that the Holocaust supplies torment and render the use of present categories even more difficult. Given the unrelenting anxiety which choked existence every moment in the Holocaust, those who seek to remember should not seek peace of mind. The moral problematics yielded by the Holocaust gnaw at one's sense of moral equilibrium; assault clear, ethical orientations; and cause great anxiety. In a sense, this is the way of identifying with those who lived in the Holocaust—a true act of daily remembrance in contrast to those who cling to the certitude and the moral security which those who live in freedom have as their privilege.

Armed with the disclaimer that no system is fully adequate in the light of the Holocaust, and with the insight that the willingness to wrest a torn and wrenching answer from the record is an authentic response to the catastrophe, we are prepared to draw and apply an analogy between the Holocaust and Omnicide. But let us take a moment to confront the methodological issue before acting. Certainly, those who choose only to remember have met their obligation and cannot be criticized. But what about those who, out of great concern for the seriousness of the Holocaust as well as the sanctity of the memory of the survivors, *oppose* the analogy? What of those who deem the application of the Holocaust record to the questions of global war a form of dilution, of cheapening discourse about the Holocaust for the sake of instant relevance?

THE UNIQUENESS OF THE HOLOCAUST IN A WORLD OF EVIL

It is essential to oppose viewing the Holocaust as similar to other evils. It is blasphemous and dishonest to compare a conscious state decision to destroy every member of the Jewish people with any policy based on judgment or rational need. The Holocaust should not be considered even with other forms of genocide. Genocide—a conscious decision to kill for rational purpose—deserves its own category and should not be conflated with Holocaust, which is total and indiscriminate killing for the sake of killing. Nevertheless, we cannot hide from the fact that there have been serious analyses of a nuclear exchange between Russia and America of 5 to 20 minutes' duration which conclude that such a nuclear confrontation would kill a minimum of 120 million people. Contemplating situations where that kind of mass death can take place, one has every right to ask: Is there any significant difference between a conscious decision and an unconscious decision? Is there any difference between a deliberate decision to kill a whole people and an "accidental" one, as for example, one that in the course of seeking to attain other goals, in fact wipes out whole peoples in the end? The question is undeniably legitimate. One should not be intimidated by the fear of "using" the Holocaust when considering it. Under these circumstances, one then has to take the possibility of analogies quite seriously.

For this reason, sensitive and deep-thinking survivors have come down on both sides of the argument. Nobel Prize-winner Elie Wiesel, who has opposed and strongly argued against the widespread use of the Holocaust analogy, has also, by the same token, spoken out on nuclear disarmament. Wiesel stated some years back that the first time it happened to the Jews, but the next time it will happen to all humanity; and he has clearly implied that nuclear arms will be the source of the next Holocaust. And international lawyer Samuel Pisar in his book *Of Blood and Hope* writes, "Standing in the shadow of the crematoria I wish to give witness to humanity that it is possible to turn the whole world into a crematorium by the use of nuclear weapons."[2]

There is no escape from drawing the nuclear analogy. There is a risk of possibly committing a terrible betrayal of the suffering and memory of the Jewish people in the Holocaust. There is a fundamental difference between holocaust and genocide and if one lumps both policies together, one is guilty of immorally breaking down categories of judgment and obliterating distinctions. To obliterate differences is to sin against the survivors and the dead. Still, in the case of Omnicide, the comparison cries out to be made—carefully, with due qualifications, without swallowing up one into the other. Therefore, recognizing that despite the similar outcome, there is a distinction between a conscious state decision to wipe out a people, and a judgment to defend humanity even at the risk of nuclear confrontation. Done properly, and continuously qualified, this analogy is an act of faithfulness to the memory of the Holocaust.

We must ascertain the telos—the end and purpose—of memory. Surely the goal is not to score moral points by telling the world how terrible it was, criticizing Christianity for having failed and modern culture for having been guilty of apathy. Surely the goal is not simply to collect the details of mass murder. The goal, in some way, must reach above and beyond the obligation to remember. Beyond memory, there is a desire and a need to prevent a recurrence. There is one overall dictum that flows from this event: *never again.*

Let the use of the Holocaust/Omnicide analogy be defended with an analogy. After World War II, Israeli Prime Minister David Ben Gurion, the key architect of the rebirth of the State of Israel,

felt that, in response to the Holocaust, the most urgent and overwhelming thing was to be for life at all costs. He feared that the very
image of the Holocaust's destructiveness, and the overwhelming
success of the mass murder, would act as a source of guilt and a
negative model that would weigh down the living Jews of Israel.
Surrounded by enemies, they could not afford the emotional luxury
of responding to or remembering the Holocaust adequately. Obses-
sion with the memory would drag them down towards death. Therefore, Ben Gurion made a conscious effort for Israel to turn its back
on that event. Indeed, he frequently portrayed the Israelis as being
distinct from those European Jews who went passively to their own
slaughter. Ben Gurion degraded the memory of the Holocaust in
order to ensure that Jewish life overcame it.

Would anyone question that Ben Gurion made the historically correct decision to give life primacy at all costs? The moral of
the Ben Gurion analogy may be stated as follows: better a wrong
application of the model of the Holocaust, but one in the service of
life, than no application, and the advancement of death. If worst
came to worst, if one is guilty of betraying or abusing the Holocaust by applying it to the nuclear issue, if the end result is that the
forces of life are strengthened, then one has committed a necessary and justified evil.

Having invoked Ben Gurion, one must add that some fifteen
years later, Ben Gurion had enough moral insight to admit that he
had made a mistake. (Still, I maintain the *right* mistake.) He concluded that the Jews of Israel inspired by this so-called negative
model had given their all to make sure they would not be destroyed.
These same Israeli Jews, Ben Gurion now felt, had drawn a yawning
distance between themselves and the Holocaust. The result was a
sense of contemptuous superiority over the victims, and sometimes
even over the survivors; this was morally wrong.

Ben Gurion saw the risk of a growing chauvinism and milita-
rist mentality among Jews divorced from their own memory.
Therefore, as prime minister he attempted a correction. He set in
motion the capture of Adolf Eichmann, the gestapo leader who
implemented the Final Solution and his subsequent trial in 1961
thereby forcing the public to face the complexity of the Holocaust,
including the nature of Jewish resistance. It had been too easy to

dismiss the so-called powerless Jew. Israelis now confronted the record of the actual resistance; they came to understand that even those who had not resisted with arms had lived with dignity and defiance—sometimes in electing to go with their families to their death. Even those who had gone quietly were now seen as human beings under the impact of suffering and total domination and were not rejected as pathetic victims who invited their own death through their passivity.

In the spirit of the Ben Gurion analogy, one must draw the comparison of Holocaust and nuclear confrontation—with fear and trembling and with a sense of limits. One must hope, as did Ben Gurion, that people are capable of moral discipline and upon reflection can correct any errors that might arise from a wrongly used analogy. But to totally avoid drawing comparisons runs the risk of trivializing the Holocaust in another way. There is a danger of making the Holocaust so sacred that it has no application to life; one can treat the event as so awesome that it becomes morally and historically solipsistic. This could easily become a cowardly, camouflaged betrayal of the Holocaust for the sake of protecting one's moral superiority or purity. That would be unworthy.

THE USE AND ABUSE OF POWER

Let us then offer some problematic lessons on the subject of the elimination of weapons of mass destruction in the light of the Holocaust. These are indeed only perceptions and not revelations or irresistible conclusions of intimidating moral standing. Faithfulness to the lessons of Holocaust calls for challenging all absolute claims—even for good causes—and placing them in a framework of proper evaluation and consideration. Furthermore, the very challenging of the proposals made in this volume would itself be a fulfillment of the obligation to consider seriously and to wrestle with the awesome event.

The first and obvious lesson is that one cannot—dare not—underestimate the tremendous force of death and evil in this world. One of the most powerful factors behind the Nazi success was its unbelievability. People could not accept that the Holocaust

was occurring. This disbelief according to historian Walter Laqueur was counted on by those who were carrying it out.[3] It
crippled Allied response even on the part of those who were well-
intentioned toward the Jews. Disbelief also disarmed the victims.
In his Holocaust chronicle, journalist Alexander Donat explained
the initial inability to fight the deportation process: "We fell victim
to our faith in mankind, our belief that humanity had set limits to
the degradation and persecution of one's fellow man."[4]

Elie Wiesel has described his disbelief when he arrived in
Auschwitz in the summer of 1944. Years after the killing process
had started—years after hearing all sorts of rumors, he and his
father stood maybe 100 yards from the crematoria and the burning pits. They were burning children alive at that time. Yet when a
prisoner told him and his father, "Poor devils, you're going to the
crematory," Elie turned to his father and said, "Can this be true?
This is the twentieth century, not the Middle Ages."[5] Wiesel, like
so many others, had become totally persuaded by the extraordinary concept of moral progress, by the conviction that human
liberation had come to characterize modern culture, by the belief
in human dignity and value which is one of the glories of democracy and has influenced the whole world, not only those living in
democracies. Even in the presence of the ultimate crime, the
victims could not believe what was being done to them precisely
because they were so convinced that human nature and human
culture were perfected. Out of an encounter with the Holocaust,
one must come to the end of the tyranny of the absolute categories (actually illusions) of modern culture. To the extent that
Christianity has not been brainwashed by modern culture, it must
draw upon its conviction that original sin taints human nature, as
a source of insight into this present moment. (Note that I do not
say that this is *the* source or the correct source, rather that the
belief in original sin is a source of insight.) Judaism must combine
its conceptions of the human capacity for both good and evil and
the human ability to be like God in order to account for this
cancerous, evil period. Secularists must critique the shallowness
of modern liberation insofar as it excessively assumes the goodness of human nature and underestimates the capacity for evil or
the likelihood of tragedy.

After the Holocaust those who romanticize—who believe
that this mass murder was "bestial" behavior, or that it took a
Svengali type like Hitler to induce such behavior, or that it was
lack of human communication that enabled the murderers to act
in this way—are guilty of reckless naivete and of failing to see the
actual record. It is true that the *Einsatzgruppen* (the killing
squads) who shot women and children daily for eighteen months,
showed higher rates of drunkenness, turnover, and nervous reactions than the general German army. But the fact is, they did not
lack for people to carry out these tasks. Nor did the SS lack
people to staff the concentration camps. For the most part, these
executioners were "normal" people, not sharply differentiated
from those who served in the regular German army. The notion
that because mass killing is evil and ugly, normal people will
instinctively recoil from participating in it must be dismissed as a
continuing illusion implanted by the pre-Holocaust culture of mod-
ernity. If anything, one might argue that the Jewish belief that
there is a cosmic struggle between life and death must be matched
by the insight that human nature enables humans to play an
important role on both sides of the battle. Therefore, the threat of
ultimate destruction must be taken very seriously.

In this regard the story of the poet Abba Kovner (1918–1988),
leader of the partisan resistance in the Vilna ghetto, is instructive.
Kovner was asked how he, a young man of 20, found the will and
stamina to organize armed resistance against the Nazis at a time
when all of Europe cowered before the German army, when
powerful generals and armies lay shattered, and when the collective wisdom of his community opposed such action. Kovner an-
swered that the key breakthrough was the recognition that they
all were going to die. He and his friends had come to understand
that the mass killing was not some bizarre behavior of the local
Nazi leadership. The killing was of such administrative and *moral*
enormity, it could only come from a major, centrally taken decision to annihilate the Jews. Therefore, in fact, all Jews were
doomed. Paradoxically, this insight liberated Kovner and his
friends. They had no further illusions. The sooner they overcame
the self-deception that the Nazis were human and therefore in
some way constrained to be humane, the sooner they understood

that they must oppose absolute evil absolutely. They realized that compassion for the other Jews would be misdirected if it paralyzed them from attempting acts of resistance. Others were morally restrained by fear of their actions' leading to the death of their families and other bystander victims. Kovner understood the merciless character of the Nazi process. There was no reason to hold back; the death process had to be opposed at all costs.

This post-Holocaust generation of humanity cannot offer the excuse of being misled by a modern faith in man's perfectibility and goodness, nor dare it depend on the purported moral limits set by human nature. The enormous capacity to choose death and to inflict it on others must never again be underestimated.

The second lesson of the Holocaust is that due to extraordinary human capacity and achievement, unprecedented concentrations of power have been created. This power represents a tremendous transformation in the balance of power between victims and oppressors. Throughout history, the oppressors have been stronger than the victims. But never has there been the kind of imbalance of available force that exists now. Power is the glory and essence of modern culture. If there is one thing modern culture stands for, it is the liberation of humanity—humanity come of age. There is no way that liberation can come or that humanity can take responsibility for its destiny without developing even more power. Science and technology have made possible the incredible human dignity created in the twentieth century. True, this is a century of unprecedented oppression; but one must be honest enough to say that the incredible destructiveness is matched in many areas by unprecedented flowerings of human culture and capability. Hundreds of millions have been released from absolute poverty; millions more have been steadily saved from sickness and causes of death that decades ago, not to mention centuries ago, totally dominated human fate.

Science and technology remain powerful forces of human liberation, so the notion that one can appeal to sentimental nostalgia or some worldwide revulsion against power and science to check the spread of nuclear force is ultimately mistaken. It is no accident that the Third World offers less resistance to pollution than developed countries. The residents of Calcutta dream of dying of smog at the age of 55—as one might in Los Angeles—instead of dying in Calcutta of hunger at the age of 25. Many poor countries lack any environmental movement because if their streams were polluted with industrial wastes, it would mean that they would have jobs and food and less starvation. We cannot expect humanity to take the easy solution of simply renouncing power.

On the other hand, that very creation of power has, for too long, been univocally affirmed as the essence of becoming human. Review the concept of the human coming of age in modern culture: Marx argues that only when humanity renounces the opiate of the masses—religion—will it take part in its own liberation. Freud offers the kind of psychological and therapeutic insight that will release human beings from the castrating father who renders them impotent. This insight, Freud promises, will enable humans to take full responsibility for their own destiny. So in many ways, taking power and expanding power by humans are at the heart of modern culture, the key to its ultimate promise of human dignity. What humanity learned in the Holocaust was that this approach was too simplistic.

The increased acquisition of power has given humans total power. Total power is equally available, in fact, perhaps *more* available for destruction than creation. The release of the atomic bomb in World War II is an appropriate climax to the Western modern culture of the last two centuries, even as the Holocaust is inescapably and strictly an outgrowth of this culture. Contrary to Wiesel's outburst in Auschwitz that "this is not the Middle Ages," the fundamental difference between this era and the Middle Ages is that, in this century, aggressors can carry out unlimited evil. In the Middle Ages, they could only fantasize and think it. What then is the resolution? There is no resolution. The Holocaust lifts the impossible moral tension to a higher level still.

To renounce power, as a policy alternative, decries the facts of human liberation. Such a solution will be rejected by the vast majority of humanity, which is prepared to take the risk precisely because it wants to be liberated. Ultimately, the Holocaust also shows that to renounce power in this era would be a victory for evil. Think of the obvious fact of Israel's condition. Had the Jews of Israel been pacifists, they would have long since been dead. The notion of pacifism as a valid response or an authentic liberating moral response to the nuclear threat is based on a self-deception, an escape for those unable to live with the absoluteness of evil. Having seen absolute death, some people—purportedly idealists—cower and blink rather than show the capacity to continually look without illusion in its face and judge what must be done. Abba Kovner wrote that his group had to continue to look at death without self-deception or unjustified hopes in order to make the proper response; the proper response was not simply to give up, but to resist.

The proper policy alternative is the "demythologization" of power. The sheer scope of unmet human needs dictates the ongoing and expanding use of power; but the glorification of power and the deification of human sovereignty must be reversed. When one glorifies power one makes it absolute. Humanity must grasp the extraordinary attraction and danger of absolute power. In the Holocaust, that power positioned the Jews as the victim. It would destroy the Jews first, but it would not have stopped with the Jews.

In the absence of a moral framework that restricts the heroic claims of power, the exercisers of power inevitably are seduced into arrogant use of the force at their command. The loss of the sense of divine partnership and of being accountable to a covenantal standard has intensified the tendency to be corrupted by power; this has led to abusive behavior toward humans and toward nature even on the part of well-intentioned people. The environment of unlimited power allowed the special enmity for Jews to be acted out to the ultimate level of evil. But once in place, such concentrations of power are available and tempting to use for evil purpose against others.

One of the most important lessons of the Holocaust is the urgency of developing a new sense of humility and self-criticism on the part of Western culture and modern man. There must be a systematic policy of the delegitimation of absolute claims—be they for democracy or dictatorship, for socialism or capitalism, for preservation of status quo or revolution. A claim that is morally unchecked is more able to summon uncontrolled power and run away with it.

Similarly, the cultural framework—philosophical, political, scientific, artistic—must operate to break up the sources of power and distribute them widely to create a "balance of forces." Power is best approached as one would deal with using cobra venom or curare for medicinal purposes; it is to be handled with great care, in a setting designed to keep alertness at maximum, and controlled for side effects. Without these checks, power, a great nurturer of life, inevitably becomes a great cause of death. Power grows in the medium of modern culture; in the absence of new antibodies, or if you will, regulators of growth, power metastasizes. There must always be serious questioning—and fear and trembling—in the very possession of infinite force. Power leads too easily to idolatry.

This, then, is another lesson of the Holocaust record. The process of the Holocaust, at some level, moved in a profoundly theological dimension, even if the theology was that of the devil rather than of God. Professor Uriel Tal and others have shown how Nazi theologians operated in their judgments about Jews. Nazism was a search for perfection. The search for wholeness in many ways drove the ideology and deepened the appeal of Nazism.[6]

The most dramatic expression of this *drang* (zeal) is Commander Otto Ohlendorf's testimony at the *Einsatzgruppen* trial. Ohlendorf was the only defendant who did not deny that he carried out the shootings—and that he wanted to. When asked by the prosecutor how he could do this, did he not see the women and children? Ohlendorf explained that of course he saw them. But he understood that to bring about the final perfection, one must make great personal sacrifices. He thought he was making a moral sacrifice for the redemption of humanity. The Jewish children, if spared, would grow up to be people who had to be destroyed. Armed with his vision of finality, Ohlendorf could do anything, even murder women and children en masse. Thus, the combination of absolute values and total power led Ohlendorf to claim the prerogatives of deity—and to operate beyond human standards of good and evil. Ohlendorf became godlike; total power led him to assume the powers of life and death. The inebriation of absolute power led to Ohlendorf becoming not God, but Moloch.

Idolatry has an enormous energy of its own. One must confront it by cutting it down to size, then mastering and controlling it. Infinite power, broken up, becomes finite and manageable. To achieve this end, the energy of idolatry must be countered with all the dedication of force and idealism in the service of humanism and the sanctity of life. Despite the necessarily partial claims and proximate tactics of those who forswear idolatry (idolatry absolutizes the relative; true faith treats all things other than the divine as partial), one can only oppose idolatry effectively by making a matching covenant with life. One must make a commitment to oppose idolatry with the same dedication as is characteristic of those who carry it out. With humility and self-criticism and full recognition of the partial claims of one's position, one must make a commitment to work for life with dedication equal to that which the absolutists, the fanatics, the idolators bring to their causes. The Nazis succeeded in the Holocaust because their level of commitment and concentration on killing the Jews was far stronger than those who opposed the destruction. Those who favor peace must learn the power of dedication; they must learn how to remain committed and active for extended periods.

So the primary application of the Holocaust record to the threat of Omnicide is to teach of the danger of absolute power. Whoever claims the right to use absolute power is idolatrous and must be checked—by a group with matching passion and commitment.

THE COVENANT OF POWER

In opposing the nuclear threat, one must work towards creating a new balance: an equivalent of the nuclear balance that has played an important role in keeping the killing reduced, up to now. Therefore, one must have the modesty to admit that the balance of terror of the postwar years has saved humanity from an all-out war. The U.S.–Russian–Cuban missile crisis in the 1960s is a classic example of how the ultimate terror that brought both sides to the brink also served to check them at the end. Had there not been such a nuclear balance, there might have been several actual world wars in the past 45 years.

The balance of power has probably saved millions of lives. In advocating nuclear disarmament, one runs a real risk of destabilizing, of creating a situation in which the balance of power shifts in a fundamental way. In 1950, such a pullback in Korea invited the North Korean invasion of South Korea. The Russian misreading of American will, and the North Korean misjudgment of the amount of power available to resist, created the great temptation to move in. After the Holocaust, Manes Sperber wrote that Jews would have to be strong; they could not afford the luxury of simply protesting what happened; Jews had a moral obligation to anti-Semites never to tempt them to such ugly behavior again.[7] The very weakness of the Jew corrupted the murderers; only Jewish strength could control the behavior of anti-Semites in the future.

The Holocaust teaches us to use power appropriately. This includes punishing enemies and rewarding friends, precisely because that encourages moral behavior. In the long run, the ability to defend oneself saves lives rather than losing them. It is true that controlled and unbalanced nuclear saber-rattling is fraught with ultimate consequences. But a restrained use of nuclear defense is within the range of legitimate policy judgment. One could argue that nuclear power should not exist, but since it does exist, it must be controlled. Unilateral disarmament, however, is not a "well-intentioned" thrust for peace; it is an invitation for destabilization, for adventurism and conflict—and for betrayal of democracy's capacity to stand against its enemies.

An alternative policy can model itself on the biblical account of the flood. The Bible teaches that God, having been angered by uncontrolled human evil, unleashed unlimited destructive power and created a flood that wiped out humanity. Then the Divine itself came to recognize that unleashing such power was no longer tolerable or acceptable. It is unacceptable because such power is dangerous to all of life, and using that kind of power or even threatening to is a total violation of respect for life. Therefore, God initiated a covenant limiting God's power; even God cannot be entrusted with absolute power.

The Holocaust demonstrated that humans have the power once reserved for God alone. That use of power started out as godlike and employed in the service of "redemption," but ended up being idolatrous and murderous. The other side of the Holocaust analogy is that humans now realize they have the powers of God, and that they should properly recognize those powers as a call by God to become partners in redemption. What is needed now is a worldwide covenental commitment to place limits on human power. One must press the governments to retreat from the brink—step by step. There was a covenant with Noah in the Bible, another covenant with Abraham, and further renewals of the covenant. The repeated covenants teach that even the Divine could not retreat from the brink in a single motion—but only step by step.

A realistic beginning to this withdrawal is distinguishing nuclear arms and biological and chemical weapons from conventional arms issues. Building up conventional forces might be one of the ways to prevent reliance on weapons of mass destruction. Those who fear American renunciation of such weapons feel there is a danger of destabilizing and unintentionally creating a situation that will lead to world war. But if the nuclear balance is replaced by conventional arms equilibrium, there would be less risk of miscalculation. Those who support nuclear disarmament as well as the destruction of biological and chemical weapons should be willing to support a buildup of conventional arms, if that would prevent destabilization and give assurance to those who support nuclear arms if only to maintain a balance of power. A conventional buildup can be combined with nuclear reduction and a chance to retreat from the brink of ultimacy.

Jewish tradition distinguishes defensive wars from preemptive wars. The Halakhah (Jewish law) puts greater limits on the tactics that one can use in preemptive wars than in defensive wars. By analogy, the concept of tactical nuclear forces, combined with a pledge of no first-strike use of nuclear arms, is also a possible policy tack. This approach emphasizes that even to the extent that nuclear arms might be used, they would only be used in a limited area, and defensively and not preemptively. This approach adds a dimension of human judgment to control the use of nuclear force—at the risk of misapplication of human judgment of the situation. It is a worthy risk if the alternative is no check on the expansion of nuclear forces.

In the same spirit, there are many specific trade-offs between nuclear powers that can reduce the level of nuclear arms on both sides. This is where concrete steps can be taken and where the pressure for nuclear disarmament is more fruitfully applied. It is important that there be perceived electoral rewards and viable policy acts that can begin to build an atmosphere of trust and progress away from the brink. These do not sound as appealing as utopian solutions, but after the Holocaust, humanity should be particularly skeptical of utopian hopes.

After years of living under the shadow of catastrophe, the current movement for nuclear disarmament is a sign of life and renewal. The movement—and its critics—must work together in each nation to prevent establishment of stereotypes of the other nations. A further lesson to be drawn from the Holocaust is the danger of separating people into different universes of moral discourse. Helen Fein in her brilliant study of response to the Holocaust suggests that the key to Jewish survival was not the Nazi murderous design, but rather the attitude of the bystanders.[8] This determined how many Jews would escape. The attitude of bystanders concerning Jews depended on whether or not they were considered to be in the group's moral universe. When the Jews were outside that moral universe of obligation, no one would take risks to save them. It was such an attitude that enabled the Nazis to carry out their murders without hesitation.

The cure to complacency vis-à-vis weapons of mass destruction is to ensure that foreign powers are not placed outside of the American universe of moral obligation. One must make extreme efforts to revive the sense of universal humanity and the need to perceive the full humanity of the other if one is to prevent Omnicide. Therefore, it is also very important to dramatize the danger of nuclear, chemical, and biological war, and the incredible damage it would inflict on humanity. One can thereby try simultaneously to break through not only the apathy and the indifference but the numbing described by Robert Lifton, that takes place under the shadow of total destructiveness.

There are no easy solutions. The human commitment to stay
alive should be absolute, but that insight must not paralyze judgment. People are able to live with fine differences and do not need
to be told that choosing life over death means giving up protection. The affirmation of nuclear power also runs the risk of unleashing absolute power, but here again, controls and fine distinctions can prevent that abuse. The ultimacy of a nuclear holocaust,
and the threat of nuclear destruction of certain areas or groups
constitute distinct categories of danger and different levels of
moral judgment. Thus, nuclear confrontation would be a holocaust only if the decision to destroy humanity were taken consciously. A nuclear exchange would be a destruction—whether
the decision is an unconscious or unintended one. The point is
that while ultimacy itself is a source of moral energy, it also tends
to undermine moral judgment. People intimidated by sheer horror
lose the power of judgment. If humanity is hanging on the brink, it
must stay as unimpassioned as possible as it edges itself back
from the brink, refraining from excessive or one-sided reactions
out of moral outrage or terror.

In the ghettos, forests, and concentration camps of Europe,
the key to resisting the Holocaust was the difficult discovery of its
total and terrible ultimacy, followed by the discovery that maintaining even limited moral resistance was also worthwhile. Jews
had to see the worst that was coming in order to recognize what
was happening to them. The Allies had to see the unprecedented
extent of the horror; those who could not admit the ultimacy
could not respond adequately. The first step for an adequate
response for inmates in the concentration camps was to recognize
that all the old rules were gone, this was total death. A person who
tried to live in the same civilized and moral way he had before
coming to the camp would surely die.

Step two was that, morale having been shattered, one must
not surrender to the camp. Perhaps the most sophisticated and
difficult moral decision in resistance was to affirm that in a flawed,
broken way, as best one can, one will uphold life and the moral
code. Those who gave in totally to the guards died as surely as
those who gave in to total hopelessness and could see no value in
resistance. With the categories of past morality now dissolved, the

key to moral survivial was to uphold what one could and to affirm the ongoing dignity of life and the importance of existence.

If humans fail to recognize the ultimacy of the threat, the threat of Omnicide becomes more imminent. If humans yield to that ultimacy by responding passively, by refusing to make the difficult decisions, and by not exercising any judgment with regard to the political efforts required to move step by step away from the brink, then humanity will not achieve its goals of universal, physical, and spiritual dignity.

The final lesson of the Holocaust is that finite human beings can show incredible moral strength: the strength to admit that if they cannot live by their established standards, they need not surrender totally; the strength to do what has to be done to stay alive without succumbing to either nihilism or apathy. That is to say, humans put limits on what they would do in order to maintain their dignity. In short, humans showed a capacity to live in tormented conflict without collapsing ethically—thereby affirming the moral power of human beings. One owes the victims no less in applying this Holocaust analogy to develop the commitment to be for peace without becoming a pacifist. To develop outrage against the threat of total destruction without becoming desensitized or hysterical will be the key to a fruitful outcome from the movement for nuclear disarmament.

The Jewish tradition constantly summons up the memories of oppression in order to stimulate efforts for liberation. The people Israel must remember that they were enslaved in Egypt in order that they will return their own bond servants to freedom and give them more help in becoming free (Deuteronomy 15:12–15). On Rosh HaShanah and Yom Kippur, an encounter with death is evoked to goad people into greater efforts toward life and to fuller living. In this generation, the memory of Auschwitz, Dora, Warsaw, and a thousand other places of death should be summoned up to drive humanity towards greater efforts in overcoming the forces of death and diverting them to the service of life.

The rabbis said that on the day of Tisha B'Av the Messiah was born, and the ultimate process of liberation started on that day of the destruction of the Temple. In the generation of Auschwitz, the Jewish people renewed Jerusalem and rebuilt the State of Israel. In a generation facing ultimate death, humanity must be daring. To oppose the ultimate potential for death by creating a major movement that asserts life—in the very same generation as Treblinka—demands a movement that works for the disarmament of weapons of mass destruction. This is a worthy response to the Holocaust. The reassertion of life must be built on proper faith in humanity, a faith that enables people to fight for peace without naivete or grasping at illusions. One has to hope that the generation in which Auschwitz functioned may yet create a triumph in which a covenant of life is renewed and applied and power is mastered for life.

NOTES

1. Albert Camus, *Resistance, Rebellion, and Death*. Trans. and introduction by Justin O'Brien (New York: Alfred A. Knopf, 1961).

2. Samuel Pisar, *Blood and Hope*, first English ed. (Boston: Little, Brown, 1980).

3. Walter Laqueur, *The Terrible Secret: Suppression of the Truth about Hitler's "Final Solution"* (Boston: Little, Brown, 1981).

4. Alexander Donat, *The Holocaust Kingdom: A Memoir* (New York: Holocaust Library, 1978).

5. Elie Wiesel, *From the Kingdom of Memory: Reminiscences* (New York: Summit Books, 1990), p. 232. See also *Night*.

6. Uriel Tal, "Political faith of Nazism prior to the Holocaust," June 14, 1978 (Tel Aviv: Tel Aviv University). "Structures of German political theology in the Nazi Era" (Tel Aviv: Tel Aviv University, 1979).

7. Manes Sperber, *Man and His Deeds*. Trans. from French and German by Joachim Neugroschel (New York: McGraw Hill, 1970). *Journey without End* (*Victi Victuri Vincendi*). Trans. Constantine Fitzgibbon (Garden City, NY: Doubleday, 1954).

8. Helen Fein, *Accounting for Genocide: National Responses and Jewish Victimization during the Holocaust* (New York: Free Press, 1977).

BIBLICAL AND RABBINIC STUDIES

3

Cataclysm, Survival, and Regeneration in the Hebrew Bible

Jon D. Levenson

In Judaism, man is always somehow a remnant. He is always somehow a survivor, an inner something, whose exterior was seized by the current of the world and carried off while he himself, what is left of him, remains standing on the shore. Something within him is waiting.

Franz Rosenzweig

THE PROSPECT OF OMNICIDE IN ANCIENT NEAR EASTERN THEOLOGY

Although ours is the first generation to have the wherewithal to eradicate human life from the planet, ours is not the first to consider this frightful prospect possible or even the first to consider it imminent. Indeed, the precariousness of life and of the whole natural order is a major theme in ancient Near Eastern literature, Gentile and Israelite alike. Whether the nuclear sword of Damocles will remain suspended over our heads or not is unclear. It is possible that technology will take the threat of Nuclear Omnicide away from us, just as it once gave it to us. That is our best hope. But if that threat, or one like it, endures, then, in the long run, the nuclear age will be seen not as the era in which unprecedented fear, pessimism, and hysteria descended upon much of humanity, but as the era in which these elements returned after the interruption of an aberrant era of optimism. Indeed, the fear that man might unleash forces that would destroy not only him but cosmic order itself has been so widespread that one is tempted to call it a constituent element of human consciousness. Modern secular persons do not see God or the gods behind the horrific devastation. But the devastation they envision is no more horrific than the devastation that the ancients at times expected of their gods, including Israel of her God, YHWH.

The best known instances of divine hostility culminating in cosmic destruction are the flood stories of the ancient Near East. In the case of the *Gilgamesh Epic*, a loosely connected cycle of Sumerian and Akkadian fragments that date to the early second millennium B.C.E. but derive from an old tradition,[1] Enlil, "Lord Wind," the forceful and terrifying counselor of the pantheon, decrees a deluge in hopes of annihilating humanity. "The uproar of mankind is intolerable," he complains to the assembled deities, "and sleep is no longer possible by reason of the babel."[2] Thus is mighty Enlil: A good night's sleep means more to him than all of human life. Fortunately, man has an advocate among the gods. Crafty Ea, the god associated with rain and subterranean waters, manages to convey the threat to the mortal, Utnapishtim, with instructions to build an ark in which to survive the deluge. The description of the deluge is surreal in its horror:

> With the first light of dawn a black cloud came from the horizon; it thundered within where Ada, lord of the storm, was riding. In front over hill and plain, Shullat and Hanish, heralds of the storm, led on. The gods of the abyss rose up; Nergal pulled out the dams of the nether waters, Ninurta the war-lord threw down the dykes, and the seven judges of hell, the Annunaki, raised their torches, lighting the land with their livid flame. A stupor of despair

went up to heaven when the god of the storm turned daylight into darkness, when he smashed the land like a cup. One whole day the tempest raged, gathering fury as it went, it poured over the people like the tides of battle; a man could not see his brother nor the people be seen from heaven. Even the gods were terrified at the flood, they fled to the highest heaven, the firmament of Anu; they crouched against the walls, cowering like curs. . . .[3]

After six days of tempest and torrent, the sea grows calm on the seventh. After six days of waiting in the ark as it holds fast to a mountain, Utnapishtim knows on the seventh that the threat has passed, for the third of the birds he released did not return. He offers a sacrifice, around which the gods gather "like flies," all except Enlil. "He shall not approach this offering," vows the goddess Ishtar, "for without reflection he brought the flood; he consigned my people to destruction." Ea, too, reproaches Enlil:

Lay upon the sinner his sin,
Lay upon the transgressor his transgression,
Punish him a little when he breaks loose,
Do not drive him too hard or he perishes. . . .[4] [cf. Jeremiah 10:24]

Here, the implication is that it was human iniquity rather than mere noisiness that prompted Enlil's nearly successful attempt at Omnicide, except that the punishment, if it fits the crime, did not fit the criminal. Man is too weak to survive his just punishment (cf. Amos 7:1–6). In the case of the *Gilgamesh Epic*, the sole survivors, Utnapishtim and his wife, receive immortality from the hand of Enlil. In this, the benevolent Ea has triumphed. Yet the rest of mankind has perished under the boundless malevolence of Enlil. All is not over, there is hope, man survives. But his survival is now known to depend upon a lucky turn of events in a bleak and unjust drama. What stands between man's life and his death are forces he cannot control.

Tablet XI of *Gilgamesh*, which we have been discussing, displays more than coincidental parallels to the flood story of Genesis 6–9, a point to which we shall return. Closer to the biblical period and as close in theme, if not in detail, to much biblical material is the *Poem of Erra*, a composition of the first millennium B.C.E., probably of Babylonian origin.[5] Išum ("fire"), the counselor, arouses his master Erra ("scorched earth") from his lethargy and his dalliance with his consort and goads him into going to war. To do this, Erra must first neutralize Marduk, king of the gods and lord of Babylon. He accomplishes this by persuading Marduk to vacate his throne in order to have his royal insignia cleaned. With Marduk dethroned and cosmic order therefore undermined, Erra is free to commence his bloodbath, carrying out slaughter in Babylon itself and in the other major cities of the region:

> Respect no god! Fear no man!
> Put to death young and old alike,
> the suckling and the babe—leave not anyone![6]

At this point, the roles of Išum and Erra reverse, as the counselor reproaches his master for killing just and unjust alike (cf. Genesis 18:23–25), and Erra first commands Išum to redirect the scorched earth policy onto Babylonia's enemies and then, pronouncing himself guilty before the other gods and forsaking Marduk's throne, orders Babylon restored. The narrative structure of the *Poem of Erra* is thus chiastic:

> At the beginning, both gods are apart: Erra in rest and Išum in violence, but with intimations of the reverse. Subsequently, they crisscross: Erra moves to violence, Išum to calm tinged by violence. At the end of the poem, they meet in harmony, in a new state of rest. . . . The effect of all this is to emphasize the intertwined nature of their personalities—something apparent even from the etymologies of their names— or more precisely, it is to show the importance of Išum in defining the range of Erra's behavior.[7]

Indeed, we may go further and question whether the superficial narrative of the poem, in which the two are represented as different gods, is best not accepted as definitive, but rather viewed as a projection into narrative of the deep psychological dynamics internal to one god, Erra-Išum. If so, then the poem represents a duality fundamental to the divine–human relationship: Divinity is both hostile and benevolent, both destructive and restorative. Neither dimension of the divine is self-sufficient; each is tinged with intimations of the other. The divine is both "for" us and "against" us. At any point, the balance may shift, but a new balance, equally short-lived, will be found. Divine hostility and its corollary destruction are real, but not unchecked by other aspects in the divine personality. The slaughter will proceed so far and then, as mysteriously as it began, it will be reversed, and its latest victim will profit from it, as his enemies suffer (cf. Deuteronomy 32:36–42).

In the *Poem of Erra*, as in Tablet XI of *Gilgamesh* and much biblical literature, the last word, or better, the *latest* word is survival, but survival under the sword of Damocles, survival after a scene of Auschwitz-like horror, with no assurance that it cannot recur. We survive only because we have been mysteriously spared. We have no inherent right to our existence.

THE PERSISTENCE OF EVIL IN CREATION

One's first impression, especially if he has had the benefit of a Jewish education, is that a great divide separates the Mesopotamian ideas discussed here from the theology of the Hebrew Bible. Indeed, in that book, although other gods are often thought to exist, it is only YHWH who is individualized and possessed of an articulated personality, and it is he to whom all power is ascribed, even by the remainder of the pantheon (for example, Psalms 29:1).[8] No other god defines the range of his behavior or restricts his power. Moreover, his goodness is intrinsic to his nature and not an aberration. Few affirmations are more abundant in the hymnic literature of the Hebrew Bible than the affirmation that YHWH is good (Psalms 73:1; 145:9, for example). In the main, his well-known wrath is only a response to sin. It is a manifestation of justice rather than petty jealousy or malice:

[I]t is noticeable that the wrath of God never acquires the characteristics of *mēnis*, that malicious hatred and envy which bulks so large in the implacability of the Greek and also of the Babylonian deities. Even if it is sometimes unintelligible, *YHWH's anger has nothing of the Satanic about it*; it remains simply *the manifestation of the displeasure of God's unsearchable greatness*, and as such is far above human conception. . . .

Unlike holiness or righteousness, *wrath never forms one of the permanent attributes of the God of Israel*; it can only be understood as, so to speak, a footnote to the will to fellowship of the covenant God.[9]

The greater benevolence of the biblical deity is inextricably associated with the more anthropocentric perspective of the Hebrew Bible generally. Whereas in some Mesopotamian stories, the gods create man only so that there will be slaves to relieve them of drudgery,[10] in Genesis 1 at least, God creates man (male *and* female) as a kind of vizier: They are to "Be fertile and increase, fill the earth and master it; and rule the fish of the sea, the birds of the sky, and all the living things that creep on the earth" (Genesis 1:28).[11] God has, in the words of a psalmist, made man

> . . . little less than divine,
> and adorned him with glory and majesty;
> You have made him master over Your handiwork,
> Laying the world at his feet. . . . [Psalms 8:6–7]

Here, as in Genesis 1, man is a godlike figure, the junior partner of the Deity in his purposive ordering and governance of the world. The partnership can persist only because of the stability of their relationship, a relationship founded upon mutual trust and respect.

It would, however, be a serious mistake to view the creation theology of the Hebrew Bible as a warrant for optimism. For Genesis 1:1–2:3, the great cosmogony with which the Torah opens, is not properly characterized as the story of God omnipotent, man his exalted plenipotentiary, and the world he created entirely according to his wishes. In fact, close inspection of the text reveals that this cosmogony is not a case of creation out of nothing, as later Jewish, Christian, and Muslim tradition has usually (but not always) conceived it. Water and darkness, symbols of the chaotic opposition to the creator-God, both in Israel and generally in ancient Near East, are primordial. God does not create them, but only brackets them with light and dry land, thus breaking up the primordial condition, limiting it but not destroying it.[12] And so when prophets employ the language of creation to describe the perfect world, the world as it should be, they often resort not to the past but to the future tense. They are describing a *better* order than that of creation as it has always been known, a *redemption* of creation in which its flaws have been corrected:

> No longer shall you need the sun
> For light by day,
> Nor the shining of the moon
> For radiance [by night];
> For the LORD shall be your light everlasting,
> Your God shall be your glory,
> Your sun shall set no more,
> Your moon no more withdraw;
> For the LORD shall be a light to you forever,
> And your days of mourning shall be ended. [Isaiah 60:19–20]

In this oracle, the setting of the sun and the disappearance of the moon, which symbolize the daily return of that frightening primordial reality, universal darkness, are overcome. God's perpetual presence will mean the definitive defeat of the negative forces checked but not destroyed by the act of creation represented by Genesis 1:1–2:3. Another oracle in the same collection as that quoted above calls this future act of redemption what it really is, a new creation:

> For behold! I am creating
> A new heaven and a new earth;
> The former things shall not be remembered,
> They shall never again come to mind.
> Be glad, then, and rejoice forever
> In what I am creating.
> For I shall create Jerusalem as a joy,
> And her people as a delight;

And I will rejoice in Jerusalem
And delight in her people,
Never again shall be heard there
The sounds of weeping and wailing. [Isaiah 65:17-19]

A wedge, in short, should not be driven between creation and redemption, as if redemption were only a historical drama that takes place within a world order immutably established at creation. What is joyfully anticipated in these oracles of redemption is rather an all-encompassing transformation, a transformation of both history and nature (including human nature), as God brings about a new order in stark contradiction to the old order in which the dark, abysmal forces and their capacity to wreak havoc have not yet been eliminated. If the vision of redemption of the prophetic and apocalyptic literature of Israel warrants any sort of optimism at all, it is optimism about the eschatological era, not about the vulnerable, fragile present which that era is to replace—in sum, a hopefulness based on radical faith in the power of God and not an optimism based on observation of things as they stand.

Other texts envision creation as the result of the victory of YHWH over chaos personified as a sea monster.[13] It is that victory that establishes YHWH's supremacy over the other gods, his universal kingship (symbolized by the Temple, his cosmic palace), and his mastery over all that is. Numerous passages allude to this primal victory over the monster, variously named Yamm, Leviathan, Rahab, Tannin, and so on. Not every such text, however, depicts the monster as destroyed. In one, YHWH commits his primordial opponent to the custody of his son and vicegerent, King David and his dynasty (Psalm 89:10-11, 26). Cosmic and political order are, once again, indistinguishable. And so when the same psalm confronts the degradation of the current dynasty of the House of David, it is as if God and the world order for which he stands have been discredited (Psalm 89:39-51). Political catastrophe is not simply the baleful result of human disobedience; it is rooted as well in the survival of primordial evil and the mysterious and painful quiescence of the God who alone can triumph over it. There is more evil and suffering in the world than can be attributed to the frailness of the human will. Hence, the passion with

which biblical suppliants call upon God to act in accordance with
the reputation he won in creation:

> Awake, awake, clothe yourself with splendor,
> O arm of the LORD!
> Awake as in days of old,
> As in former ages!
> It was you who hacked Rahab in pieces,
> That pierced the Dragon. [Isaiah 51:9]

And, indeed, some texts go farther still, speaking of that combat
and that victory as yet to be:

> In that day the LORD will punish,
> With his great, cruel, mighty sword
> Leviathan the Elusive Serpent—
> Leviathan the Twisting Serpent,
> He will slay the Dragon of the sea. [Isaiah 27:1]

The prominent role of the combat myth of creation in Jewish
apocalypticism (including clear reflections of the myth in rabbinic
apocalyptic visions) is powerful testimony that creation in ancient
Judaism is not simply a report from the past, but a hope for the
future, a hope rooted in the grisly fact that the present state of
things can more closely resemble chaos than creation, or, to put it
more directly, that we are living before rather than after creation,
and the world that perfectly corresponds to God's wishes, though
solemnly promised, is yet to be.

In some midrashim, this strange set of circumstances is interpreted to mean that God is not yet fully God:

> Rabbi Levi said in the name of Rabbi Acha bar Chanina: As long as
> the descendants of Amalek are in the world, neither the name [that
> is, YHWH] nor the throne is complete. When the descendants of
> Amalek will have perished, both the name and the throne will be
> complete.[14]

To the rabbis, the tribe of Amalek personified genocidal anti-
Semitism. So long as such as they remain in the world, the world

is not really God's, or to put the point differently, God is not yet
master of the world, though tradition and Jewish practice proclaim him so. Underlying this curious midrash is the unusual
wording of Moses' vow in Exodus 17:16:

> He said, "It means, 'Hand upon the throne [kēs] of the LORD
> [Yāh]!' the LORD will be at war with Amalek throughout the ages."

If kēs means "throne," then it lacks the last letter of the usual form
of this word (kissē'), just as Yāh [YH] lacks the last two letters of
the more usual form of God's name (YHWH). Rabbi Acha played
on the apocopated form of these two words to affirm that so long
as Amalekites survive, the full measure of God's divinity and
sovereignty are unrealized. Here again, the omnipotence of God
and the goodness of his world are elements of the faith in a future
transformation, one that will blast inimical forces from the world.
Such faith is not passive or quietistic. On the contrary, the rabbis
made much of the biblical injunction upon Israel to wipe out
Amalek (Deuteronomy 25:17–19): Man can and must contribute
to God's self-realization, to the establishment of the heavenly
kingdom on earth. But until those consummations devoutly to be
wished have been brought about, the Jews remain vulnerable to
all the horrific barbarities that Amalek symbolizes. Here, too, a
nondialectical affirmation of God's omnipotence and sovereignty
cannot do justice to the theology of the foundational texts of the
Jewish tradition. And this was true long before the horrors of the
Holocaust made the inadequacy of the nondialectical affirmation
so glaringly obvious to modern man.

We have been examining ways in which the Hebrew Bible
personifies the negative forces identified with chaos, death, exile,
and the like as a sea monster or a people whom YHWH must
overcome, even as he has at moments of redemption in the past.
Not always, however, is the negative dimension personified as an
adversary of YHWH. Sometimes, it—or, at least, some aspects of
it—are seen as a side of God himself, in a theology that is surely
less dualistic but hardly more comforting than the combat myth.
This negative side of God is the demonic dimension, the aware-

ness that YHWH can be "uncanny, ghastly, ferocious, hostile, and nearly Satanic."[15] It is to this dimension, so frightening that its very existence, then as later, was often denied, that we now turn.

THE AMBIVALENCE OF THE DEITY
IN ISRAELITE MONOTHEISM

Even when, as usual, it is transgression that activates YHWH's wrath, the fact remains that the mere elimination of the transgressor or his repentance often does not suffice to placate the enraged Deity. In the case of Noah, the Israelite Utnapishtim, it is the savor of the burning bodies of dead animals and birds that activates YHWH's favor after the deluge:

> The LORD smelled the pleasing odor, and the LORD said to Himself: "Never again will I doom the earth because of man, since the devisings of man's mind are evil from his youth; nor will I ever again destroy every living being, as I have done." [Genesis 8:21]

In other words, man has not improved: Noah and his descendants are no less afflicted with the infirmities of human nature than the rest of humanity (Genesis 6:5) who have just perished. The inclination to evil remains; a superior race lacking it has not appeared. What induces YHWH to vow never to repeat his near-omnicide (thus implying the irrationality of the plan all along) is not morality, but the "pleasing odor." If YHWH's omnicidal rage in the Israelite flood story is more ethical in character than Enlil's or Erra's, his final turn to benevolence is no less mysterious than theirs.

In Exodus 4:24–26, YHWH attempts to kill Moses on his way back to Egypt, in spite of having just commanded him to return in order to confront the Pharaoh. He relents only after Moses' wife circumcises their son and touches the bloody foreskin to "his legs." The antecedent of the possessive is unclear; it could be the child, Moses, or YHWH. In any event, the passage is bizarre and does not lend itself easily to moralization. It does, however, fit nicely with the tendency in biblical thought that sees the shedding of blood as the effective antidote to God's homicidal impulses. One can compare the etiology of the Passover sacrifice: the blood from the paschal lamb on the Israelite houses signals to YHWH which ones to spare as he carries out his final plague, the killing of all the first-born of Egypt (Exodus 12:13). Similarly, blood-manipulation is central to the rite of the sin-offering. Here, forgiveness does not follow immediately upon the sinner's discovery of his wrongdoing and his consequent remorse. It is rather the sprinkling of the blood and the burning of the fat of the sacrificial animal to create a "pleasing odor" that secures divine forgiveness (Leviticus 4). Again, although divine disfavor is an interruption created by transgression, YHWH must still be *appeased*. In the cultic legislation, sin is more than juridical guilt. It is also a miasma that must be removed in mysterious ways.

In Numbers 17:8–15, YHWH proposed to annihilate all Israel with the exception of Moses and Aaron. Only the quick thinking of Moses secures deliverance, as he instructs his priestly brother to put altar-fire and incense into a pan and ". . . make expiation for them. For wrath has gone forth from the LORD: the plague has begun!" (Numbers 17:11). Aaron does so: "He stood between the dead and the living until the plague was checked" (Numbers 17:13). Once again, the near-omnicidal rage of God far outruns its moral provocation, and the curb upon it is aromatic smoke, this time from kindled incense. The sinning majority survives only because of the extraordinary act of appeasement undertaken by the priest. Elsewhere in the Torah, YHWH is biased toward life (Deuteronomy 30:19), and some of the prophets, most memorably Ezekiel, insist that God does not desire the death even of the wicked, but only their repentance, so that they may live (Ezekiel 18:23).[16] But in passages like Numbers 17:8–15, we see revealed another side of YHWH's character, the side that lacks this bias to life and that is induced to relinquish homicidal campaigns not by repentance, praise, or argument, but by cultic intercession. The priest does what Ea and Išum do: he turns divine wrath into benevolence, lethal fury into life-enhancing favor. If divine malevolence is the exception, it is still defeated only by exceptional actions which are the sacred rites. But for the cult, passages like this tell us, we would all be dead.

In the instances that we have been discussing (with the possible exception of Exodus 4:24–26), human sins are the provocation for the deadly rage of YHWH, although it is a rage that is dissipated only by a sacrificial offering. In other instances, YHWH is seen as the actual cause of a person's sin, for which the human agent is still held responsible. The best known example of this latter pattern is the "hardening" of Pharaoh's heart throughout the early chapters of Exodus: YHWH orders Moses to perform miracles so as to induce Pharaoh to let Israel go, but he also stiffens Pharaoh's heart so that the miracles will not have the desired effect (Exodus 4:21). From the point of view of narrative technique, the pattern makes perfect sense in the Exodus story. It would hardly do to have Pharaoh capitulate after one miracle, but neither would it do to have the miracles of YHWH appear ineffective before the iron will of Pharaoh. The narrative resolves the dilemma by having Moses work overpowering marvels against Pharaoh and having YHWH insure that yet another marvel is needed. In this way, YHWH demonstrates to Pharaoh "that there is none like Me in all the world" (Exodus 9:14). Here, as is usual in the Hebrew Bible, the interests of narrative technique and of theological teaching dovetail. They are, in the last analysis, inextricable: even the opposition to YHWH comes from YHWH himself. Nothing is outside his control, ". . . I have spared you for this purpose: in order to show you My power, and in order that My fame may resound throughout the world" (Exodus 9:16).

The resolution of the narrative dilemma through this particular theology, however, is purchased at the price of another precious theological affirmation: the goodness of God. For God is here portrayed as an author of evil. To be sure, he does not inflict the evil upon an innocent person. Pharaoh has sinned, and one punishment for his sin is that God takes away his capacity to hearken to the warnings that God continues to send, so that even his contrition is ephemeral (Exodus 9:27–35). Other narratives suggest that in spite of all the hymnic affirmations of the goodness of YHWH, he could still be seen as the instigator of evil and without the extenuating circumstance of the narrative challenge posed by the plague stories. King Saul's putative depression and paranoia, for example, are ascribed to "an evil spirit from the

Lᴏʀᴅ" (1 Samuel 16:14). There is no indication that the narrator regarded this expression as a contradiction in terms. Indeed, YHWH can be depicted elsewhere as the author of specific sins, even sins that result in the deaths of thousands, although, again, there is almost always an implication that it is human misdeeds that start the catastrophic chain of events. In 2 Samuel 24, for example, YHWH, angered for some obscure reason, "incited David against [Israel]" by ordering him to take a census (2 Samuel 24:1-2). David's aide, Joab, finds the order strange, but David is insistent, that is, until he is overcome by guilt feelings (2 Samuel 24:10). His confession, however, does not altogether avail; a pestilence fells 70,000 Israelites before David placates YHWH through sacrifice (2 Samuel 24:15, 25). Here, the assumption seems to be that YHWH needs a pretext to carry out the destruction that he desires. Rather than wait for the pretext, he creates it by commanding an action that he condemns.

The assumption is the same but more explicit in Ezekiel 20:25-26:

> Moreover, I gave them laws that were not good and rules by which they could not live: When they set aside every first issue of the womb, I defiled them by their very gifts—that I might render them desolate, that they might know that I am the Lᴏʀᴅ.

It is too simple to say that Ezekiel condemns child sacrifice as an offense to YHWH. Rather like some other biblical texts,[17] he views child sacrifices as a solid old YHWHistic practice, commanded by God himself—but no less evil as a result of this. God commands what he abhors so as to desolate its practitioners and to bring them thereby to an eerie recognition of his majesty.[18] He uses evil as a means to accomplish his purpose, which is beyond good and evil, good in a mysterious sense that is not impaired by his use of evil. In texts like these, divine sovereignty takes precedence over divine goodness. God's goodness is subordinate to his greatness and not identical with it. Man's task is to accept humbly the lordship of God without subjecting him to moral critique. In Job's words, "Should we accept only good from God and not accept evil?" (Job 2:10). This counsel is, like the God of Israel himself, simultaneously terrifying and comforting.

The theology that attributes both good and evil to God and therefore accepts both as somehow right is a theology that upholds God's providence at the expense of his goodness. He, the lord of all there is, decrees even that which opposes his good purpose. In this way, the monotheistic faith remains intact, for nothing that exists lies beyond God's power. To attribute autonomy and self-sufficiency to evil is to accept a kind of dualism, in which God is nothing more than deified goodness, unable, to all appearances, to eradicate evil. In that case, God's greatness would be subordinate to his goodness: in order for any event to be seen as an act of God, it would have to pass the test of goodness. Since so much reality would fail that test—the Nazi Holocaust and the prospect of Nuclear Omnicide come immediately to mind—one would be driven to wonder whether it is not the evil side of the great duality that is the more powerful and thus the more worthy of worship and imitation. By affirming God's sovereignty over evil and even his providential use of it, the theology under discussion is able to avoid many of the problems of its dualistic competitor.

On the other hand, the theology that accepts the notion that God can be the author of evil pays a dear price for its upholding of the interrelated classical ideas of monotheism, providence, and divine sovereignty, for it calls into doubt the existence of an absolute basis for the preference of good over evil. Indeed, it undercuts the very basis of trust in God, for if God's laws are not necessarily good and his revelations may not be in our best interests, then we must be ever on guard against the Deity himself. And if we are to practice the commandment of *imitatio Dei*, how are we to know which set of divine actions to imitate?[19] Are we to go into homicidal rages, deceive, and kill because God sometimes does? Surely, if our norms originate in God's will, he must want to observe them no less than we. "Shall not the Judge of all the earth deal justly?" (Genesis 18:25).

In the light of the problems involved in attributing evil to God under any circumstances (problems as imposing as those of never attributing evil to God in any way), it is not surprising that the tradition should have made efforts to soften some of the passages that we have been discussing. For example, when the Chronicler retells the story of David's census (2 Samuel 24) in 1 Chronicles 21, it is no longer YHWH, but Satan who "incited David to number Israel." (1 Chronicles 21:1) Here in this late book, the figure of Satan clearly is the result of a hypostatization of the evil side of YHWH: Those actions that one is squeamish about attributing to God are attributed to this maleficent angelic being. The goodness of God has been upheld at the expense of his sovereignty. Evil comes not from him, but from another divinity. But, if Satan is under YHWH's control, as he always is in the Hebrew Bible, then YHWH still cannot be altogether exonerated. A similar movement in the direction of the exculpation of God, somewhat more successful, can be seen in the way the rabbinic liturgy changes the biblical verse in which God boasts that He "makes peace and creates evil" (Isaiah 45:7).[20] In the first blessing before the morning *Shma'*, the words have been deliberately changed to "makes peace and creates *everything*." We read *everything* as a euphemism, as it is stated in the Talmud.[21] The euphemism qualifies the ostensible legitimation of evil in the verse without slipping into a dualism which would ascribe independence to evil. It upholds the goodness of God without making God into the deification of goodness, inspiring but powerless.

We have seen that the idea of God's goodness and the idea of his absolute sovereignty are in contradiction. Affirm either, and the other is cast into doubt. *It is characteristic of Judaism that it tends to accept the contradiction as tolerable rather than to reject it as fatal.* That is, Judaism generally sees it as a *paradox*, a mystery of the faith, if you will, or a creative tension, and it refuses to allow either idea to eradicate the other. Instead, the two are related dialectically. The passages in the Hebrew Bible that see God as a possible author of evil are real; they must not be explained away. But the passages that affirm his goodness without qualification, "that the Lord is upright,/my rock, in whom there is no wrong" (Psalm 92:16), are no less real and, in fact, far more numerous. The first set of passages keeps the second from becoming saccharine and escapist. The second set keeps the first from becoming the basis of a Jewish dualism or diabolism.

This dialectical theology of divine goodness and total sovereignty, in which each is read in light of the other, underscores our awareness of the eerieness, the uncanniness, the otherness of the God of Israel. It does not destroy this awareness. The "will to fellowship of the covenant God" is a large part of the theology of the Hebrew Bible. It is not the entirety of that theology. It is the truth, but not the whole truth. YHWH displays not only the benevolence of Ea; he also exemplifies the ambivalence of Enlil and Erra-Išum. Indeed, the tendency to depict the Deity as the *coincidentia oppositorum*, "the coincidence of opposites," is an ancient one, by no means unique to Israel. One thinks of the Hindu myth of the battle of the god Indra with the dragon Vritra, symbol of darkness and chaos, who is, in fact his brother.[22] Or one thinks "of Iranian Zervanism, according to which [the good] Ohrmazd and [the evil] Ahriman were both born of Zervan, the god of boundless time. Here we face the supreme effort of Iranian theology to transcend dualism and postulate a single principle that will explain the world."[23] The pre-Socratic philosopher Heraclitus, who flourished late in the sixth century B.C.E. in Ephesus, brings the idea to the level of self-consciousness: "Day (and) night, winter (and summer), war (and) peace, satiety (and) hunger—(all this together) is the god."[24] "For him," writes a noted historian of philosophy, "the conflict of opposites, so far from being a blot on the unity of the One, is essential to the being of the One. In fact, the One only exists in the tension of the opposites: this tension is essential to the unity of the One."[25]

The One of Israel has not uprooted the destructive forces that terrorized some ancient civilizations. He has opposed them or absorbed them in a divine nature that can be experienced, but cannot be characterized univocally. In the latter instance, the debate within the pantheon becomes an ambivalent monologue within the one God, although a monologue deeply affected by man's deeds and arguments. After the alleged "monotheistic revolution of Israel," we may still speak of destructive, homicidal forces, cosmic in scope. Only we must recognize that those forces are in tension with the benevolent, creative, and life-affirming dimension of God, a dimension that many of the texts believe will definitively emerge triumphant—though so far it has not.

DECIMATION AND REGENERATION

The most prominent interpretation of divine hostility in the Hebrew Bible, indeed in all Judaism, is the covenant theology. This is
the theology that correlates blessing with virtue, and curse with
transgression. Long lists of blessing and curses in the Torah make
it clear that if Israel keeps faith with her God and performs his
commandments (without exception), she will have health, wealth,
natural abundance, fertility, long life, and sovereignty, but that if
she breaks faith with her God and violates or neglects his commandments, then she will come to know disease, impoverishment,
famine, sterility, premature death, and exile (Leviticus 26 and
Deuteronomy 28).[26] It is this theology of correlation that underlies
the prophetic interpretation of history. The prophets were able to
interpret history moralistically because they were usually confident that people get what they deserve.

The covenant theology is in tension with the idea of a personal God. The God of the covenant can easily become a divine
change-machine: Put in a dollar bill, and you get out a dollar in
change—never more, never less. God becomes totally predictable, in fact unfree. Whereas man can choose his deeds, God's
are predetermined. He responds to us as a perfect machine
responds to its operator. That this mechanistic model of divinity is
false to the experience of this world was recognized in some
circles and in some periods in biblical times themselves. Complains a psalmist:

> All this has come upon us,
>   yet we have not forgotten You,
>   or been false to Your covenant.
>
> It is for Your sake that we are slain all day long
>   that we are regarded as sheep to be slaughtered.
> Rouse Yourself; why do You sleep, O Lord?
> Awaken, do not reject us forever! [Psalm 44:18, 23–24]

After the Holocaust, these words have a special poignancy. But
the problem of a God who retains sovereign freedom over his

covenant obligations and who may choose to neglect or even reverse them, making the chosen into the slaughtered, was recognized long before Auschwitz. In raising it, the Holocaust was anything but unique.

In passages like the one just cited, God's freedom from covenantal justice is terrifying. In us, as in the biblical authors, it provokes indignation. In other instances, however, God's deviation from the correlation stipulated in the covenant is bracing, and it evokes gratitude. Two examples should illustrate the point. The first is the covenant with Abraham and the other Patriarchs, Isaac and Jacob (Genesis 17:1–21). In this covenant, no conditional blessings are mentioned. On the contrary, the Patriarchal Covenant serves as a reservoir of grace to an Israel punished severely under the Covenant of Sinai:

> When I, in turn, have been hostile to them. . . . then at last shall their obdurate heart humble itself and they shall atone for their iniquity. Then will I remember My covenant with Jacob; I will remember also My covenant with Isaac, and also My covenant with Abraham; and I will remember the land. . . . Yet, even then, when they are in the land of their enemies, I will not reject them or spurn them so as to destroy them, annulling My covenant with them; for I the LORD am their God. I will remember in their favor the covenant with the ancients, whom I freed from the land of Egypt in the sight of the nations to be their God; I, the LORD. [Leviticus 26:41–45]

The oath to the Patriarchs cannot be retracted, the promise of the land is inviolable, and even the worst breaches of covenant on the part of Israel cannot bring her relationship to her God and suzerain to an end. YHWH's mysterious love for the people Israel and his oath to their ancestors is mightier than their worst imaginable sins. Grace limits justice: "He has not dealt with us according to our sins/nor has He requited us according to our iniquities" (Psalm 103:10).

Our second example of the pattern of God's benevolent suspension of justice is the insistence in much biblical literature upon the perdurable availability of repentance and God's unending willingness to accept penitents. Overtones of this idea can be heard in the passage from Leviticus cited above: The self-humbling of "their obdurate heart" induces God to remember the Patriarchal Covenant. In this instance, contrition plays the role of aromatic smoke in Genesis 8:21 and Numbers 17:12–13, changing hostility into favor. It removes God's attention from the conditionality of the Mosaic and fixes it instead onto the unconditionality of the Patriarchal Covenant. Elsewhere, repentance alone, without the Patriarchal Covenant, brings about the same restoration:

> When all these things befall you—the blessing and the curse that I have set before you—and you take them to heart amidst the various nations to which the LORD your God has banished you, and you return to the LORD your God, and you and your children heed His Command with all your heart and soul, just as I enjoin upon you this day, then the LORD your God will restore your fortunes and take you back in love. [Deuteronomy 30:1–3]

Here, although Israel's deeds are essential to her relationship with God, his love for her survives the corruption of those deeds and insures her a second chance at faithfulness and observance. Love does not provide exemption from law, nor grace from works. Rather, God's love and his grace insure the eternal availability of the laws to Israel and the eternal existence of an Israel to obey them. Even a justified cataclysm is not final.

Given human nature (which even chosenness does not overcome), these gracious extenuations are essential to human survival. Without them, the human propensity to evil would destroy the race, and justice untempered by grace would prove a death sentence:

> If you keep account of sins, O LORD,
>   LORD, who will survive?
> Yours is the power to forgive
>   so that You may be held in awe. [Psalm 130:3–4]

Unremittingly just, YHWH would soon lack worshippers. Therefore, although justice is essential both to the divine nature and to the divine–human relationship, both God and man have an interest in cultivating other aspects of the divine nature that can counteract it. A talmudic statement in the name of the Babylonian master Rav (third century C.E.) portrays God himself as offering this prayer:

> May it be My will that My mercy may overcome My anger and prevail over My [other] attributes and that I may deal with My children through the attribute of mercy and that I may, for their sake, stop short of the strict limit of justice.[27]

In rabbinic theology, the attribute of justice (*middat haddin*) is at odds with the attributes of mercy (*middat harachamim*). Here God prays that the latter will prevail. To be sure, its opponent in the divine monologue, the attribute of justice, is not to be identified with the demonic dimension of YHWH's personality discussed earlier. But although it is not demonic, divine justice shares with the demonic the fact that unchecked, it leads to human annihilation. "If you seek justice," a talmudic sage imagined Abraham to say to God, "there is no world, and if you seek a world, there is no justice."[28] Omnicide would result if God's prayer were not granted. The underlying assumption seems to be that we have no compelling claim upon divine mercy. (Indeed, mercy on which there is a compelling claim is no longer mercy, but justice.) The survival of the world appears here as unmotivated. It originates in the mystery of the unfathomable personality of God. In spite of our best efforts, which God not only desires but commands, we exist by his grace alone—so precarious is life. We survive only because of his inexplicable preference for mercy over justice.

Mediating between God's just annihilation of man, or at least of his covenant people, and his commitment to mercy is the idea of the remnant.[29] At times, prophets see the remnant of the coming cataclysm as hopeless. Indeed, occasionally they deny that it will exist at all:

> If they burrow down to Sheol
> From there my hand shall take them;
> And if they ascend to heaven,
> From there I will bring them down.

If they hide on the top of Carmel,
There I will search them out and seize them;
And if they conceal themselves from My sight
At the bottom of the sea,
There I will command
The serpent to bite them.
And if they go into captivity
Before their enemies,
There I will command
The sword to slay them.
I will fix My eye on them for evil
And not for good. [Amos 9:2–4]

Some prophetic texts, however, view the imminent catastrophe as a purgation: God is inducing Israel to repent, or he is cleansing them of their wicked:

But I will leave within you
A poor, humble folk,
And they shall find refuge
In the name of the LORD.
The remnant of Israel
Shall do no wrong
And speak no falsehood;
A deceitful tongue
Shall not be in their mouths.
Only such as these shall graze and lie down,
With none to trouble them. [Zephaniah 3:12–13]

As in the case of the Israelite flood-story and its Mesopotamian antecedents, the cataclysm is real but not final. A seed of life is preserved, and a new beginning is possible. Neither God's justice nor his promise is thwarted. He punishes transgressions and does not allow his mercy to overwhelm his justice, as if man's deeds were of no account and God did not hold obedience dear. But, at the same time, he bears with the nation and promises not to "sweep away the innocent along with the guilty" (Genesis 18:23). Indeed, the purpose of an oracle like that excerpted above is to provide an inducement for repentance: those who behave like the humble remnant will survive and find peace after the debacle. As in the case of the flood story, in which God finally renews the original blessings and mandates of creation (Genesis 9:1-3), so in the case of the remnant prophecies, God often promises to leave not merely a pathetic, if pure, little band, but to make of them the seed of restored glory:

In that day
—declares the LORD—
I will assemble the lame [sheep]
And gather the outcast
And those I have treated harshly;
And I will turn the lame into a remnant
And the expelled into a populous nation.
And the LORD will reign over them on Mount Zion
Now and forever more. [Micah 4:6-7]

Again, we must note that contrary to what is often asserted, Judaism is not optimistic; it is redemptive. Nothing in the present order of things can be identified as the seed out of which the new and better age to come will grow inevitably. The glorious new era that the prophets envisioned is not an evolutionary development, but rather a miraculous restoration after catastrophe—peace after war, mercy after justice, hope after hopelessness. In the prophetic vision things will get worse before they get better. But they *will* get better.

This curious mixture of optimism and pessimism is not unique to prophetic eschatology. It conforms to a more general biblical pattern in which the focus of divine favor is continually narrowing. The Torah illustrates the pattern nicely. At first, God pronounces all mankind to be "very good," and he blesses and sanctifies the crown and consummation of all creation, the Sabbath (Genesis 1:31; 2:3). But after the flood, it is only Noah and his family who are blessed, and the rights and responsibilities of creation continue in them alone (Genesis 9:1-2). Still, the new humanity, the humanity that emerges from Noah, is the recipient of a divine covenant (Genesis 9:8-17). Ten generations later, the themes of blessing and covenant reappear, only now fixed on one

man, Abram, from whom a whole nation is to appear (Genesis
12:1–3; 15:17–20). Yet the Patriarchal Covenant is not the birth-
right of all Abrahamites, but only of Isaac and his descendants
(Genesis 17:21), and then not of all Isaac's descendants, but only
of the line of Jacob/Israel, the others becoming slaves to Israel
(Genesis 27:28–29). "After all"—declares the LORD—"Esau is
Jacob's brother; yet I have accepted Jacob and have rejected Esau.
I have made his hills a desolation, his territory a home for beasts of
the desert" (Malachi 1:2–3). Even within God's covenant partner
Israel, the focus narrows, as Phinehas is granted the priesthood,
and David the throne, by eternal covenant (Numbers 25:10–13;
Psalms 89:20–38). In short, the Hebrew Bible displays a Chinese
doll effect of covenants within covenants. The scope of God's
focus is continually narrowing and then enlarging. Elections evoke
rejections. The prophetic identifications of the hopeful remnant
with the poor or the righteous or those faithful to YHWH (1 Kings
19:18) or the Diaspora (Jeremiah 24) are all manifestations of the
same pattern. The underlying theology is one that regards catastrophe as possible, imminent, and in most cases, just, yet refuses
to dwell on catastrophe or to see it as terminal and irreversible.
The positive word is last, but the last word is positive.

    Franz Rosenzweig (1886–1929), perhaps the profoundest reli-
gious mind that modern Judaism has as yet produced, observed
that:

> If the Messiah should come "today," the remnant will be ready to
> receive him. In defiance of all secular history, Jewish history is the
> history of this remnant; the word of the prophets, that it "will
> remain," even applies to it. All secular history deals with expansion.
> Power is the basic concept of history because in Christianity revela-
> tions began to spread over the world, and thus every expansionist
> urge, even that which consciously was purely secular, became the
> unconscious servant of this expansionist movement. But Judaism,
> and it alone in all the world, maintains itself by subtraction, by
> contraction, by the formation of ever new remnants. . . . In Judaism,
> man is always somehow a remnant. He is always somehow a survi-
> vor, an inner something, whose exterior was seized by the current of
> the world and carried off while he himself, what is left of him, remains
> standing on the shore. Something within him is waiting.[30]

That these words were written a generation before the Holocaust and by a man with no premonition of it but with a huge psychic investment in German Jewry is remarkable. They convey in modern language the exquisite sense of loss, but also hope and confidence that characterizes the remnant-theology. Only a remnant greets the messiah, yet it is the messiah whom the remnant greets.

It is in apocalyptic literature that the pattern of destruction followed by renewal reaches cosmic proportions. Indeed, some of the descriptions of the expected catastrophe in Jewish apocalypticism (including its Christian coda) bear an eerie resemblance to the nightmare of Nuclear Omnicide often conjured up today:

> Behold,
> The LORD will strip the earth bare,
> And lay it waste,
> And twist its surface,
> And scatter its inhabitants.
>
> The earth is withered, sere;
> The world languishes, it is sere . . .
> For the earth was defiled
> Under its inhabitants;
> Because they transgressed teachings
> Violated laws,
> Broke the ancient covenant.
> That is why a curse consumes the earth,
> And its inhabitants pay the penalty;
> That is why earth's dwellers have dwindled,
> And but a few men are left. [Isaiah 24:1, 4–6]

Although the modern secularist will doubt that the ancients had the capacity to provoke such a catastrophe, he still must not doubt that the apocalypticists thought they did. Moreover, unlike most modern secularists, the apocalypticists saw these horrific events as the prelude to the definitive and consummative victory of God, a victory that would not only restore the ruined past, but inaugurate a radically new and superior future. It is in that turn from hostility to benevolence, in that pivotal apocalyptic moment, that God overcomes, at long last, the persistent forces of evil, or, to change the metaphor, it is only then that he achieves a definitive integration of his ambivalent personality, as the living and the dead together enjoy the new age:

> The LORD of Hosts will make on this mount
> For all the peoples
> A banquet of rich viands,
> A banquet of choice wines—
> Of rich viands seasoned with marrow,
> Of choice wines well refined.
> And He will destroy on this mount the shroud
> That is drawn over the faces of all the peoples
> and the covering that is spread
> Over all the nations:
> He will destroy death forever.
> My LORD God will wipe the tears away
> From all faces
> And will put an end to the reproach of His people
> Over all the earth—
> For it is the LORD who has spoken.
>
> Oh, let Your dead revive!
> Let corpses arise!
> Awake and shout for joy,
> You who dwell in the dust!—
> For Your dew is like the dew on fresh growth;
> You make the land of the shades come to life. [Isaiah 25:6–8; 26:19]

God's victory is a victory over death itself: corpses rise. It is not simply that a remnant survives and replenishes the people and the world. Rather, the generation of the cataclysm lives to see the losses of all the generations made good. The destruction and desolation of the first phase of the apocalyptic era are not final. Indeed, from the perspective of the pivotal moment, that phase seems, amazingly, to have been a small interruption:

In slight anger, for a moment,
I hid My face from you;
But with kindness everlasting
I will take you back in love
—said the LORD your Redeemer. [Isaiah 54:8]

God triumphs over the destruction and the desolation and re-
deems the dead, who participate in the consummation of history.
It is in this apocalyptic eschatology that we find the origin of the
central rabbinic doctrine of *techiyat hammetim*, the resurrection
of the dead,[31] which becomes the last of the Thirteen Principles of
Judaism formulated by Maimonides and adapted into the liturgy.

The rabbis and Jewish philosophers recognized that the doctrine of the future resurrection of the dead was not simply a piece
of inherited lore, but a bearing beam in the edifice of Jewish faith.
What rests upon it finally is the issue of whether life is tragic or
comic, whether the real and gigantic horrors of this world are
ultimate or penultimate. If they are ultimate, then the Jewish
redemptive vision is false, and we must face our fate with stoic
resignation and with the tragic hero's dignity and resolve in the
face of hopelessness. If they are only penultimate, the "birth pangs
of the messiah," in the rabbinic idiom (only almost unbearably
prolonged), then life is comic in the highest and most serious
sense of the word, and the redemptive vision of the Hebrew Bible
and rabbinic literature is not an evasion, but a manifestation of the
awareness of the eternal and supernatural validity of hope. For
those who believe this world is the only world, the prospect of
Omnicide will only fortify their stoic resolve, even as they work to
avert doom. For those who have intimations of a world-to-come
and who allow themselves to trust those intimations, the prospect
of Omnicide is no less horrific and no less to be struggled against,
but neither is it the final world in God's surprising plan:

For behold! I am creating
A new heaven and a new earth;
The former things shall not be remembered,
They shall never again come to mind. [Isaiah 65:17][32]

NOTES

1. On the interpretation of Gilgamesh, see Thorkild Jacobsen, *The Treasures of Darkness: A History of Mesopotamian Religion* (New Haven and London: Yale University Press, 1976), pp. 195–219. But note that the flood-story is an interpolation into Gilgamesh from another tale, such as *Atra-Hasis* (see no. 10).

2. N. K. Sandars, *The Epic of Gilgamesh* (Harmondsworth, England: Penguin, 1964), p. 105. This is an elegant translation prepared from less elegant translations.

3. *Ibid.*, p. 107.

4. *Ibid.*, p. 109.

5. See Peter Machinist, "Rest and Violence in the Poem of Erra," *Journal of the American Oriental Society* 103 (1983), pp. 221–226. On the meaning of the names of the protagonists, see pp. 223–224, no. 16. An English translation and discussion of the text is Luigi Cagni, *The Poem of Erra* (Sources from the Ancient Near East 1/3; Malibu: Undena, 1977).

6. This is Jacobsen's (*Treasures*, p. 228) translation of Tablet IV, lines 6–12.

7. Machinist, pp. 223–224.

8. On this, see Jon D. Levenson, *Sinai and Zion: An Entry into the Jewish Bible* (San Francisco: Harper & Row, 1987), pp. 56–70.

9. Walther Eichrodt, *Theology of the Old Testament* (Philadelphia: Westminster, 1961), pp. 261–262. (This is a translation of Eichrodt's sixth edition [1959]; the first edition came out in 1933–1939.) I have transliterated the Greek word. Throughout the study, I have devocalized the tetragrammaton in quoting from authors where it appears with vowels.

10. See W. G. Lambert and A. R. Millard, *Atra-Hasis: The Babylonian Story of the Flood* (Oxford: Oxford University Press, 1969), pp. 55, 57.

11. Unless otherwise noted, all translations from the Hebrew Bible are taken from the new version produced by the Jewish Publication Society of America (Philadelphia), *The Torah* (1962), *The Prophets* (1978), and *The Writings* (1982). Permission to quote is gratefully acknowledged.

12. In these remarks, I am summarizing the more extensive discussion in Jon D. Levenson, *Creation and the Persistence of Evil: The Jewish Drama of Divine Omnipotence* (San Francisco: Harper & Row, 1988), pp. 78–127.

13. On this, see Levenson, *Creation and the Persistence of Evil*, pp. 3–50.

14. *Tanh., Kî tēsē'* 11.

15. I have translated this list of synonyms from P. Volz, *Das Dämonische in YHWH* (Sammlung gemeinverständlicher Vorträge und Schriften aus dem Gebiet der Theologie und Religionsgeschichte 110; Tübingen: J. C. B. Mohr/Paul Siebeck, 1924), p. 4. Volz's honest little book was a great aid to me in preparing all of the third section of this essay.

16. But note that the humane and rational ethic of chapter 18 cannot be generalized even throughout Ezekiel. See this horrific oracle three chapters later:

> Say to the land of Israel: Thus said the
> LORD: I am going to deal with you! I will
> draw My sword from its sheath, and
> I will wipe out from you both the righteous
> and the wicked. [Ezekiel 21:8]

17. Genesis 22:2 and Exodus 22:28. See also Micah 6:7.

18. See also 1 Kings 22, in which YHWH authorizes "a lying spirit" to enter the prophets so as to give Ahab the positive war-oracle that will bring about his death in combat (1 Kings 22:22–23).

19. The imitation of God appears occasionally as the warrant for a human practice, for example, the Sabbath (Exodus 20:8–11) or the pursuit of sanctity (Leviticus 19:1). But the biblical ethic would seem to prohibit the imitation of many other divine attributes.

20. Here, the JPS version (see no. 11) has not been used, as "create woe" does not quite convey the full measure of the statement. Of course, words like *ra'* ("evil, woe") can indicate either the quality of the agent's will or the effect upon the victim. The ambiguity seems to be deeply rooted in the Israelite worldview.

21. *Bavli Berachot 11b.*

22. Mircea Eliade, *The Two and the One* (London: Harvill; New York: Harper & Row, 1965), pp. 92–93.

23. *Ibid.*, p. 83.

24. The translation is taken from Felix M. Cleve, *The Giants of Pre-Socratic Greek Philosophy: An Attempt to Reconstruct Their Thoughts* (The Hague: Martinus Nijhoff, 1973), p. 57. The fact that Heraclitus was a younger contemporary of the anonymous Exilic author of Isaiah 40–55 may not be coincidence (see Isaiah 45:7).

25. Frederick Copleston, *A History of Philosophy, Volume I, Part I: Greece and Rome* (rev. ed.; Garden City, NY: Doubleday, 1962), p. 56.

26. On covenant, see Levenson, *Sinai and Zion*, pp. 23–86.

27. *Bavli Berachot 7a.* Since Babylonia in Rav's time was in the control of a zealous Zoroastrian dynasty, the resemblance of this prayer to the Zervanic dualistic monotheism already mentioned (see no. 23) is unlikely to be coincidence.

28. *Bereshit Rabbah* 49:9; *Leviticus Rabbah* 10:1; *Pesikta de-Rav Kahana, Nachamu* (Buber Edition), p. 125. (This is my translation.)

29. See Gerhard F. Hasel, *The Remnant: The History and Theology of the Remnant Idea from Genesis to Isaiah*, Andrews University Monographs V. (Berrien Springs, MI: Andrews University, 1982).

30. Franz Rosenzweig, *The Star of Redemption* (New York: Holt, Rinehart, and Winston, 1970), pp. 404–405. This is a translation of the second edition (1930). The first edition was published in 1921.

31. See Leonard J. Greenspoon, "The Origin of the Idea of Resurrection," in *Traditions in Transformation: Turning Points in Biblical Faith*, ed. Baruch Halpern and Jon D. Levenson (Winona Lake, IN: Eisenbrauns, 1981), pp. 247–321.

32. I thank Professors I. Tzvi Abusch, Robert L. Cohn, and Dr. Ronald A. Pascale for reading this paper and lending me their sage counsel. Any errors that remain are my responsibility.

4

Torah and Weapons of Mass Destruction: A View from Israel

Pinchas H. Peli

I call heaven and earth to witness against you this day, that I have set before you life and death, the blessing and the curse: therefore choose life that both you and your descendants may live (Deuteronomy 30:19).

Torah is clear and explicit when it speaks about life. Life is looked upon not only as a God-given blessing, but also as a challenge.

One cannot simply recline and wait passively for life to go one's way; one has "to choose life so that you and your descendants may live." There has never before been a time when this challenge of "choosing life" has confronted us more acutely and directly than it does now. Death has rallied the bulk of human skill and intellectual and material resources to produce its best and most efficient instrument ever: weapons of mass destruction. How does the Torah, also known as *Torat Hayim*, "a teaching for life," tell us how we should face this gravest challenge to life itself?

Of course, our dilemma could ideally be resolved by eliminating nuclear weapons completely. This would follow the eschatological visions of peace and harmony, which the prophets of Israel so poignantly expressed (Isaiah 2:3–4; Micah 4:1–7) and to which we unwaveringly cling, awaiting their eventual fulfillment.

There is much in Jewish tradition in praise of peace, and in denunciation of war or bloodshed in any form. This attitude confronting the enormity of nuclear, chemical, and biological warfare could instantly produce a vehement condemnation of the arms race. However, Torah deals not only with desirable or wishful thinking, but also and oftentimes specifically, with appalling reality. What, then, is the stand of Torah vis-à-vis the realities of the possession and use of weapons of mass destruction?

WHAT DO WE MEAN BY TORAH?

A French proverb says that "Only the details are really important." This is not true as far as the overall attitude of Torah to war and peace is concerned. In this case, details are crucial in providing us with a better understanding of the Torah's view of the actual situation which troubles us.

At this point let us define the concept of "Torah" for the purpose of this presentation. It is comprised of two integral and inseparable parts: *Halakhah* or "law," and *Aggadah*, or "lore." While *Halakhah* tells us *what* to do and *how* to perform the will of God as expressed in *Mitzvah* (precept or commandment), *Aggadah* tells us *why* we are supposed to behave in the manner thus prescribed. The two perspectives—the "how" and the "why"— must always be viewed together. Any attempt to view Torah (or for that matter, Judaism as a whole) through only *one* perspective—either as a "legal," or "legalistic," system or as a "prophetic" moralistic call—is doomed to fail. The very roots of the words emphasize this fundamental duality: *Halakhah* is from the root which connotes "walking," or "a way", and the root of *Haggadah* and *Aggadah* is "to tell." The way a Jew is called upon to follow must be accompanied with the Tale that is told about the Way.

Halakhah and Aggadah, which together make up the body and soul of Torah, require a *third* component: History. The greater part of the books of Torah which teach us the Halakhah and Aggadah of Judaism deals with a story—the story of the trials and tribulations of the people of Israel. The verses in the Pentateuch, covering the detailed itinerary of the children of Israel traveling through the desert on their way out of Egypt, are just as important and are read in the synagogue with the same solemnity as the verses "Hear, O Israel, the Lord our God is One" or "Thou shall not steal."

The history of the Jewish people thus becomes a vital component of Torah. When Ruth, the Moabite, expresses her desire to accept the God of Israel, she does not only say "your God will be my God," but precedes that statement with: "Your people will be my people," and follows it up with: "Wherever you die, I will die" (Ruth 1:16–17). She thereby joins the history of the people of Israel and declares her readiness to share its fate, not only its faith.

In the light of this definition of Torah, as law, lore, and Jewish history, let us examine the subject at hand.

ALL IN THE SAME BOAT

Indeed, we are not dealing with an abstract situation, but rather one reflected in the actual life of the people of Israel. This state in the midst of the historical process of restoration of its homeland has been assaulted seven times militarily and is threatened with destruction and annihilation. Even so, we must not ignore the fact that nuclear war is a universal and fatal threat to humankind as such. No isolation can save the State of Israel from sharing the fate of the world. We are all in the same boat. And that is why I believe that the view of Torah in regard to nuclear weapons, and to a lesser extent, biological and chemical armaments, also is not divisible, although it would have to take into consideration the particular historical circumstances which prevail regarding the people and the State of Israel.

As to the universal threat of destruction of the world through the weapons of mass destruction, the view of Torah is crystal clear: The world created by God was meant for life; it was given over to Man to rule, to preserve and cultivate, and not to destroy and mutilate. Man is committed to the construction of the world, and under no circumstances to its destruction. This founding principle is well established both in Halakhah and Aggadah.

The very story of creation of heaven and earth by a purposeful and free-willed Creator are the opening words of Torah. It reaches its climax with the introduction of the Sabbath which in a way transfers the task of creation from God alone to God with Man as his faithful partner. Thus the word la-asot at the end of the passage introducing the Sabbath—"for on it He desisted from all his work which he created la-asot (and made)" (Genesis 2:3)— was interpreted by Jewish commentators to read: "which He (God) created la-asot"—to continue-to-be-done by God and Man as partners. The prophet Isaiah stresses this point clearly: "The Creator of heaven Who alone is God, Who formed the earth and made it, Who alone established it, did not create it for a waste, but formed it for habitation" (Isaiah 45:18).

The rabbis in their peculiarly picturesque language put it this way in the Midrash:

> When the Holy One encountered the first human being, He took it before all the trees in the Garden of Eden and said "See how lovely and excellent My works are. All that I have created, I have created for you. Consider this carefully, do not corrupt or desolate my world. For if you corrupt or desolate it, there is no one to set it aright after you." [Kohelet Rabbah 7:28]

God himself trusted that this world was never to be destroyed. Thus, the rabbis interpreted the verse in Deuteronomy (32:4), "A God of trust and not iniquity," as "a God who trusts his world and goes on creating it." Thereafter, he binds himself with an oath in covenant with Man not to wreck the world (Genesis 9:8–17). The rainbow remains forever the sign of this irrevocable covenant.

This is the voice of Aggadah. In the Tale we have been told about the meaning and the preciousness of the world created by God and our own responsibility for its preservation and cultivation. This understanding, however, cannot remain merely in the realm of the abstract. The genuine way of Torah demands its proper translation via Halakhah into actual life realities.

TRANSLATED INTO PRACTICE

One is not allowed to willfully destroy any created being. This prohibition is known in Halakhah as *bal tash'hit*—Do not destroy, or corrupt. The rabbis, of course, derive this prohibition from Scripture: "When thou shalt besiege a city a long time, in making war against it to take it, thou shalt not destroy the trees thereof by wielding an axe against them: for thou mayest eat of them, and thou shalt not cut them down" (Deuteronomy 20:10).

The rabbinic interpretation of the above verses stresses the fact that Torah deals here with the extraordinary circumstances of war when normal laws are usually suspended. Yet *even then* we are to watch out for trees, which are not to be destroyed; so *how much more* may we not destroy trees, or anything else that is useful in normal times. This has been codified into law (*Avodah Zarah* 11; *Baba Metzia* 32; Maimonides Code, section Kings). A heretic, one who does not believe in God and in his purposeful creation is called "a destroyer of trees" (*Tosefta Hagigah* 2:3).

Certainly Halakhah and Aggadah join hands when it comes to the preservation of human life. Human life belongs to God, not to Man; one must, therefore, watch over it carefully, directly and indirectly, both in peace and in war. This concept of the priceless value of human life is expressed often in Aggadah as well as in Halakhah, which again has to deal with real situations rather than with ideal aspirations. The two perspectives are often invoked to emphasize the importance of this subject. As for instance in the following *Mishnah* (*Sanhedrin* 37a–37b):

> How were the witnesses inspired with awe? Witnesses in capital charges were brought in and intimidated (thus): Perhaps what you say is based only on conjecture, or hearsay, or is evidence from the mouth of another witness, or even from the mouth of a trustworthy person. Perhaps you are unaware that ultimately

we shall scrutinize your evidence by cross examination and inquiry?

Know then that capital cases are not like monetary cases. In
civil suits, one can make monetary restitution and thereby effect
his atonement: but in capital cases one is held responsible for the
blood of the accused, and the blood of his (potential) descendants
until the end of time, as we find in the case of Cain, who killed his
brother. Thus, it is written: "The bloods of thy brother cry unto
me": not the blood of thy brother, but the bloods of thy brother, his
blood and the blood that is, of his (potential) descendants. For this
reason was man created alone, to teach you that whosoever destroys a single soul, Scripture imputes (guilt) to him as though he
had destroyed a complete world, and whosoever preserves a single
soul, Scripture ascribes (merit) to him as though he had preserved
an entire world.

After cautioning the witness on the grave responsibility he
bears, the Mishnah continues:

Perhaps you will say, why get into this anxiety? [Know then:]
Is it not already written, he being a witness, whether he has seen
and known, if he does not utter it—he becomes a partner to the
crime. And should you say: Why should we bear guilt for the blood
of this [man], why testify? Surely, however, it is said (Proverbs
11:10) "when the wicked perish, there is rejoicing."

A careful reading of this Mishnah teaches us three lessons:
(1) How seriously human life is to be taken. (2) How great the
value is of the life of one individual: This principle is borne out by
many other halakhic rulings which presuppose that, when dealing
with human life, quantity does not matter at all, and that the life of
one person cannot be weighed against the welfare of many. (3)
The third lesson comprises the conclusion, which is arrived at as
follows: If taking the life of a person is so serious (and the Mishnah
earlier in the same source lists many other restrictions on capital
punishment which practically amount to its total abolishment),
why should the potential witness not shun testifying and thereby
perhaps save a human being from prosecution? No, says the
Mishnah, you are not allowed to play the role of the "nice,"

moralistic person. It is sinful to stay "clean" and "not get involved." When justice is executed it may often cause pain, but
there is also enjoyment of the good in this pain, asserts the
Mishnah, basing itself on Scripture (Proverbs 11:10), "When the
wicked perish there is rejoicing."

HIGH-POWERED TENSION OF AMBIVALENCE

This brings us to the crux of the tension that is inherent in the
view of Torah on all problems related to evil. Evil must be combat-
ted relentlessly and yet one must beware not to cause damage to
the image of God that is imprinted upon us, nor wreck the world
created by God and entrusted to us as its guardians.

Only one chapter, forty-seven verses in the text of Torah,
separates the unconditional commandment "Thou shall not kill"
(Exodus 20:13) from the text (Exodus 22:37) whence the rabbis
learn the rule that "if someone comes to kill you—be prepared to
kill him first." Human life being sacred and precious, the Torah
enjoins us not only not to kill others but also not ourselves; suicide
is considered a grave sin. By the same token there is no virtue at
all in the eyes of Torah to allowing yourself to be killed by others,
or in passively allowing a would-be aggressor to reach the point
where he could carry out his intent to kill you.

Torah realizes the high-powered tension into which this ambivalence places us. In the light of Torah, Halakhah tries to offer
practical solutions to dilemmas liable to arise from this dual attitude, which basically stems from one source: the sacredness of
human life, every individual human life. To cite one example: All
prohibitions promulgated by Torah are abrogated in face of a
threat to one's life. If the fulfillment of a precept of Torah is to risk
one's life, the ruling is clear: Torah is to be put aside and human
life saved. There are, however, a few exceptions to this rule. Three
transgressions must never be committed even though it may
mean the ultimate sacrifice of one's own life. These are idolatry,
incest, and murder. By murder, we mean that if a person is
ordered to murder someone else and threatened that if he refuses
to do so he will be killed himself, the latter is to be preferred. The

obvious case that arises is the one in which one's own life is viewed as a much more valuable asset to society than that of the fellow to be slain. In this case, it is still a situation of one life against another. The rabbis' response (*Sanhedrin* 74a) is, after all is said and done, "Who says your blood is sweeter, perhaps his is sweeter?" In other words, one cannot save one's own skin at the price of sacrificing another person. On the other hand, if one sees a person pursuing another person with the intention of murdering him, one is supposed to kill the would-be murderer and save the person that is being pursued—in this case not himself, but a third person. Further, when an entire town is besieged under threat of being annihilated unless it hands over one particular person, the entire town should die rather than deliver to death the one person demanded. Again, the reason is the same: life can never be measured quantitatively.

This is the kind of reverence and responsibility for life that is rooted in Torah, and preached and practiced in both Halakhah and Aggadah as they are reflected in Jewish history and throughout the generations.

BETWEEN "POSSESSION" AND "USE"

The position of Torah towards both world and life sheds ample light on the subject of Omnicide. We must remember to distinguish between the powerful thrust of the Torah point of view, which clearly abhors the demonic destructive power of weapons of mass destruction and the possible solutions to actual problems incurred by the "possession" and "use" of such weapons in a given imperfect historical situation. There is, of course, quite a distance between "possession" and "use," but their proximity and interdependence are obvious and need not be elaborated upon here.

Even when the purpose of possessing nuclear arms is to serve as a "deterrent" to preserve the "balance of terror" and thereby restrain the "other side" from carrying out its "evil designs," would Torah consider the very possession of lethal weapons as "evil?"

The answer to this question in the light of Torah is not one-sided. While the great dream of the prophets of Israel is a time of perfect peace, when swords should be beaten into plowshares and spears into pruning hooks, when nation would not raise sword against nation and "they shall learn war no more"—one might say without hesitation that Torah is *not* pacifistic and the use of weapons is not always abhorrent. It is unquestionably worse *not* to possess weapons when clearly faced with a murderous aggressor. Moses, the greatest moral lawgiver of all time, was also a warrior and even began his career as the "killer" of an evildoer. Singing God's praises, Moses calls God himself "a man of battle" (Exodus 15:3), one who used a "strong hand" to deliver His people from the tight claws of their evil oppressors. David, the sweet singer of Israel, is perhaps less pleasant when he sings "Blessed be the Lord my rock, who teaches my hands how to battle, to use my fingers for war" (Psalms 144:1). From Moses and David down to the last of the rabbis, weapons (alas, not always in their possession due to the helplessness of Diaspora living conditions) were looked upon at the very least as a "necessary evil," at most as an ornament that befits a man. Thus, we find in the Mishnah's discussion of the laws of carrying on the Sabbath the following controversy between Rabbi Eliezar and the sages:

> A man may not go out on the Sabbath with a sword or a bow or a shield or a club or a spear. If he goes out with any of these he is liable to a sin-offering. Rabbi Eliezar says: They are his adornments. But the sages say they are only a reproach, for it is written (Isaiah 2:4): "And they shall beat their swords into plowshares and their spears into pruning hooks; nation shall not lift sword against nation, neither shall they learn war anymore." [*Shabbat* 6:4]

Here Halakhah and Aggadah converge; the practical and the ideal inform each other. The great Hebrew poet Hayyim Nahman Bialik (in his famous essay "On Halakhah and Aggadah") sees this as a striking example how the lofty ideals of Judaism are encased in the shell of laws and rules, how the prophet Isaiah appears on the scene as the rabbis are discussing a minute detail of law.

"BLOOD UPON THY HOUSE"

When we ask whether the possession of weapons of mass destruction even for the sake of a "good" purpose is permissible, as its very existence may trigger the worst imaginable consequences, we have to deal with this question in the typical way of rabbinic study of Torah. Where there is no direct answer to a certain question, analogous principle is applied to examine the question at hand.

Here is a possible analogy to the question of right and wrong in the act of the possession of these globally lethal weapons which may lead to using such weapons. We read in the Torah (Deuteronomy 22:8): "When thou buildest a new house, then thou shalt make a parapet for the roof, so that thou bring not blood upon thy house, if any man falls from thence."

In expounding this passage, Rabbi Nathan (a second-century sage) said: "Whence is it derived that a man may not breed a vicious dog in his house nor place a shaking ladder in his house? (From Scripture), where it is said, 'that thou bring not blood upon the house.'"

The very fact of (passively) not building a railing on the roof of your new house or (actively) bringing a vicious dog or a shaky ladder into your house makes you liable "to bring blood upon your house." You did not set the dog to bite anyone, nor force anyone to climb the shaky ladder, but by being in possession of such harmful things, you become responsible, perhaps even guilty, if anything happens.

Following this line of thought from Torah, which is expressed in many other writings as well (cf. Exodus 21:33; Leviticus 19:14), one should take a clear stand against the possession of weapons of mass destruction. Once in the house, who knows when one will come to use it by design or by mistake. However, here too, when faced with certain realities, the "vicious dog" is not always barred from the house. Halakhah suggests a number of exceptions to the rule against the possession of a "vicious dog." For instance, one is allowed to keep the dog as long as he is kept chained (Mishnah, Baba Kama 7:7). Even this restriction does not apply equally in all situations. In a town close to the border, the vicious dog is to be kept chained during the day only, and unchained at night for security reasons. Possession of dangerous materials could easily "bring blood upon thy house"; one should therefore not have them in the house. If, however, they have to be in one's possession, one must take the necessary precautions and make sure to have the proper "chain" and lock in order to curb escalation from "possession" of the dreadful stuff to its "use."

THE REALITY FROM THE "OTHER SIDE"

The dreadful descriptions of the possible results of a nuclear holocaust defy the most outrageous science fiction. They border on the mysterious, on that which is beyond our human grasp, and loom "on the other side" of our human existence. The enormity of the concept may be part of the reason why it is far from easy for us to relate to the subject. "Holocaust" is a term that belongs to the "other side," to "another planet," and yet we know that it is nevertheless painfully real. Who knows this more than the Jewish people? While others talk with dread of a possible holocaust—we are sensitized to it after experiencing it on our own flesh. We, too, are unable to confront it. Even for us it lies beyond comprehension; it is the great mystery. How shall we deal with it? The rabbis in the Talmud (*Hagigah* 14b) tell us of four great men of the early second century who dared to penetrate the great mystery. The "four who entered the orchard" are Ben Azai, Ben Zoma, Aher (Elisha Ben Abuya), and Rabbi Akiva (an early second-century sage from the Land of Israel). What happened to them? Ben Azai, we are told, looked and died. Ben Zoma looked and became demented. Aher mutilated the roots. Only Rabbi Akiva entered and departed safely.

The examples of Rabbis Ben Azai, Ben Zoma, Aher, and Akiva represent different ways of responding to Omnicide. One response is death: You cannot fight it—be prepared to die. The second response is to lose one's sanity and stamina in face of the crisis. The third alternative, the one chosen by Aher, is to join the forces of evil, following the old maxim of political pragmatists: If you cannot beat them—join them. The only one who came out of the "orchard" unhurt was Rabbi Akiva—the one who was ready to face the forces of evil, he alone overcame them.

The Jewish people are alive today because they followed in the footsteps of Rabbi Akiva. Coming out of the Holocaust prepared for us by the Western Christian world, we decided that we are not dead, as some of our enemies would like us to be. We did not lose our wits, but managed to emerge from the ashes and decided to go on rebuilding our homeland. And we certainly did not survive by joining the forces of evil. In any case, we so often find ourselves abandoned by others, defending ourselves against forces which, in many different disguises, are trying to annihilate the Jewish people.

THE VIEW FROM ISRAEL

Of course, we are bound by Torah and tradition to make every effort to save the world from a nuclear holocaust. Yet, we who experienced a terrible Holocaust, which victimized many millions of innocent people know very well that to preach piously against it is to expose ourselves again to the agents of evil. If Hitler had been taken more seriously four decades ago, perhaps we could have stayed the forces that implemented the Holocaust.

If anyone has a right to possess nuclear weapons in order to deter murderous aggression, Israel is the country that irrefutably should have such a right. It is, after all, the only state in the world that is threatened openly and constantly with total destruction. Such threats have to be taken seriously. Auschwitz and Treblinka are still with us. To the Jewish people "Final Solutions" through annihilation are not a nightmarish fairy tale.

I do not know if Israel has developed the ultimate weapon (the old adage still prevails: Those who know don't talk; those who talk don't know). But again, if Torah is a practical guide it may offer a way—Halakhah—of translating an ideal—Aggadah—into day-to-day reality. Israel must offer safeguards that will keep the "vicious dogs" chained, as it is so strongly concerned with the preservation of the world and with the survival of human life.

"When God created iron (on the third day of creation) the trees began to weep, and when God asked the reason for their tears, they said: We cry because Thou hast created the iron to uproot us therewith. All the while we had thought ourselves the highest of the earth, and now the iron, our destroyer, has been called into existence. God replied: *Your yourselves* will furnish the axe with a handle. *Without your assistance* the iron will not be able to do anything against you."[1]

It is true that the threat of nuclear weapons is unprecedented and endangers us all. But it is equally true that it is up to us to save ourselves and the world from possessing weapons of mass destruction. Nothing will be done to us—if we would not do it. Torah tells us that we are capable, as well as commanded, of doing the right thing.

NOTES

1. Louis Ginzberg, *The Legends of the Jews*. Trans. from the manuscript of Henrietta Szold (Philadelphia: Jewish Publication Society of America, 1966), vol. 1, p. 19.

5

A Jewish Understanding of War and Its Limits

Reuven Kimelman

Jewish teachings on war focus on two issues: When can war be waged; and how can war be fought. Classical Jewish teachings distinguish between "mandatory wars" and "discretionary wars." Mandatory wars (*milhemet mitsvah/hovah*) refer to biblically commanded wars. Discretionary wars (*milhemet reshut*) are wars undertaken at the discretion of the Sanhedrin or a duly constituted representative body.

It is generally agreed that there are three types of mandatory wars, such as: (1) Joshua's war of conquest against the seven Canaanite nations; (2) the war against Amalek; and (3) a defensive war against an already launched attack. It is also generally agreed that an expansionary war undertaken to enhance the political prestige of the government or to secure economic gains is clearly discretionary.[1]

Not all three categories of mandatory war are of current concern. The Canaanite nations, having lost their national identity in ancient times, are removed from current considerations. The Talmud attributes this to the Assyrian policy of mass deportation and exchange of populations.[2] This judgment coheres with a pronounced tendency to blunt the impact of the seven-nation rulings. According to 1 Kings 9:20 ff., these policies were not implemented even during the zenith of ancient Israel's power. Maimonides is quite adamant that all trace of them has vanished.[3] A midrash is at pains to guarantee that the rulings with regard to the seven nations not be extended to the other nations that then resided in Canaan.[4] Limiting the jurisdiction of the seven-nation material to a particular time and place renders it inoperative for subsequent times. The result is that the directives to Joshua vis-à-vis the seven autochthonous nations of Canaan cannot serve as precedent for contemporary practice. Amalek has generally been transformed into a metaphor for sheer evil or rendered operationally defunct by making it a category of the premessianic struggle.

The two remaining categories, defensive and expansionary wars, are neatly classifiable as mandatory and discretionary respectively. So, for example, King David's war against the Philistines is termed mandatory,[5] while his wars "to expand the border of Israel" were termed discretionary.[6] Intermediate classifications such as preventive, anticipatory, or preemptive are not as neatly drawn. Not only are the classifications debated by the rabbis,[7] but major talmudic commentators, such as Rashi and Meiri, disagree on the meaning of the differing positions.

According to Rashi, the majority rabbinic position holds preventive action to be discretionary while Rabbi Judah considers a preemptive war to be mandatory.[8]

According to Meiri,[9] a preemptive strike against an enemy from whom an attack is feared or who is known to be preparing for war is considered mandatory by the majority of the rabbis, but only discretionary by Rabbi Judah. According to Meiri, Rabbi Judah considers a counterattack mandatory only if the enemy has already launched an attack.

The position codified by Maimonides also limits the mandatory classification to a defensive war launched in response to an attack.[10] The remaining part of this discussion of war and its limits deals with the significance of the terminological distinction between mandatory and discretionary wars. There are four basic questions involved: May the mandatory classification of a defensive war be extended to include preemptive strikes? Which branch of government makes the decision to wage war? How may the war be conducted? And finally who is subject to the draft?

PREEMPTIVE STRIKES

There is a widespread consensus that the right to national self-defense is as much a moral right as is self-preservation. One does not have to be Machiavellian to view the security and survival of the state as "hors de discussion." The question is whether the inalienable right of self-defense is limited to an already launched attack. This apparently is the position of the majority, according to Rashi, and that of Rabbi Judah, according to Meiri. This position has also been accepted in Article 51 of the United Nations Charter, which reads "Nothing in the present Charter shall impair the inherent right of individual or collective self-defense if an armed attack occurs against a member. . . ." On the other hand, Rabbi Judah, according to Rashi, and the majority, according to Meiri, hold that a preemptive strike against an enemy who is preparing for attack, even though it has not yet gone beyond its borders, is sufficiently similar to a defensive counterattack to be considered "mandatory."

This position holds that to wait for an actual attack might so jeopardize national security as to make resistance impossible. Such an argument was championed by Lord Chancellor Kilmuir before the House of Lords when he remarked with reference to Article 51: "It would be a travesty of the purpose of the Charter to compel a defending state to allow its opponents to deliver the first fatal blow."[11]

The United States House Appropriations Committee endorsed the concept of a preemptive attack in the following report:

> In the final analysis, to effectively deter a would-be aggressor, we should maintain our armed forces in such a way and with such an understanding that should it ever become obvious that an attack upon us or our allies is imminent, we can launch an attack before

the aggressor has hit either us or our allies. This is an element of deterrence which the United States should not deny itself. No other form of deterrence can be relied upon.[12]

This understanding of anticipatory defense allows a counter-attack while the initial attack is being mounted. Under the terms of modern warfare, for example, if an enemy were to launch a missile attack, the United States could strike back even if their missiles had not yet penetrated the airspace of the United States or its allies. Such a counterattack is clearly within the limits of self-defense and justly deemed mandatory.

The doctrine of anticipatory defense would allow for a preemptive strike even if the missiles were still in their launching pads, as long as the order had been issued for their launching.

THE AUTHORIZATION OF WAR

The second major difference between a mandatory war and a discretionary war lies with the branch of government empowered to authorize war. A mandatory war is an executive decision. A discretionary war requires the advice and consent of the Sanhed-rin[13] or its judicial/legislative equivalent.

The obligation to participate in a mandatory defensive war flows from three assumptions. The first two assume that national defense is based on an analogue of individual self-defense[14]; and that national defense is required by the verse "Do not stand idly by the blood of your neighbor"[15] (as Leviticus 19:16 was under-stood). The implication is that the duty to come to the rescue of countrymen under attack is comparable to the duty to intervene in order to rescue one from an assailant.[16]

These two assumptions alone are inadequate. After all, if es-cape is available, self-defense is optional. Moreover, classical legal opinion is divided on the obligation of risking life for another.[17] The result is that the domestic analogy alone remains insufficient for extrapolating the right of national defense from the right of home defense.

To justify the risk of life in the name of national defense, an added consideration must be called for, namely the assumption that in order to save the community,[18] obligations to the collective mandate the risk of life. Thus, responsibility to the security of the community assumes added weight when the community is entrusted with the protection of the total citizenry.

In a defensive war when the enemy has attacked, the lives of the citizenry have already been placed in jeopardy. The counter-attack constitutes an effort to diminish the risk, not increase it. Such is not the case in wars that aim at extending the political or economic influence of the government. Even in a preemptive attack, according to one school of thought, the lack of imminent danger to the population prevents the executive from risking on his own the lives of the citizenry. Whether a policy of war should be endorsed or not is left to the discretion of the Sanhedrin.

There are several reasons for involving the Sanhedrin in the decision-making process of a discretionary war. The Sanhedrin is considered the legal embodiment of popular sovereignty, the "adah" in biblical terms.[19] Maimonides held the high court to be the legal equivalent of "the community of Israel as a whole."[20] He used interchangeably the phrases "according to the majority of Israel" and "according to the high court."[21] In fact, former Chief Rabbi Shlomo Goren has argued that the requirement to secure the Sanhedrin's approval in a discretionary war derives from its representative authority.[22]

The Sanhedrin is also the authoritative interpreter of the Torah-Constitution. Since the judicial interpretation of the law is structurally separate from its executive enforcement, the Sanhedrin can serve as a restraint on executive power.

It may be concluded that the role of the Sanhedrin in a discretionary war is to safeguard the lives of the citizenry without the approval of those who represent them, and whose role it is to interpret the original contract wherein the duties of citizenship are stated. This assumes a type of social contract between government and the people. The people commit themselves to the state as long as the state does not unnecessarily risk their lives. This type of covenantal relationship can be traced back to a biblical perspective which assumes that mutual agreement interlocks the people and the monarch.[23]

The following analysis suggests that before granting authorization, it is incumbent upon Sanhedrin to weigh the probable losses, to consider the chances of success, and to assess the will of the people. Since war always costs lives, the cost in lives has to be measured against the chance of success. These calculations are made by that deliberative body which sees itself as most representative of the people and which is most likely to be objective.

A chief executive who may perceive war as an opportunity for enhancing his personal prestige or for consolidating his political base would not be sufficiently disinterested to qualify for rendering such life-endangering decisions. It is too easy for a head of state to confuse, in all sincerity, his interests, or those of his administration, with the national interest. All the more so, if he is purposely masking his intentions. Josephus underscores this concern by noting that the biblical laws of warfare are intended to prevent war "wage(d) for self-aggrandizement," indeed, "they deter them (Israel) from war for sake of conquest."[24]

THE CONDUCT OF WAR

Despite the requirement to calculate chances of success, victory alone is not decisive; the price of victory must be considered. This is difficult to weigh in advance, for while theorists may predict outcomes, combatants are struck by the all-pervasive unpredictability of the course of events. This awareness apparently lies behind Rabbi Eleazar's statement that "any war which involves more than sixty thousand is necessarily chaotic."[25] Indeed, Mar Samuel allowed a regime to lose up to one sixth of its fighting forces before being charged with criminality.[26]

Since preventive warfare is unwarranted if the number of lives saved does not significantly exceed the number of lives jeopardized, it is incumbent upon the Sanhedrin to undertake a cost analysis. This role of the Sanhedrin is spelled out by J. David Bleich: "The Sanhedrin is charged with assessing the military,

political and economic realities and determining whether a proposed war is indeed necessary and whether it will be successful in
achieving its objectives."[27]

Estimating one's own losses is insufficient. The whole destruction ratio required for victory must be considered. This
assessment involves a "double intention," that is, the "good" must
appear achievable and the "evil" reducible.

Thus, for example, prior to laying siege to a city, there is a
need to assess whether it can be captured without destroying it.[28]
There is no warrant for destroying a town "in order to save it."

The other rules for sieges follow similar lines of thought.
Indefensible villages may not be subjected to a siege. Nor may
peace terms be exacted from the enemy before negotiations have
begun, by subjecting a city to a blockade of hunger, thirst, or
disease. Messengers of peace must be sent to a hostile city for
three days. If the terms are accepted, well and good, no harm will
befall any inhabitants of the city. Even if the terms are not accepted, the actual siege is not to begin before the enemy has
opened hostilities. Only then may the siege begin with all rigor and
severity. A city may even be subjected to a blockade of hunger,
thirst, or disease with the intention of securing its capitulation or
fall. No direct cruelties, apparently, against the inhabitants may be
inflicted, even under siege. One side must be left unbesieged in
order to permit people to escape.[29]

Although Philo assumes that the city subjected to siege had
reneged on its treaty obligation, his rendition of the biblical material is in the same spirit of the aforementioned midrashic material.
He writes:

> They must . . . send heralds to propose terms of agreement and at
> the same time point out the military efficiency of the besieging
> power. And if their opponents repent of their rebellious conduct
> and give way and show an inclination to peace, the others must
> accept and welcome the treaty, for peace, even if it involves great
> sacrifices, is more advantageous than war.[30]

Nonetheless, Philo continues: "If the adversaries persist in their
rashness to the point of madness, they [the besiegers] must

proceed to the attack invigorated by enthusiasm and having in the justice of their cause an invincible ally."[31]

What is common to both Philo and the rabbinic tradition is the assumption that although armies are entitled to try to win wars, they are not entitled to deploy all means that seem to them necessary to win. Even military necessity must be balanced by some notion of proportionality. Armies are generally entitled to do what they must to win, indeed, with all due haste to bring the hostilities to a close. Justified acts of destruction are limited, however, to those that advance the goal of victory. Purposeless violence or wanton destruction is ruled out.

The biblical balance between military and moral considerations is spelled out by Philo:

> All this shows clearly that the Jewish nation is ready for agreement and friendship with all like-minded nations whose intentions are peaceful, yet is not of the contemptible kind which surrenders through cowardice to wrongful aggression.[32]

Lack of cowardice, though, does not imply lack of moral distinctions between combatants as legitimate military targets and noncombatants as illegitimate ones. As Philo notes:

> When it takes up arms it distinguishes between those whose life is one of hostility and the reverse. For to breathe slaughter against all, even those who have done very little or nothing amiss, shows what I should call a savage and brutal soul.[33]

Philo, referring to Deuteronomy 20:19–20, extends the doctrine of the immunity of noncombatants to explain the prohibition against vandalizing the environs of the besieged city:

> Indeed so great a love for justice does the law instill into those who live under its constitution that it does not even permit the fertile soil of a hostile city to be outraged by devastation or by cutting down trees to destroy the fruits. . . . Does a tree, I ask you, show ill will to the human enemy that it should be pulled up roots and all, to punish it for ill which it has done or is ready to do to you?[34]

Maimonides, codifying an expansion of the prohibition against cutting down fruit-bearing trees to include almost all wanton destruction, states, "Also one who smashes household goods, tears clothes, demolishes a building, stops up a spring, or destroys articles of food with destructive intent transgresses the command "You shall not destroy."[35]

Similarly, Josephus, expanding on the biblical material, mentions a prohibition against burning the countryside,[36] thereby expressing a repugnance to a scorched-earth type policy.

The case for the immunity of noncombatants takes the form of two a fortiori arguments. Deuteronomy explains the prohibition of destroying trees by asking rhetorically, "Are trees of the field human to withdraw before you under siege?" (20:19). It follows that just as a tree, having fled, would not be chopped down, so a person, were he to flee, should not be cut down. Furthermore, the ruling that a fourth side of a besieged city be left open indicates that if (unarmed) soldiers have the right to become refugees, all the more so do noncombatants and other neutrals.

This extrapolation is made explicit by Josephus. He says the legislator commands Jews to:

> show consideration even to declared enemies. He . . . forbids even the spoiling of fallen combatants; he has taken measures to prevent outrage to prisoners of war, especially women.[37]

The Israel Defense Forces refers to this as the "purity of arms" doctrine. It has been maintained under wartime conditions.[38] These ethical intrusions into the waging of war have two foci: the moral character of the soldier; and humanity of the enemy. With regard to the former, Philo, as cited above, feels the Torah is worried about the brutalization of the soldier's soul; Nahmanides thinks the Torah is concerned with the soldier "learn(ing) to act compassionately with our enemies even during wartime."[39]

The second focus, the humanity of the enemy, forms the basis of Philo's explanation for the biblical requirement of expiation for those soldiers who fought against Midian:

For though the slaughter of enemies is lawful, yet one who kills a man, even if he does so justly and in self-defense and under compulsion, has something to answer for, in view of the primal common kinship of mankind. And therefore purification was needed for the slayers, to absolve them from what was held to have been a pollution.[40]

In sum, it does not automatically follow that just because an army is legitimately violating the territorial integrity and political sovereignty of the aggressor state, it may violate the life of enemy civilians. Not to make a distinction between the citizenry and the state is to concede the totalitarian argument that the citizen is a tool of the state.

These factors seem as applicable to mandatory wars as they are to discretionary wars. Indeed, the overlap of considerations figures prominently in the classical discussion.[41]

Indeed, since the statement by Rabbi Eleazar (see p. 87) about the chaotic nature of warfare derives from the numbers involved in the conquest of the Land of Israel, it may be assumed that mandatory wars require a weighting of victory against losses not unlike that of discretionary wars. In the biblically mandated war against Amalek, it is explicitly stated, in 1 Samuel 15:6, that neutrals were given a chance to clear out of the battle area before Israel attacked.

The Midrash traces the blurring of the distinction between the two types of war back to the Torah. The following dialogue serves to counter the assumption that the requirement of offering peace before attacking be limited to discretionary wars.

God commanded Moses to make war on Sihon, as it is said, 'Engage him in battle,' but he did not do so. Instead he sent messengers . . . to Sihon . . . with an offer of peace (Deuteronomy 2:26). God said to him: 'I commanded you to make war with him, but instead you began with peace; by your life, I shall confirm your decision. Every war upon which Israel enters, they shall begin with an offer of peace.'[42]

Even a divinely commanded war must be predicated on an overture of peace. Accordingly, as the above midrash goes on to point out, Joshua adopted this policy in the conquest of Canaan. It has also been pointed out that Joshua, in assessing his chances of victory, applied to the priestly Urim and Tumim before battle.[43] The significance of this lies in the fact that even in mandatory wars, the chief executive is not at liberty to commit the population to war without proper approval.

The move to impose upon mandatory warfare the procedural or moral restraints of discretionary warfare serves to counter the "sliding scale argument," namely, the belief that "the greater the justice of one's cause, the more rights one has in battle."[44] The move from convictions of righteousness to feelings of self-righteousness is slight. The subsequent move, namely regarding the enemy population as beyond the pale of humanity, is even slighter. Since this tendency is especially pronounced in ideological and religiously motivated wars, any countermovement is especially salutary.

Of course, if the country is already under attack, the aforementioned procedural or assessment demands make little sense. Within the war powers of the executive branch of government, the exclusive prerogative to initiate war may be activated only to counterattack in hostilities already commenced. But then it is the enemy who has initiated hostilities.[45]

The third consideration that the Sanhedrin must weigh before granting its approval to commence hostilities is the will of the people. This issue is problematic, since it is not clear whether the people, in reality, retain any semblance of sovereignty once they have transferred their authority to their representative leaders, who legally express their collective identity.

In general, even those who maintain that sovereignty rests with the community hold that during the tenure of their representatives, the people have no alternative recourse.[46] Representative government is not government by the people, but government by the *agents* of the people.

During the tenure of the representatives, the agents of the majority rule. Concurrent with theories of majority rule, however, Jewish political theory has made provision for minority rights.[47]

THE DRAFT

Do provisions for minority rights apply in war? Presumably not. Apparently, once the proper procedure has been complied with, the individual has no recourse but to fight. If the duly constituted authorities have determined the necessity of war, who is the individual to review the government's decision? Moreover, if it is a defensive war, how could anyone be exempt from the need of self-defense, the duty to rescue others, and the defense of the state whose existence serves to protect all?

These considerations for individual as well as collective defense surely obtain in a mandatory war. Whether they do so in a discretionary war as well is not as certain.

A prominent peculiarity of the rules of warfare is the exemptions from military service. According to the Torah, the officials shall address the troops, as follows:

Is there anyone who has built a new house but has not dedicated it . . . or planted a vineyard but has never harvested it . . . or spoken for a woman in marriage but has not married her . . . let him go back home, lest he die in battle and another . . . [do] it.

The officials shall go on addressing the troops and say, Is there anyone afraid and tenderhearted? Let him go back to his home, lest the courage of his comrades flag like his. [Deuteronomy 20:5-9][48]

Those in the above categories are first required to report for duty before being assigned alternative service.

There is another category of individuals who, in addition to being exempt from reporting for duty, are also exempt from all alternative service, such as provisions and weapon supply, road repair, special security expenditures, and even oversight of defensive installations.[49] This category derives from the following verse: "When a man has taken a bride, he shall not go out with the army or be assigned to it for any purpose; he shall be exempt one year for the sake of his household, to give happiness to the woman he has married" (Deuteronomy 24:5). According to the Mishnah, the absolute exemption for one year of one who has consummated his marriage applies also to "one who has planted a vineyard and harvested it."[50]

The purpose of the exemptions is not made explicit. It might be to minimize unnecessary deaths, to mitigate individual hardship, to reinforce those who remain, to maintain the sanctity of the camp, or even to prevent depopulation of urban areas.[51]

At any rate, the rabbis understood each case as illustrative of a principle and extended the exemptions to cover four categories of handicaps. They are economic, familial, psychomoral, and physical.[52] Claims for economic or familial exemptions had to be substantiated. The other two were assumed to be self-evident.[53]

Although the psychomoral exemption is assumed to be self-evident, the nature of the exemption is debated. The Torah mentions two categories; "afraid and tenderhearted."

According to Rabbi Yose HaGelili, "afraid" means apprehensive about his sins; "tenderhearted" means fearful of war lest he be killed. According to Rabbi Akiva, "afraid" means fearful of war; "tenderhearted" means compassionate—apprehensive lest he kill.[54]

Besides having to be substantiated, the economic and familial exemptions share another common denominator. Projects such as starting a house, beginning a vineyard, or getting engaged most often affect men in their prime—the age of maximum combat readiness. A large number of exemptions for this age group could hamper mobilization efforts to an extent that would impair the military effort. Nahmanides says it in so many words: "Were it not so [the requirement of substantiation], a majority of the people would seek exemption on false pretenses."[55]

Precisely! There is a loophole in the war legislation. A loophole so gaping that it allows those unconvinced of the validity of the war to reassert their sovereignty through legal shenanigans. Doubts about the validity of the war would create their own social momentum and influence the numbers seeking exemptions. Thus, a situation has been created where albeit the executive declares war with the approval of the Sanhedrin, the efficacy of conscription still depends upon the ability of the authorities to persuade the people of its necessity.

Mobilization will fail without a high degree of popular support. When their lives are at stake, the populace retains a semblance of sovereignty. They indirectly end up passing judgment on whether the military venture is indeed necessary and whether it serves legitimate political ends.

The resort to military force, in a discretionary war, requires a moral as well as a political raison d'être. Otherwise the war effort risks being undermined by the morale of that community which constitutes the resource of power. Military success is as much a function of "staying power" as it is of "striking power." Striking power is subject to both quantitative and qualitative assessments of military resources. Staying power is, however, a correlative of the strength of motivation which itself derives from unity of purpose and popular consensus with regard to national aspirations. The result is that victory is not only a function of military might, but also a product of the social fabric, national will, and national resources.[56]

In sum, the issue is not just the proper use of force, but also the proper means of assessing whether to resort to force. Such calculations exceed formal military considerations. Thus, official responsibilities for assessment lie with the Sanhedrin. Nonetheless, since large numbers of lives are at stake, there exists a legal technicality in the mobilization process which allows for discerning popular sentiment. As the justification for the war loses credibility, and the war itself loses popularity, so grows the likelihood of mass petitions for exemptions on dubious grounds. In the final analysis, the endorsement of the people may weigh as heavily as the approval of the Sanhedrin.

EPILOGUE

The Midrash asks why the Torah records those occasions when God's orders were rescinded in favor of Moses' counsel of restraint in the conduct of war. It answers, "Even war is recorded for the sake of peace."[57] Restraint in, and of, war creates openings for peace.

NOTES

1. See *Bavli Berakhot* 3b, *Bavli Sanhedrin* 16a, and Maimonides, *Hilkhot Melakhim* 5:1.

2. *Berakhot* 28a.

3. Maimonides, *Hilkhot Melakhim* 5:4.

4. See David Hoffman in *Midrash Tannaim* ad Deuteronomy 20:15 (Berlin: Ittskovski, 1908–1909).

5. *Midrash Samuel* 22:2.

6. *Midrash Lekah Tov*, Deuteronomy, p. 35a.

7. The loci classici are *Bavli Sotah* 44b, and *Yerushalmi Sotah* 9:10, 23a.

8. This is also his position in *Yerushalmi Sotah* 9:10, 23a as correctively recorded in the Vatican Ms; see Saul Lieberman, *Tosefta Kifeshutah, VIII–Sotah* (New York: Jewish Theological Seminary, 1961) p. 696, no. 43.

9. Ad *Bavli Sotah* 43a.

10. Maimonides, *Hilkhot Melakhim* 5:1, following *Hazon Ish Al HaRambam*, B'nei Brak 5729, p. 841.

11. E. Lauterpacht, "The Contemporary Practice of the United Kingdom in the Field of International Law—Survey and Comment, III" (1957) 6 I. Comp. L.Q. 330, quoted in Barry Feinstein, "Self-Defense and Israel in International Law: a Reappraisal," *Israel Law Review* II (1976), p. 531.

12. *Ibid.*, p. 533.

13. *Mishnah Sanhedrin* 1:4.

14. See *Midrash Tanhuma, Parshat Pinhas*, sect. 3.

15. See Reuven Kimelman, "Torah against Terror—Does Jewish Law Sanction the Vengeance of Modern-Day Zealots?" *The B'nai Brith International Jewish Monthly* (October 1984), pp. 16–22.

16. See Avraham Avidan, "HaHistaknut BeHasalat HaZolat LeOr Ha-Halakha—The Risk in Saving Another in the Light of the Halakha," *Torah SheBa'al-Peh* 16 (Jerusalem, 5734), p. 130. The debate revolves around the opinions of David ben Zimra (*Teshuvot RaDBaZ* III, no. 1052) and Joseph Karo, *Kesef Mishnah, Hilkhot Roseah* 1:14.

17. See *Avidan*, no. 17, p. 133.

18. Abraham Kook, *Mishpat Kohan* (Jerusalem, 5726), sec. 142–144.

19. See *Bavli Sanhedrin* 16a.

20. Maimonides, *Commentary to the Mishnah, Horayot* 1:6 (ed. *Kafah, Nezikin,* p. 309).

21. See Gerald Blidstein, "Individual and Community in the Middle Ages," in *Kinship and Consent: The Jewish Political Tradition and Its Contemporary Uses,* ed. Daniel J. Elazar (Philadelphia, 1981), p. 247, no. 26.

22. Shlomo Goren, *Mashiv Milhamah* I, Jerusalem 5743, pp. 127*ff.*

23. See 2 Kings 11:17; 2 Chronicles 23:3; and Josephus, *Antiquities* IX, 7, 4–153.

24. Josephus, *Contra Apion* II, 272 and 292.

25. Song of Songs *Rabbah* 4:4.

26. *Bavli Shavuot* 35b.

27. J. David Bleich, "Preemptive War in Jewish Law," *Tradition* 17:25 (1983).

28. See *Sifre* Deuteronomy section 103, ed. Finkelstein (New York: Jewish Theological Seminary, 1969) p. 239, with *Midrash HaGadol* ad Deuteronomy 20:19, ed. Fisch (New York, Jerusalem: Mossad Harav Kook, 1972) p. 451.

29. This listing, based on the sources in the previous note, follows almost verbatim that found in David S. Shapiro's "The Jewish Attitude towards Peace and War," Israel of Tomorrow, ed. Leo Jung (New York: 1946), p. 239. A more comprehensive and analytic treatment of this material is found in Laurence K. Milder's unpublished rabbinic thesis, "Laws of War in the Bible and Formative Rabbinic Literature" (New York: HUC-JIR, 1983).

30. Philo, *The Special Laws,* IV, 221.

31. *Ibid.,* 222.

32. *Ibid.,* 224.

33. *Ibid.,* 225.

34. *Ibid.,* 226–227.

35. Maimonides, *Hilkhot Melakhim* 6:10.

36. Josephus, *Contra Apion* II, 212.

37. Referring to Deuteronomy 21:10*ff.*, see Josephus, *Contra Apion* II, 212–213.

38. *The Seventh Day: Soldiers Talk about the Six Day War,* ed. Avraham Shapira, English trans. by Henry Near (London: Deutsch, 1970).

p. 132. According to Meir Pa'il, this doctrine has vindicated itself. He writes: "There can be no doubt that the turning toward extreme and consummate humanism can endanger the I.D.F.'s ability to function, but experience has proven that the proportions of this danger are extremely small and that it does not constitute a phenomenon that really endangers the operative capacity and the efficiency of the defense forces." "The Dynamics of Power: Morality in Armed Conflict After the Six Day War," *Modern Jewish Ethics: Theory and Practice*, ed. Marvin Fox (Columbus, OH: Ohio State University Press, 1975), p. 215.

39. See above, Chap. II, no. 36, fifth mitzvah, p. 246. For variations of this theme, see SHaDal—S.D. Luzzatto's *Commentary to the Pentateuch* (Tel Aviv, 1965)—ad Deuteronomy 20:19.

40. Philo, *Moses* I. 314. Lamentations *Rabbah*, Introduction 14, condemns King Amaziah for his brutal killing of the enemy.

41. For Rashi and Ramban, see Yehudah Gershuni, *Sefer Mishpat HaMelukhah*, Jerusalem 5784, pp. 130–134; for Maimonides, see *Hilkhot Melakhim* 6:1, 6:7, and 7:1 [following Gerald J. Blidstein, *Political Concepts in Maimonidean Halakha* (in Hebrew) (Tel Aviv: Bar-Ilan University, 1983), p. 221, no. 34, and Yosef Dov Soloveitchik, *Koves Hidushei Torah* (Jerusalem, 5734), pp. 128–131].

42. Deuteronomy *Rabbah* 5, 13.

43. Numbers 27:21.

44. The expression and definition are Michael Walzer's in his *Just and Unjust Wars: A Moral Argument with Historical Illustrations* (New York: Basic Books, 1977), p. 246.

45. See Eliezer Waldenberg, *Sefer Hilkhot Medinah* (Jerusalem, 5712), II, p. 105.

46. See Blidstein, no. 21, pp. 225–227; and Samuel Morell, "The Constitutional Limits of Communal Government in Rabbinic Law, Jewish Social Studies 33 (1971), pp. 87–119. On referendums, see Waldenberg, no. 44, III, pp. 90–97.

47. Blidstein and Morrell.

48. According to *Maccabees* 3:56, these exemptions hold also in a defensive war, see infra.

49. See Maimonides, *Hilkhot Melakhim* 7:11.

50. *Mishnah Sotah* 8:4.

51. *Sifre* Deuteronomy, sect. 192, p. 233.

52. See Shlomo Goren, *Torat haShabbat VehaMoed* (Jerusalem, 5742), p. 359.

53. *Sifre* Deuteronomy, sec. 192, p. 233.

54. Based on David Halivni, *Mekorot UMesorot, Nashim* (Tel Aviv, 4729), ad *Sotah* 44a, pp. 473–474.

55. Ramban ad Deuteronomy 20:8, see *Bekhor Shor ad loc.* In fact, when Gideon made provisions for the psychomoral exemption, he lost two-thirds of his fighting force (Judges 7:2–31).

56. See Reinhold Niebuhr, "The Limits of Military Power," in *The World Crisis and American Responsibility*, ed. Ernest V. Lefever (New York: Association Press, 1958), p. 116; and General Israel Tal, "The Concept of National Security," in *New Outlook Middle East Monthly*, vol. 26/2, March/April 1983, p. 44.

57. Midrash *Tanhuma Tzav* 3.

6

Nuclear War and the Prohibition of Wanton Destruction

David Novak

METHODOLOGY

When dealing with the question of whether it is permitted or forbidden to wage nuclear war, it would seem that if an authentically Jewish answer is to be found, the place to look for it would be in the speculations of Aggadah more than in the precedents of Halakhah.[1] For, according to virtually all the experts dealing with this question, nuclear war would radically alter human life and society in a totally unprecedented way; indeed, it might very well destroy all life on this planet. Halakhah is a system of precedent and rules derived from precedent. Even though the system itself is subtle enough to adequately treat unusual, even bizarre, cases, it is an axiom of that system that its general rules are formulated for what will usually obtain in human affairs, not for what might happen but never has.[2] If, as the experts maintain, nuclear war entails the probability of the end of the world as we know it, then, it would seem, we should examine Jewish eschatology which, although entailing some halakhic issues, is essentially an exercise in speculation about the "end of days," and how human expectations and hope are to be constituted in relation to it. In an earlier study I engaged in such aggadic speculation about the scriptural and traditional descriptions of God's lordship over His creation and the true character of His promise of created continuity made to Noah and his descendants, that is, to humankind, and what the loss of faith in that promise entails in terms of responsible human action.[3] Such speculation indeed might be one of those subjects that Maimonides regarded as ultimately more important than the more mundane analysis of what is usually forbidden and permitted (he'asur ve-ha-mutar).[4]

BAL TASH'HIT

Nevertheless, there is one area of Halakhah which might provide some directly normative guidance to Jews agonizing over this very real question facing all of humankind, and that is the prohibition of "wanton destruction" (bal tash'hit).[5] I shall analyze the various interpretations of the meaning of this prohibition in an attempt to derive at least some guidance for an authentically Jewish approach to the question of waging a nuclear war.

The prohibition of wanton destruction is found in a passage in the Pentateuch which presents a very clear prohibition and then connects it with a very unclear reason:

> When you lay siege to a city for many days, battling against it in order to capture it [le-tafsah], do not destroy [lo tash'hit] its trees, wielding the ax against them, for (ki) from them you do eat and you may not cut them down. For [ki] are the trees of the field human to withdraw from before you in a siege? [Deuteronomy 20:19]

From this specific prohibition is derived the general prohibition of destroying anything for no good reason. According to some authorities, this general prohibition is directly prescribed by the passage quoted above, and the specific case mentioned there is simply an example of a larger class of prohibited acts (*binyan av*).[6] According to at least one other authority, however, the scriptural prohibition is confined to the case at hand and the more general prohibition, mentioned frequently in the Talmud, is a decree of the rabbis which they associated with this relevant scriptural passage (*asmakhta*).[7]

On the surface this dispute would seem to only affect the number of lashes to be administered to a person convicted of the crime of wanton destruction, as would be the case with anyone else convicted of violating a negative commandment.[8] If all wanton destruction is a direct violation of a scriptural command, then the convicted violator is to be given up to thirty-nine lashes as prescribed elsewhere by Scripture.[9] If, on the other hand, only the wanton destruction of fruit trees violates the explicit scriptural prohibition, then one convicted of any other act of wanton destruction is only to be lashed according to rabbinic discretion (*makkat mardut*), which is considered a lesser penalty.[10] However, there is another effect of this exegetical dispute and that pertains to the reason given in the last part of the verse from Deuteronomy 20:19. If the prohibition of wanton destruction is directly scriptural, then the reason supplied in the last part of this verse grounds and thereby limits the entire prohibition. Nevertheless, if the prohibition of wanton destruction is rabbinic, with the specific exception of the destruction of fruit trees proscribed by Scripture explicitly, then the reason given in Scripture in connection with this proscription only applies to it alone and does not, therefore, ground and thereby limit the more general prohibition. As such, one can thus supply a more all-encompassing and thereby more sufficient reason for it.[11]

THE UTILITARIAN VIEWPOINT

The reason for the commandment given in Scripture is enigmatically worded, but most of the commentators seem to follow the Septuagint which translates this second part of the verse as "perhaps [*me*] the trees in the field are human [*anthropos*] to come [*eiselthein*] from before you into the fortified place [*ton charaka*]?[12] Thus Rashi (following Onqelos) writes, "perhaps the trees of the field are human to be punished with hunger and thirst like the people of the city [*k'anshay ha'ir*]; why do you destroy them [*lamah tash'hiteno*]?"[13] This reasoning seems to entail an ethic of retribution, namely, you may not harm what has not harmed you, unlike those who have harmed you, whom you may indeed harm. Furthermore, according to this interpretation, this even entails an ethic of retribution by anticipation, namely, you may not harm what will not harm you *later*, unlike those who will harm you *later* whom you may indeed harm *now*.[14] All of this is based on the fact that the earliest rabbinic sources place this commandment in the context of a permitted offensive war (*milhemet ha-reshut*).[15] Thus, following this the line of reasoning, the sixteenth-century Italian exegete, Rabbi Obadiah Sforno, wrote in his commentary:

> For is it indeed so that the trees of the field are human to surrender themselves over [*li-msor et atzmam*] into your hand because of the force of the siege? And inasmuch as this is not so, and that it is right [*ra'uy*] to harm the inhabitants of the city with weapons of war . . . to bring the city under siege, and this will not be accomplished [*she-lo tasig zeh*] by the destruction of the trees, hence it is not right [*ayn ra'uy*] to destroy them as it is right [*she-ra'uy*] that you destroy the human inhabitants of the city.[16]

In other words, not only does this type of interpretation entail an ethic of retribution by anticipation (in today's military parlance, a "preemptive strike"), but it seems to entail placing a higher value on trees than on the lives of human beings, even if they happen to be your enemies.

What emerges from this is an ethic of rather extreme utilitarianism where all arguments must satisfy the demands of immediate self-interest in order to be valid. Thus Philo writes:

> One the contrary, it benefits [*ophelei*] you by providing the victors with abundance both of necessities [*anankaion*] and of the comforts which insure a life of luxury. For not only men but plants also pay tributes to their lords [*pherousi tois kyriois*]. . . . and theirs are the more profitable [*tous ophelimoterous*] since without them life is impossible.[17]

And Josephus follows the same line when he concludes that trees "were created for the service of men [*ep' opheleia . . . ton anthropon*]."[18]

This line of reasoning has proven to be quite consistent in its logic. In fact, it is able to solve the apparent contradiction between the commandment against wanton destruction in Deuteronomy 20:19 and the later commandment of the prophet Elisha to the kings of Israel and Judah, namely, "You shall smite every fortified city and every choice city, and every good tree you shall fell and all of the sources of water you shall stop up and every good field you shall ruin with stones" (2 Kings 3:19). Instead of trying to explain away the prophetic text which seems to contradict the text from the Pentateuch, the advocates of this line of reasoning, consistent with their utilitarianism (at least in this case), turn the commandment from Deuteronomy into a hypothetical imperative (to use Kant's helpful terminology and conceptuality)[19] rather than a categorical imperative. Thus, the nineteenth-century Rumanian exegete, Rabbi Meir Leibush Malbim, writes:

> Battling against it to capture it [*le-tafsah*]"—this is added because siege may be made against the city in order to destroy it and make it uninhabitable [*u-le-hashbitah*] as a city. Therefore, the explanation is that the intention [*ha-kavvanah*] should only be to capture the city that it be yours . . . but this consideration is eliminated [*l'afuqay*] if they want [*im rotzim*] to destroy the city as in the case of Moab. [2 Kings 3:19][20]

In other words, Malbim makes the efficacy of the earlier commandment contingent on prior human choice, namely, *if* you only want to capture a city, then do not wantonly destroy its fruit trees; but, if you do want to destroy a city, then you may do so as indicated by the commandment of Elisha regarding Moab.[21] Earlier, the fifteenth-century Turkish exegete, Rabbi Elijah Mizrahi, argued, on the basis of the same rabbinic comment in the *Sifre* later used by Malbim, that the whole restriction was confined to an authorized offensive war (*milhemet reshut*), but "if it were in a defensive war [*be-milhamah shel mitzvah*], the city is to be made uninhabitable and not to be captured."[22] One could indeed see this very same type of reasoning employed by the United States in the 1945 atomic bombing of Hiroshima, a major city of Japan, which had attacked the American fleet at Pearl Harbor in 1941.

Even if one were to follow this whole line of reasoning to the logical conclusions I have attempted to draw from it heretofore, a case could still be made for declaring the waging of nuclear war in our day to be immoral. For now, unlike 1945 when nuclear weapons were a United States monopoly, an ever-growing number of nations do have nuclear weapons. Thus, even if a nuclear-powered nation were to wage nuclear war against a nonnuclear-powered nation, considering the balance of power in the world of realpolitik today, it is inevitable that the nonnuclear-powered nation would ally itself with another nuclear-powered nation which would come to its defense in its own self-interest, inasmuch as weaker nations invariably fall within the sphere and power of stronger nations. Thus, it seems most likely that the initiation of any nuclear hostilities in today's world would quickly trigger a worldwide conflagration whose results would soon prove to be disastrous for any and all nations. In other words, the qualification of the prohibition of wanton destruction, based on utilitarian considerations of immediate self-interest, would not apply in a situation where an act of nuclear aggression would result in suicidal consequences.[23] Clearly, the logic of ordinary warfare, in which there is an obvious and sustained difference in kind between the victors and the vanquished, does not apply to a nuclear war. The advantage of delineating the utilitarian point of view in classical Jewish sources is that utilitarianism is the most minimal moral point of view possible and is seemingly the easiest to defend[24]; and even on the grounds of this minimal moral point of view, there is no justification for waging a nuclear war in the world today.

THE THEOCENTRIC VIEWPOINT

Although utilitarianism is an easy moral point of view to defend, it is based on an egocentricity, which is rather atypical in the light of Judaism's theocentricity and the human self-transcendence (some call it "altruism") it so frequently requires. Thus, the nineteenth-century Italian exegete and theologian, Rabbi Samuel

David Luzzatto (*Shadal*), criticized the whole utilitarian line of reasoning we have been examining, noting that in his opinion this commandment "was not given to teach human beings to make calculations [*heshbonot*] for their own benefit [*le-hanaat at atz-mam*] but, on the contrary, it was given to strengthen in our hearts compassion [*ha-hemlah*] and graciousness and opposition to our own purposes [*ve-ha-mitnagdut le-toelatenu*].[25] Further-more, the second part of the verse might not be a reason at all, but rather the second part of the commandment itself by inference, namely, in your wartime panic do not look upon the fruit trees of your enemies as being enemies themselves. In other words, the full two-part commandment might very well be: Do not cut down the fruit trees of your enemy, *and* do not regard them as you would your human enemy.[26] Thus, the first part of the command-ment prescribes action, the second part attendant attitude. If so, then the sufficient reason for the commandment is not found in this verse at all.[27] Moreover, if the general norm against wanton destruction is actually rabbinic in origin, then we can avoid all the exegetical problems we have seen in Deuteronomy 20:19 and immediately look for the sufficient reason elsewhere, a reason evident to our intellect (*atio quod nos*) and one grounded within the objective moral order of creation itself (*ratio per se*).[28] Indeed, one could argue that the very technology that has had only to answer to minimal utilitarian criteria of immediate use is itself the very cause of the dilemma of nuclear weapons, where the work of human hands now transcends and dominates its makers. Technol-ogy can only be contained when a transcendent realm of value is affirmed, inasmuch as technology is manifest as power for power's sake alone. Technology for its own sake is ultimately purposeless and, therefore, without limit.[29]

The explicit appeal to an objective moral order to explain the prohibition of wanton destruction seems to have been made by the eleventh-century Spanish exegete, Rabbi Abraham Ibn Ezra:

> For the trees of the field are humanlike [*u-kemohu*] because he is injuring (*hovel*) human beings [*nefesh*] by injuring the means of human life [*hayay nefesh*]. . . . You shall not destroy fruit trees which are a source of life for humans [*hayyim le-ven adam*]. It is

only permitted [*muttar*] to eat from them and it is forbidden [*asur*] for you to destroy them in order to lay siege against a city.[30]

The important point to note in this explanation is the emphasis on the priority of human life—all human life—even over considerations of military advantage. For Ibn Ezra, the destruction of the food-producing trees is no longer a hypothetical imperative contingent upon the fulfillment of a subjective aim; rather it is a categorical imperative, namely, food-producing trees are not to be destroyed, even when their destruction would contribute to your own military advantage, because they are *necessary for human life in general*. The prohibition thus absolutely eliminates from the realm of the permitted what, in the twentieth century, came to be termed the "scorched earth policy." For Ibn Ezra, destruction of an enemy is not an end in itself, thereby justifying any means whatsoever. Conquest is never allowed to entail destruction for the sake of destruction. Any destruction, even in wartime, must be both temporary and partial in order to be justifiable. Cutting down fruit trees, especially in an arid region such as the ancient Middle East, results in both permanent and widespread damage.[31]

Ibn Ezra's anti-utilitarian line of reasoning was picked up in the fourteenth century by the Spanish exegete, halakhist, and theologian, Nahmanides:

> Rabbi Abraham [Ibn Ezra] explained it well . . . but the opinion of the rabbis is that it is permitted to cut down fruit trees to build a siege . . . fruit trees are only mentioned to indicate that one should use a non-fruit tree first [*she'ilan sereq qoden*]. If so, then the explanation of this passage in their view is that the Torah prohibited [*she-hizhirah*] . . . cutting them down destructively [*derekh hash'hatah*] not for the sake of a siege, as is the practice of military expeditions [*ke-minhag ha-mahanot*] . . . as it is said in 2 Kings 3:19, and every good tree you shall fell, etc. . . . and you shall not do this to destroy them, but you shall trust in the Lord that He will deliver them into your hand.[32]

Nahmanides only allows an exception to this rule in the case where fruit trees will be used for military purposes by your enemies against you there and then, even if that requires cutting them down.[33] However, cutting them down may not be a matter of long-term strategy inasmuch as destruction for the sake of some remote goal might very well be, in truth, destruction for its own sake. This would be directly contrary to faith in God as Creator and Deliverer. In other words, the long-term goal might be a rationalization for present nihilism. This type of pseudomoral reasoning was termed by the rabbis "a transgression for the sake of a commandment" (mitzvah ha-ba'ah b'averah), which is, of course, a contradictio in adjectu.[34] The means must be consistent with the end; if not, the end cannot justify them.

Nahmanides' problem is how to deal with Ibn Ezra's seeming departure from the rabbinic interpretation of this commandment. For the line of utilitarian reasoning we saw from Philo to Malbim seems to arise directly out of the rulings of the sages in Halakhah. Thus the Sifre on Deuteronomy 20:19 rules, "to withdraw from before you in a siege—if they prevent you [im m'akevekha] by coming before you in a siege, then cut them down [qatza-tzehu]."[35] In dealing with the general prohibition of wanton destruction, the Talmud rules:

> Rabbi Hyya bar Abin said in the name of Samuel that if one lets blood and becomes chilled, a fire is made for him even during the summer. A teak chair was broken up for Samuel [for firewood] . . . A footstool was broken up for Rabbah. Abaye said to Rabbah that this was a violation of the prohibition of wanton destruction [bal tash'hit]. He replied "my own body is more important [de-guf'ay adif]!"[36]

Now this type of reasoning must be carefully delineated because it seems to be of the "slippery slope" variety, namely, virtually any destructive act can be justified on the basis of the most meager subjective reason. One can see an example of such subjective reasoning in the law of Sabbath observance. There, according to the Mishnah, only constructive acts are considered within the category of the scripturally prohibited thirty-nine labors (avot mel'akhah).[37] However, the Talmud includes one who tore his clothes in anger because he "assuaged his feelings (de-ke'avad nahat ruah le-yitzro]."[38] In Maimonides' words, "he is like one performing a constructive act [ve-haray hu ke-metagen]."[39] Thus, the only person who would not be guilty of committing a scripturally proscribed constructive act on the Sabbath would be a person who did it in a totally dispassionate way, which is a rather remote possibility in a psychologically normal person where emotions and actions are evidently correlated.

However, there is a difference in the law of wanton destruction and the law of constructive activity on the Sabbath, and the contrast between them will better explicate the former. The Sabbath was given to place a limit on man *qua homo faber* in both a social and an individual sense. Objective constructive acts (even those which initially entail some destructive preparatory work), which the rabbis modeled after the building of the Sanctuary in the wilderness by Moses and the Israelites, have tangible, socially beneficial, results.[40] Subjective constructive acts, such as acting out one's anger, only have an emotional significance, but lack these tangible, socially beneficial results. Nevertheless, both are forms of "labor" (*mel'ak-hah*) which interfere with the Sabbath as a full human celebration of the creativity of God. Regarding wanton destruction, on the other hand, any kind of constructive act which entails some destructive "ground breaking" must have some immediately socially beneficial, tangible results, like the thirty-nine labors connected with the construction of the Sanctuary in the wilderness. If the act does not have this social value, if it is only to satisfy some private subjective aim, then it is considered destruction for its own sake. Even Rabbah's burning a stool to keep warm was a socially justifiable act in that his bodily need could be the bodily need of anyone else in the same situation. However, the institution of the Sabbath indicates that even such temporary destruction for the sake of immediate construction, that this whole continuum itself must not become co-equal with human life and activity itself.[41] It too must be limited, whereas wanton destruction must be eliminated altogether.

IDOLATRY AND WANTON DESTRUCTION

The fact that wanton destruction cannot be justified on subjective emotional grounds is brought out in the following talmudic passage:

> Rabbi Huna tore silk garments in the presence of Rabbah, his son,
> saying, "I am going to see whether he will become angry or not."
> . . . And did he not violate the prohibition of wanton destruction?
> No, because he tore them on the seams.[42]

Now the interpretation of this episode is that tearing the silk
garments on the seams would enable them to be so easily repaired
and restored to their original quality so as not to constitute
destruction at all.[43] However, were this not the case, then Rabbi
Huna would have been in violation of the prohibition. What is
important to note here is that the Talmud does not suggest that
Rabbi Huna would have been exonerated on the grounds that he
was gaining some kind of emotional satisfaction by so testing his
son's patience. That would have been an insufficient justification
precisely because it is too subjective and too private. Furthermore, it is clear from the questions the Talmud raised about this
bizarre incident, its authors did not approve of Rabbi Huna's
conduct at all.

Indeed, this very unjustifiable destruction is considered to be
ultimately idolatrous. Thus, the sixteenth-century halakhist, Rabbi
Joseph Karo, connects the prohibition of wanton destruction as
codified by Maimonides with a talmudic text that follows the
talmudic text that designated destruction out of anger as a positive violation of the Sabbath, a text[44] we examined earlier:

> One who tears his clothes in anger, and who breaks his things in
> anger, and who scatters his money in anger, he should be considered
> as an idolator in your eyes. For such is the craftiness [umanuto] of
> the evil inclination [yetzer ha-ra]: today it says to him, "do such and
> such," tomorrow it says to him, "do such and such," until it says to
> him, "worship idols," and he goes and does so.[45]

It is important to note that Maimonides uses the language of this
aggadic passage to codify the halakhah of wanton destruction,
found in various places in the rabbinic sources.

What emerges from all of this is that idolatry is the very
epitome of wanton destruction. If so, then the service of God the
Creator is the essential opposite of this. In our century it was

Sigmund Freud who most insightfully designated the human capacity for nihilation as the "death wish," contrasting the term
thanatos (death) with his earlier reduction of all human thought
and action to *eros* (sensual desire).[46] Unfortunately, although
Freud was a Jew—and a proud one at that—he was also an
atheist, and being an atheist, he missed the theological truth that
the drive for *thanatos* and the drive for idolatry (*avodah zarah*)
are in essence the same.[47] This is what Nahmanides was trying to
express in his attempt to harmonize the theological insight of Ibn
Ezra with the precedents of halakhah. For Nahmanides' own
insight was that wanton destruction is performed precisely when
faith in God's future saving action is lost.

     If this is the case, then even destructive action rationalized as
being in the ultimate interest of the state—even the Jewish state
constituted by the Torah itself—cannot be justified.[48] For nationalism per se, where the life and activity of the political community
are posited as being ends in themselves, requiring no further
justification and admitting no transcendent source of criticism, is
itself idolatry—indeed it is *the* idolatry of the twentieth century, a
century that has witnessed more bloodshed and more wanton
destruction than the whole history of humankind before it. Jews,
especially, as the victims of the greatest program of mass murder
and destruction in human history, should realize that the Holocaust was the ultimate example of wanton destruction, serving no
constructive purpose even for the Nazi murderers themselves.[49]

     It was the prophets of Israel who in God's name challenged the
nationalist pretensions of the kings and the people of ancient days.
Even though the Talmud sees the actual prophetic experience as
ending with the destruction of the Second Temple in 70 C.E., it still
regards some residue of prophetic insight left in the people of Israel
and their historical experience.[50] Thus the prophetic critique of the
ultimate nihilism of absolute ethnocentricity can still be spoken
today—indeed with some very current illustrations.

     This critique of ethnocentricity and the nihilism it inevitably
entails, comes out in the treatment of this whole issue in the
scriptural exegesis of the fifteenth-century Spanish exegete, theologian, and statesman, Don Isaac Abrabanel. In commenting on
Deuteronomy 20:19, he writes,

> This means that they should not cut down the fruit-producing trees which are in the city like the practice of the warriors whose purpose [she-magamatam] is to destroy and annihilate everything, as it states in 2 Kings 3:19. . . . Therefore, it is not right [ayn ra'uy] to destroy them for it is not good [ayn ne'ot] that man should destroy what benefits himself [she-yo'llehu].[51]

It seems that what Abrabanel means by "man" (ha'adam) is what Ibn Ezra meant by "it," namely, humankind in general, whose life and well-being depend on care and nurture of the created order of nature.

An earlier medieval source emphasized this objective and universal criterion by stating,

> The root of this commandment is known and that is to teach us to love the good and the purposeful [ha-tov ve-ha-to'elet] and to cleave to it, and from this the good will cleave to us and we will remove from ourselves anything destructive [mi-kol davar hash-'hatah]. . . . It is not so with the wicked, the brothers of destructive demons [maziqim], who rejoice in the destruction of the world and who destroy themselves.[52]

Along these lines, the fourteenth-century Provençal exegete and theologian, Gersonides, went so far as to emphasize that this commandment reflects God's providence (hashgahah) even over plants, proscribing the destruction of those which benefit others, especially.[53] It is the emphasis of an objective moral order, which is part of a created universal order presided over by Divine providence, which provides the ontological grounding for the altruism—the self-transcendence—which this commandment seems to require of us. The integrity of the moral realm involving fellow humans presupposes the integrity of the larger created realm of nature. One cannot work to improve the moral quality of human life and society without working to improve the quality of creation.[54] In our day the concern for nuclear disarmament and the concern for ecology complement each other and ultimately coalesce into the concern for God's creation itself.

We have seen earlier that the most utilitarian treatments of Deuteronomy 20:19 had treated the "scorched earth policy" of 2 Kings 3:19 as being on a par with the former; that is, one has the choice of either approach, depending on how one—in this case how one nation—judges its own immediate self-interest. However, in his commentary on 2 Kings 3:19, Abrabanel, on the basis of a midrashic text, declares this to be an emergency measure for that time only through prophetic dispensation [*bi-dvar Ha-Shem le-fi sha'ah*].[55] Although his justification of this emergency measure as being due to the incorrigible corruption of the Moabites begs the question in this particular case, his isolation of it by this means does remove it from being a precedent for any such action at any other time. Thus, the contradiction he rightly sees between these two scriptural norms is solved, in the sense that the prohibition of absolute destruction is taken as the categorical imperative, and the commandment of Elisha to the kings of Israel and Judah is taken as the lone exception *sui generis*. This is the traditional Jewish method of interpretation used in resolving seeming contradictions between the Pentateuch and the Prophets.[56]

THE PROHIBITION OF TOTAL DESTRUCTION

It should be noted that, following the line of interpretation developed by Ibn Ezra, *Sefer Ha-Hinukh*, Nahmanides, Gersonides, Abrabanel, and Luzzatto, the enigmatic reason presented in Deuteronomy 20:19 is a sufficient grounding not only for the specific prohibition of wanton destruction of fruit trees but for the general prohibition of wanton destruction per se. For by comparing trees (*etz*) and humans (*adam*), it indicates that destruction of the environment and destruction of human society go hand in hand. Ultimately, even self-interest requires a transcendent frame of reference.

If, on the other hand, we follow Maimonides' interpretation that the general prohibition of wanton destruction is rabbinic, then we need not concern ourselves with the minute analysis of

Deuteronomy 20:19b and all its problematics, and we can simply see this general prohibition as being based on the general scriptural affirmation of the sanctity of all created beings, perhaps best expressed by the prophet, "He did not create it to be a wasteplace [*tohu*], but He formed it to be a dwelling [*la-shevet*]" (Isaiah 45:18).[57] Furthermore, this also precludes the problem we saw earlier in the comment of Rabbi Elijah Mizrahi, namely, that the whole scriptural prohibition of wanton destruction only applies in an authorized offensive war (*milhemet reshut*), but in a defensive war (*milhemet mitzvah*), wanton destruction is not only permitted but is actually its goal. If, however, the general commandment, with which we are concerned as a source of guidance about the waging of nuclear war, is rabbinic, then it does not really matter whether or not the specific scriptural commandments only pertain to an authorized offensive war, which, according to the Talmud, could not be legally waged after the destruction of the First Temple in 586 B.C.E.[58] Moreover, even if the commandment now only applies to a defensive war, the requirement of offering peace terms (Deuteronomy 20:10) to combatants (even to Canaanite combatants for whom Deuteronomy 20:16 mandates unconditional massacre), which seems to only apply in an authorized offensive war, was extended by the rabbis to also apply in a defensive war, which is the only authorized war today.[59] Now, if we are not to unconditionally destroy our enemies, then we are not to unconditionally destroy their environment, based on the analogy of trees and humans in Deuteronomy 20:19b. This is certainly the case in a situation like the nuclear threat today, where our own destruction entails the destruction of our own environment which would inevitably follow in its wake.

NUCLEAR WAR

After this analysis of the prohibition of wanton destruction, arguing for the line of interpretation which sees its rationale as being grounded in an objective moral order within an objectively good created order of nature, I would like to draw some tentative normative points from it which pertain to the question of nuclear war.

1. The evil of nuclear war, which cannot be justified by any of the usual criteria of temporary destruction for the sake of ultimate victory, is to be emphasized continually. Those who advocate otherwise are like those fools who the Talmud said love their property (symbols of their technical power) more than their own lives.[60] Such fools, especially when they occupy positions of political, military, or economic power, are not only foolish, they are dangerous. Therefore, it seems to me, normative Jews, who live by the Torah's ideas and precepts, should participate with those who work to publically expose these dangerous delusions of nuclear victory.[61]

2. It seems that bilateral, not unilateral, disarmament is what is required. Unilateral disarmament on the part of the Western nations would mean that their enemies would have all the nuclear weapons. This would be like the situation, noted earlier by Nahmanides, where not cutting down the fruit trees would enable the enemy himself to use them as offensive weapons of destruction. We must never forget that the unilateral disarmament of the Western nations after World War I led to a state of military impotence which encouraged Mussolini and Hitler to engage in unlimited aggression. Therefore, universal disarmament must be pursued to lessen the likelihood of nuclear aggression. For Americans, especially, this means working to eliminate the bellicose rhetoric too often used by our leaders, rhetoric which exacerbates international tensions and makes disarmament even more remote.

3. Since war and aggression begin in the stubborn and arrogant pride of human beings, which the prophets and sages saw as the source of all sin,[62] normative Jews should endeavor in their individual lives and in their various societies to banish from their hearts all arrogance and hatred among themselves and toward others, and pray that God will purify our hearts and enable us to be a light to the nations who in our day are groping in the darkness of the nuclear threat which hangs over all the earth like a terrible sword.[63]

NOTES

All translations, unless otherwise noted, are by the author.

1. For the notion that Aggadah can be normative when it does not contradict Halakhah, see Rabbi Zevi Hirsch Chajes, *Darkhay Ha-Hora'ah*, sec. 2, *Kol Kitvay Maharatz Chajes* (Jerusalem: Divri Chakhamim, 1958), 1:251–252.

2. See *Bavli Eruvin* 63b and parallels; *Bavli Sanhedrin* 52b and Tosefta s.v. "hilkhata"; *Zevahim* 45a; *Bavli Yoma* 13a, Tosephta, s.v. "halakhah."

3. *Halakhah in a Theological Dimension* (Chico: CA, 1984), ch. 7, "The Threat of Nuclear War: Jewish Perspectives."

4. *Hilkhot Yesoday Ha-Torah* 4:13 re: *Bavli Sukkah* 28a.

5. See *Encyclopedia Talmudit* 3:335b-, s.v. "bal tash'hit."

6. *Semag*, neg., no. 229; *Semaq*, no. 175.

7. Maimonides, *Hilkhot Melakhim* 6:10 (also, *Sefer Ha-Hinukh*, no. 529). This follows Maimonides' method of limiting scriptural (*d'Orayta*) commandments to those explicitly stated in Scripture, or those inferences the rabbis themselves designated as "essentially Toraitic" (*guf Torah*). See *Sefer Ha-Mitzvot*, introduction, no. 2. Nevertheless, in *Sefer Ha-Mitzvot*, neg., no. 57 Maimonides designates all wanton destruction (*kol hefsed*) as violations of *bal tash'hit d'Orayta*.

8. See *Mishnah Makkot* e.1*ff.*

9. Deuteronomy 25:2–3. See *Sifre: Devarim*, no. 286; *Mishnah Makkot* 3.10.

10. See Rabbi Isaac Lampronti, *Pahad Yitzhaq*, ed. Leghorn (1840), 4:119b. s.v. "makkat mardut."

11. For the notion that all rabbinic legislation has evident reasons (*ta'ama*), see *Bavli Gittin* 14a and Tosefta, s.v. "ke-hilkhata." For the notion that a reason (*telos*) is a limitation (*peras*), see Aristotle, *Metaphysics*, 994b15.

12. Alfred Rahlfs, *Septuaginta; id est Vitus Testamentum Graece iaxta ixx, interpretes* (Stuttgart: Privilegierte Wuerttembergische Bibelenstalt, 1935, 1952), p. 323.

13. *Payrush Rashi Al Ha-Torah*, ed. C. B. Chavel (Jerusalem, 1982), 563.

14. See *Mishnah Sanhedrin* 8:5 and D. Novak, *Violence in Our Society*,

Some Jewish Insights (New York: American Jewish Committee, Institute of Human Relations, 1983), 11*ff.*

15. *Sifre: Devarim,* no. 203.

16. In *Miqra'ot Gedolot* (New York, 1951) thereto.

17. *De Specialus Legibus* 4:226, 228, *Philo,* trans. F. H. Colson (Cambridge, MA: Loeb Classical Library, 1939), 8:148–149.

18. *Antiquities,* 4.299, *Josephus,* trans. H. St. John Thackeray (Cambridge, MA: Loeb Classical Library, 1930), 4:620–621.

19. See *Fundamental Principles of the Metaphysics of Morals,* trans. Thomas Kingsmill Abbott (New York: Liberal Arts Press, 1949), 31*ff.*

20. *Sefer Ha-Torah Ve-Ha-Mitzvah* (Jerusalem, 1957) thereto. See, also, Rashbam thereto.

21. *Cf.* Maimonides, *Hilkhot Berakhot* 11:2.

22. *Sefer Otzar Ha-Payrushim Al Ha-Torah: Mizrahi* (New York, 1965) thereto. For the difference between *milhemet reshut* and *milhemet mitzvah,* see *Mishnah Sotah* 8:7 and *Bavli* and *Yerushalmi* thereto; Maimonides, *Hilkhot Melakhim* 5:1; *Sugyat Ha-Milhamah,* ed. J. Copperman (Jerusalem, 1962).

23. One should compare the compromising stand of Rabban Johanan ben Zakkai, the transitional figure between pre-70 C.E. Rabbinic Pharisaism and post-70 C.E. Rabbinic Judaism (halakhic Judaism), as recorded in the famous passage in *Bavli Gittin* 56b, with the endorsement of mass suicide for reasons of national pride made by the Zealot leader, Eleazar ben Jair, as reported by Josephus in *Bellum Judaicum* 7:334–336. See also D. Novak, *Law and Theology in Judaism* (New York, 1974), 1:83*ff.* For similar moral reasoning, see Pope John XXIII, *Pacem in Terris* (Washington, DC: 1963), p. 30.

24. For a classic statement of utilitarianism, see Jeremy Bentham, *An Introduction to the Principles of Morals and Legislation* (London: Printed for W. Pickering, 1823), chap. 1.

25. *Payrush Shadal Al Hamishah Humshay Torah,* ed. P. Schlesinger (Tel Aviv, 1965) thereto, 537. See also his comment on Exodus 22:20. Later on (538–539), however, in order to justify the command of Elisha in 2 Kings 3:19, Luzzatto provides what seems to me to be an interpretation which contradicts his critique of the utilitarian interpretation of Deuteronomy 20:19. Nevertheless, he concludes (539) with the suggestion that the reason for this norm is to show gratitude to anyone or anything which has benefitted us. Gratitude per se cannot

be justified on utilitarian grounds (see *Bereshit Rabbah* 96:5 re. Genesis 47:29).

26. The conjunction *ki* in this verse probably functions as "a neutral interrogative . . . expecting a negative answer." Brown, Driver, and Briggs, *A Hebrew and English Lexicon of the Old Testament* (Oxford: Oxford University Press, 1966), 472a. For a similar interpretation of a two clause verse connected by the conjunction *ki*, note Exodus 22:20— "You shall not oppress the sojourner (*ger*) or persecute him, for (*ki*) you were sojourners (*gerim*) in the land of Egypt." Ibn Ezra interprets the second clause as itself a command, viz., "*and* remember (*u-zekhor*) that (*ki*) you were like him (*kemohu*)." (On Deuteronomy 20:19 Ibn Ezra also uses the key term *kemohu*.) Here, too, the first part of the command prescribes action; the second part an attendant attitude. For the argument that the second clause is an insufficient reason (*ta'am*) per se for the first, see Nahmanides thereto; *cf.* Rashi, however.

27. The same line of reasoning is employed by the Talmud (*Bavli Sanhedrin* 21a) in explaining the fact that Rabbi Simon (*Mishnah Sanhedrin* 2:4 and *Bavli Baba Metzia* 115a) opines that even when reasons seem to be given for specific norms in the Torah itself, these reasons are themselves norms (*darish ta'ama de-qra*), and the true and sufficient reasons are not revealed in the text but, if possible, are inferred from the text. See E. E. Urbach, *Emunot Ve-De'ot Hazel* (Jerusalem: Magnes Press, 1971), 328.

28. See Thomas Aquinas, *Summa Theologia*, 1–2, q. 94, a. 2.

29. See Jacques Ellul, *The Technological System*, trans. Joachin Neugroschel (New York: Continuum, 1980), 129, 256.

30. In *Miqra'ot Gedolot* thereto.

31. If one follows the line of reasoning that sees Deuteronomy 20:19 as a general prohibition exemplified by the prohibition of cutting down fruit trees, then this is a case of "Scripture taking a contemporary example" (*dibber ha-Katuv be-hoveh*), but the norm is not limited to that example (*ba-meh matzinu*). See *Mishnah Baba Kama* 5:7; *Sifra*, intro., 13 *Principles*, no. 3; *Encyclopedia Talmudit* 2:1ff., s.v. "Binyan av."

32. *Payrush Ha-Ramban Al Ha-Torah*, ed. C. B. Chavel (Jerusalem, 1963) thereto. See *Bavli Baba Kama* 91b. In his addenda to Maimonides, *Sefer Ha-Mitzvot*, pos. no. 6, Nahmanides designates *bal tash'hit* as only prohibiting "purposeless destruction" (*hash'hatah be-hinam*). Moreover, he restricts the prohibition to the time of invasion of an enemy land, but during the time of retreat "all is permitted" (*kol zeh muttar*). In his Torah

commentary, written many years later in his career, he does not mention this qualification. It seems to me that this is because he moved closer to the more categorical position of Ibn Ezra. See also Maimonides, *Hilkhot Melakhim* 6:8.

33. *Ibid.*

34. See *Bavli Sukkah* 30a and parallels; *Payrush Hallah* 1:5/58a; LXX and Targum Pseudo-Jonathan on Deuteronomy 16:20; also, *Bavli Sanhedrin* 74a.

35. No. 203, ed. Finkelstein, 239.

36. *Bavli Shabbat* 129a.

37. *Mishnah Shabbat* 7:2.

38. *Mishnah Shabbat* 13:1; *Bavli Shabbat* 105b.

39. *Hilkhot Shabbat* 8:8 and 10:10.

40. See *Bavli Shabbat* 49b, 97b re: Exodus 35:1; *P. Shabbat* 7:2/9b; *Mekhilta: Vayaqhel*, ed. Horovitz-Rabin, 345.

41. See Exodus 36:4–7.

42. *Bavli Kiddushin* 32a.

43. See Rashi, *ibid.*, s.v. "be-fombay."

44. *Kesef Mishneh* on Maimonides, *Hilkhot Melakhim* 6:10.

45. *Bavli Shabbat* 105b. See Maimonides, *Hilkhot De'ot* 2:3.

46. See Sigmund Freud, *Beyond the Pleasure Principle*, trans. J. Strachey (New York: Liveright, 1961), 70*ff.*

47. See Psalms 115:2–8; *Mekhilta: Yitro*, 223 and no. 8 thereon.

48. See Shalom Spiegel, *Amos versus Amaziah* (New York: Jewish Theological Seminary of America, n.d.).

49. See William L. Shirer, *The Rise and Fall of the Third Reich* (New York: Simon & Schuster, 1960), pp. 1432–1434.

50. See *Bavli Baba Batra* 12a–b; *Bavli Pesahim* 66a.

51. *Payrush Ha-Torah*: Abrabanel, ed. (Warsaw, 1862) thereto.

52. *Sefer Ha-Hinukh*, no. 529 (New York, 1966), 78b.

53. *Payrush Ha-Ralbag Al Ha-Torah*, Deuteronomy 20:19, ed. Venice (1547), 129b, no. 5.

54. See Genesis 2:15, 8:22–9:8.

55. Ed. Leipzig (1686) thereto. The midrashic text is *Tanhuma: Pinhas*, printed ed., no. 3. There the Midrash also indicates that in the campaign

against Midian (Numbers 25:17), the prescription of Deuteronomy 20:19 did not apply. The reason given for this exception is self-defense. See *Bavli Berakhot* 62b and *Bavli Sanhedrin* 72a re: Exodus 22:2.

56. See, e.g., *Bavli Yebamot* 90b and Tosefot, s.v. "ve-li-gmar"; *Bavli Sanhedrin* 89b and Tosefot, s.v. "Eliyahu"; *Bavli Kiddushin* 43a re: 2 Samuel 11:11 and Tosefot, s.v. "mored." See also Gersonides and Abrabanel on 2 Samuel 1:15.

57. See *Mishnah Gittin* 4.5.

58. See *Bavli Berakhot* 3b–4a and *Bavli Sanhedrin* 16a–b re: 1 Chronicles 27:34; also, *P. Sanhedrin* 1:3/19b re: 2 Samuel 24:19, 2 Chronicles 3:1 and Deuteronomy 32:7, and *P. Shabbat* 2:6/5b re: Numbers 27:21. Today the prerequisites of a Sanhedrin (*Mishnah Sanhedrin* 1:5 and 2:4; *Bavli Sanhedrin* 41a and parallels) and the *Urim ve-Tumim* (*Mishnah Sotah* 9:12; see *Mishnah Yoma* 7:5), necessary for waging a *milhemet reshut*, are no longer extant. Although Maimonides follows the Talmud in indicating that a *milhemet reshut* is to be waged according to the example of King David (see his comment on *Mishnah Sanhedrin* 1:5), he does not indicate that the *Urim ve-tumim* are a conditio sine qua non for such a war. See *Hilkhot Melakhim* 5:1.

59. *P. Shevi'it* 6:1/36c and Maimonides, *Hilkhot Melakhim* 6:1, 5; also, *Bavli Gitten* 46a, Tosefot, s.v. "kayvan"; Nahmanides on Deuteronomy 20:10.

60. *Bavli Berakhot* 61b re: Deuteronomy 6:5.

61. See *Bavli Sanhedrin* 108a–b; *Bereshit Rabbah* 30:7.

62. See *Mishnah Avot* 3:1.

63. See, esp., R. P. Turco, O. B. Toon, T. P. Packerman, J. B. Pollack, and C. Sagan, "Nuclear Winter: Global Consequences of Multiple Nuclear Explosions," *Science* (December 23, 1983).

DIALOGIC
REFLECTIONS

7

The Human Situation
and the Nuclear Threat

Maurice Friedman

The nuclear threat brings human values into crisis as never before in human history, thereby challenging, evoking, and illuminating them in an unprecedented fashion. For human values are not Platonic ideals shining untroubled in an eternal sky. They are earthbound, dying in each conflagration and, like the phoenix, springing up from their own ashes to live anew in the face of fresh situations that call them forth.

In the context of the English civil war in the seventeenth century, the political philosopher Thomas Hobbes held man to be evil and life in nature to be nasty, raw, brutish, and short—a war of all against all. In the eighteenth century, in the context of the deteriorating French monarchy and the need to point toward the revolution which he helped at least indirectly to set in motion, Jean-Jacques Rousseau held exactly an opposite position to Hobbes's, that man is good but that it is civilization that has changed him and made him evil.

PSYCHOLOGICAL AND
PHILOSOPHICAL APPROACHES

Sigmund Freud, the father of depth psychology, took a position between these two. He believed that civilization produces individual and collective neuroses and "discontents." But in his later thinking he also held that along with Eros—the love instinct—there is Thanatos—the death instinct. People are aggressive and destructive, not as a secondary result of frustration of the libidinal drive, but rather as a primary given of humankind. People take advantage of others, and the more helpless others are, the more harm they inevitably do them without even thinking of the cruel advantage they are taking. *Homo homine lupus*, Freud concluded—man is a "wolf to man." Who in the face of recorded history and his or her own experience would have the courage to deny it? In the years since Freud made this statement, as much new evidence has accumulated to support his thesis as had been recorded in the whole of human history up to that time.

This double attitude toward civilization and individuals led Freud, in his classic exchange of letters with Albert Einstein a half century ago, to hold that war is inevitable. Albert Einstein, pacifist, idealist, and universalist, held in contrast to Freud that war was not inevitable, that we can and should do things that will lead to overcoming the need for armed conflict. Einstein retained this attitude until his death.

However, Einstein had himself ushered in the age of atomic physics and thus the nuclear age with the discovery of relativity in 1905. Einstein was the first to warn President Roosevelt that the Nazis were probably developing an atomic bomb, and thus set this country on its own road to making one. On President Roosevelt's desk, at the time of his death, was a letter from Einstein and other nuclear physicists begging him not to use the atomic bomb that had been created partly as a result of Einstein's own initiative.

Martin Buber, the great Jewish philosopher, told me that Einstein could have had an operation that would have saved his life, but that he was so depressed and discouraged about the consequences of nuclear arms that he did not undergo it. Einstein stands as a tragic figure—the man of peace who ushered in our nuclear age, but is all too humanly aware of its catastrophic possibilities.

A quarter of a century ago I moderated a dialogue between Martin Buber and Carl Rogers, the noted American psychologist who has been very active in the fight against nuclear arms. Central to that dialogue was the same question of Hobbes and Rousseau and of Freud and Einstein—the question of what and who we are. In conscious contrast to Sigmund Freud, Carl Rogers held that people are not evil by nature. Were a person to be accepted, for example, by his therapist with unconditional positive regard, we would have a socially constructive result. Martin Buber suggested a third position: that people are polar. "That which you say can be most trusted in people can be also least trusted in them." By this Buber meant that we have a movement toward direction and also a refusal to take direction, a yes and a no, and that both are part of every person. This is why Buber could not agree with Rogers, who equated accepting persons with confirming them. "I have to struggle with people, for them, because of this polar nature," Buber said.

The classic question remains: Is human nature good or evil? Modern philosophical anthropology, for example, does not imagine, as Hobbes and Rousseau did, that you can define a human being without taking into account the world in which he or she lives. Philosophical anthropology looks to the wholeness and uniqueness of the human as someone who lives under certain conditions, who has possibility, who knows that she or he will die, and who is a social being. In *The Knowledge of Man*,[1] Buber's philosophical anthropology, man sets man at a distance, making his fellow into an independent other who is over against him. This fact enables man to enter into relations with those like himself but as an individual. Through this "interhuman" relation, men confirm one another, becoming a self along with the other. Individualization is indispensable, not as a goal, but as a stage on the way to meeting with others. What we call our "I" is neither some inner essence nor the mere product of social conditioning, but the ground from which we go out again and again to meet the Thou.

Mutual confirmation is essential for us on our way to becoming a *self*—a person who realizes her uniqueness precisely in relation to other selves whose distance from her is completed by her distance from them. True confirmation means that I confirm my partner as this existing being even while I oppose her. I legitimize her over against me as the one with whom I have to engage in real dialogue. This mutual confirmation of persons is most fully realized in what Buber calls "making present," an event which happens partially wherever persons come together, but in its essential structure only rarely. Making the other present means to "imagine the real," to imagine quite concretely what another person is wishing, feeling, perceiving, and thinking. This is not empathy or intuitive perception, but a bold swinging into the other which demands the most intense action of one's being. The inmost growth of the self is not induced by man's relation to himself, as people like to suppose today, but by the confirmation in which one person knows herself to have been made present by her uniqueness to the other. In making present we add something of our will to what is imagined of the other and thus participate in the other's inmost self-becoming.

The sphere of the between comes to its fullness in the life of dialogue. "All real living is meeting," as Buber says—the going out to meet others and holding our ground when we meet them. Genuine dialogue is two-sided, beyond the control of the will. We attain personal wholeness when we respond to the other without thinking of ourselves, and we attain genuine dialogue not by aiming at it but by allowing the other to exist in her otherness and not just as a content of our experience and thought. We can perceive the other person as whole and unique only through the attitude of a partner and not through that reductive, analytical, and derivative look that prevails today.

The relation between persons takes place not only in the "I–Thou" of direct meeting but in the "We" of family and community. The essential We includes the Thou potentially; for only persons who are capable of truly saying Thou to one another can truly say We with one another. This We is not of secondary or merely instrumental importance; it is basic to human existence. To make real our human existence together, we must join with others in building a common world of speech and a common order of being. We have our experiences and thoughts as I, but it is as We that we construct and develop a world out of our experiences and lift the ideas that we have transplanted into the firmament of the spirit into being itself, "the between." Thus our common world is built by the common speech-with-meaning, the human cosmos by the common logos.

Speech, from this point of view, is no mere function or tool, but is itself of the stuff of reality, able to create or destroy reality. Speech may be falsehood and conventionality, but it is also the great pledge of truth. Whether one takes refuge in individualism or collectivism, the person who flees answering for the genuineness of her existence is marked by the fact that she can no longer really listen to the voice of another. The other is now only an object that she observes. But true dialogue means that the other has not only ears but a mouth. She can say something that will surprise one, something new, unique, and unrepeatable for which the only adequate reply is the spontaneous response of the whole being, and nothing that can be prepared beforehand. Only if real listening as well as real speaking takes place has there been the full possibility of mutual confirmation of *present* in family, community, and society. Only thus, and not through any mere *feeling* of group unity, will the full potentiality of the group *as a group* be realized.

We need to be confirmed by others in our uniqueness and not as their extension. Yet, all too often what significant others offer us is what I call the "contract"—confirmation with strings attached. Such "strings" again and again make the emergence of the self through confirmation problematic. For our need for confirmation is so great that we not only accept this contract but even succumb to the temptation of seeming to be what the other wants. This invisible, unspoken contract reads: "If you are a good boy or girl, student, churchgoer, citizen, or soldier, we shall confirm you as lovable. If you are not, not only will you not be confirmed but you will have to live with the introjected knowledge that you are fundamentally unlovable." This is a contract that most of us buy, more or less, and there is no human way to be wholly free of it.

THE IMAGE OF THE HUMAN

To go a step beyond philosophical anthropology, or rather to make it more concrete, we must look at the image of the human as something that is not a concept, nor even an analysis of the existential conditions of human existence, but the image of what it is, can, and should mean to be a human being.[2]

This means that we cannot take human values for granted; rather we have to seek their source in the basic attitudes toward reality in which they are rooted. Human values are not self-sufficient; on the contrary, they presuppose an image of the human—an image of a meaningful direction of personal and social existence—a basic life-stance from whose ground we go forth to meet what comes to meet us. Man, said Nietzsche's Zarathustra, is a valuing animal: without valuing, even the shell of existence is hollow. To live means to make value choices, to hold in tension tradition and the unexplored future. We need, therefore, an image of the human to help us go beyond the mere realization of potentialities to the discovery of what the human can be in each one of us and in every family, community, and society. It must be revealed anew in every situation. It can never be revealed once and for all.

Thus, another important link between the human situation and the nuclear threat, and one that is integrally related to the life of dialogue, is the image of the human. The image of the human implies a meaningful personal and social direction, a response from within to what one meets in each new situation, standing one's ground and meeting the world with the attitude that is rooted in this ground. It is at one and the same time concern for what is authentic *human* existence and concern for what is authentic for us in particular; for it is with others that each of us realizes what the human can become in us. We come to awareness of ourselves as selves not just through our individuality, and not only through our differences from others, but in our dialogue with other selves—in their response to us and in the way they call us into being. Because we live as separate selves, yet also in relation to other persons and to society—present, past, and to come—we need an image of the human to aid us in finding a meaningful way of life, in choosing between conflicting sets of values, and in realizing our own unique potentialities.

The image of the human distinguishes between our potentiality and the direction we give to it. Terms such as self-actualization and self-realization leave unanswered the question of what direction we must take to "realize" or "actualize" our selves. Our need is to give our potentialities direction, not some abstract ideal but a constantly changing, flowing direction of movement that is at one and the same time a response to the present, a choice between possibilities in a given situation, and a line of advance into the future.

Prometheus was a Titan, one of the earth gods who were conquered by the Olympian sky gods. Prometheus rebelled against Zeus, the most powerful god in the Greek pantheon, and he had knowledge and foresight with which to do so. Prometheus has come down to us as a great symbol of a proud rebel, who defied in the name of the human, and who expanded the realm of the human in the face of jealousy of Zeus, so that each successive generation could have ever greater possibility and hope. What we tend to forget, however, is that Prometheus was also a tragic figure. He did not rebel against the order; he rebelled on the basis of it, because he was a god, he was immortal, and he had foreknowledge that Zeus did not have. As the sly, cunning god who gave man civilizing tools, Prometheus is indeed the father of modern science. Yet, if we go back to the Greek origins, we can also understand the ambiguity of that science. It not only wrests a place for humans in the teeth of the hostility of Zeus, but it leads to hubris, the Greek notion of people bringing about their own destruction through the overstepping of limits. Such destruction became a realistic possibility when the atomic bomb and the potential for nuclear war were created. We now stand at the place where Prometheus can simultaneously bring us forward to the most undreamt-of advances of science—and in so doing destroy the human.

When we consider the peril we face, we have to look again critically at the Renaissance creed of Francis Bacon: that the way to the realization of one's humanity is through the knowledge that gives one power over nature. Today we stand precisely at the point where our humanity is endangered through that very power over nature. As Einstein put it, the atomic age has changed everything but our way of thinking; therefore we are in danger of destroying ourselves. Perhaps that is why Captain Ahab in Melville's *Moby-Dick* throws the quadrant down on the deck and says, "Science, curse thou vain toy." It no longer does for him what it was supposed to have done.

If we look at the figure that I call the Modern Promethean, we find the carrying forward, not of the god—there is no god anymore—not of the immortality of the original Prometheus, not of the foreknowledge, but of that desire to give people something, to rebel in the name of people. This is a heroic, even romantic rebellion under which, I suspect, often lies desperation and despair. This expresses itself again and again, in an either/or stance. We now know ourselves not in a secure order like that of the Middle Ages, but face-to-face with the same infinity that terrified Pascal, the infinite spaces between the stars. We feel it will destroy us, and so we have to destroy it. We say what Nietzsche says in *Thus Spake Zarathustra*: "If there were gods how could I bear to be no god; therefore there are no gods." Along with Captain Ahab, we feel the White Whale to be the incarnation of all evil, an evil that destroys not just Ahab but all humankind. If Ahab can destroy Moby Dick, he imagines that he will automatically establish good. In the process he becomes evil and destroys himself and all the crew except Ishmael, who is saved only to tell the story.

The image of the human is a basic attitude, a way of responding. I won't ever be St. Francis, Albert Camus, or Abraham Lincoln, but my dialogue with them can enter into the way I respond to situations they did not face.

The image of the human stands in need of revelation. Like a face, it both conceals and reveals, and it must be revealed anew in every situation. The human image is hidden: It can never be revealed once and for all, because what the human can be we will only discover in each new situation.

But there is another meaning of the hiddenness of the human image in our time. That is the obliteration of the human, the eclipse of the human, the destruction of the human image which we have witnessed in Auschwitz, in Hiroshima, in Biafra, and in the millions who were killed in the Soviet slave labor camps of the Gulag Archipelago.

Erich Fromm held that the nineteenth century was the death of God, while the twentieth century is that of the death of man. But actually both deaths are the same. For the death of God is the loss of any basis for movement, for living, for values in our life. The death of man—the loss and destruction of the human image—is a consequence of the death of God. I agree with Elie Wiesel that with the Holocaust, the extermination of six million Jews and five million others, the Nazis paved the way for the nuclear holocaust. In *One Generation After*, Elie Wiesel writes, "If the human race should perish by the nuclear bomb, this will be the punishment for Auschwitz, where in the ashes the hope of man was extinguished. At Auschwitz not only man died, but also the idea of man"[3] (or, I would say, the image of man). The Nazi Holocaust was the first great scientific extermination of people. No one ever protested effectively or tried to stop it. No plane ever bombed the train tracks carrying 10,000 lives a day to Auschwitz. The possibility arose that the human image would indeed disintegrate.

In the eighteenth century, Thomas Jefferson could confidently declare: "We hold these truths to be self-evident, that all men are created equal." Today, it is not self-evident to anyone that all men are created equal, because the *inequality* of men has been made a fact of history, and the existence of that fact makes it all too probable that other such "facts" will occur. It is in the teeth of that manifested inequality that we must affirm the true equality of men—in the teeth of the monstrous consequence with which the Nazis declared some races inferior to others, in the teeth of the atomic bomb dropped upon the Japanese, in the teeth of man's readiness to turn human beings into cakes of soap, and to condemn others to a horrible death, fast or slow, by radiation.

Is the hidden image in our day so "hidden" that it can no longer be revealed? The crisis of human values in which we find ourselves means that we no longer know what it means to be human and that we are becoming aware that we do not know this. This is above all a crisis of trust—or of confidence—in man, in eternity, in existence itself. The eclipse of the human means the loss of courage to address and to respond, which is the heart of existential trust. If we can no longer summon the resources to meet a new situation in whatever form it takes, then our image of the human—our stance as human beings—is imperiled. The waning of genuine dialogue between persons is the symptom, taught Martin Buber, but a pervasive "existential mistrust," such as has never before existed, is the disease itself.

When we try to anticipate concretely what it will be like when a nuclear bomb hits, it is abundantly clear how the nuclear threat is a cause of the hiding of the human image in our time. But I think it is also an effect of the human image in the sense of the attitude of the modern Promethean. The nuclear war threatens hope, it threatens our very communication, which makes us human beings. In our day, more than ever before, there is the *death* of a dialogue in which language is abused and perverted. One nuclear bomb is called "peacemaker," and all our language betrays a massive denial and a massive self-deception.

THE COMMUNITY OF JOB

There is an alternative—a response to the challenge of the nuclear threat that would bring about a decisive change in our image of the human. What is the direction of that change, and how would that in turn help to overcome the nuclear threat?

In the era of the "death of God," the era of alienation and of exile, there have been two types of rebellion: that of the modern Promethean and that of the modern Job. An unprejudiced reading of the Book of Job shows not the submissive, humble figure that people always imagine Job is, but, on the contrary, perhaps the person in all religious history who issues the strongest challenge to God. Job combines trust and contention in dialogue with God. This is no blind faith. "It is all one, I despise my life. Therefore I say, He mocks at the calamity of the guiltless, if it be not He, then who is it?" The attitude of Job can remain in the modern Job even if that person, like Albert Camus, is an atheist. That attitude of openness, of readiness to enter the dialogue, of contending within the dialogue—this is the response to the challenge of the nuclear threat that could help to overcome it, and perhaps the only response that can. It could be a revelation of the hidden human image in a time when the Dialogue with the Absurd may be our most meaningful stance. We must contend with the absurdity of trying to live and prepare for the future when, for the first time in human history, there may be no future. Even the small nations, in the future, will have the atomic bomb and be able to hurl the world into nuclear war and total destruction. Then, too, there is the absurdity of the statement, it is "impossible to win a nuclear war," and the incredible denial that underlies the whole notion that there could be meaningful civil defense for Los Angeles or San Diego or San Francisco.

So what is our possibility, applied concretely? It is what Martin Buber called dialogue and confirmation. The modern Promethean stance is to say *Carthaga delenda est*: Our opponents are evil and must be destroyed; we can do it and we can survive with 35 percent of our population and become rich. The alternative of the modern Job is to say we live together in this world, for better and worse. It doesn't even matter whether our opponents are good or evil, the real question is, "How can we live together?" There is no meaningful ethic of self-interest any more, and there is no meaningful ethic of nationalism. Human conflict must be arbitrated through the very dialogue that combines trust and contending. This is the true alternative to the either/or of the modern Promethean.

The contract[4] which confirms us with strings attached necessitates a distinction that is not usually made between two different types of community: the "community of like-mindedness," or "affinity," and the "community of otherness." The community of like-mindedness is made up of people who huddle together for security—sons or daughters of the American Revolution, or Communists, or Jews, or Catholics, or Protestants, or born-again Christians. They imagine that they are safe and secure because they use the same slogans and the same language, even though they may not have much real relation with one another. It's the "Godfather" mentality, which led R. D. Laing to say, "The family is a protection racket." Communities, too, are often protection rackets and so are nations. Nonetheless, such a community will always be a false community, for it is only concerned with that coloration that makes these people feel secure because they are so afraid of conflict and opposition.

The community of otherness is no mere ideal. It is a direction of movement—one for which we discover the resources in each new situation. The community of otherness means the recognition that any community is really made up of the people who are there, even if only two friends, a husband and wife, or a family. If the members of any such group claim that there is only one point of view, then this reveals a collusion in which people are pretending not to have more. Marriage is the exemplary bond, says Buber, because in it we learn that the other has not just an opinion or point of view, but a different touch from the regions of existence, a different soil, and a different faith. It is the otherness that has to be confirmed for us to become human and for us to find a way forward. This is not at all a matter of individualism; on the contrary, it is a matter of the only way the community can be made real. That has to begin with friendship; it has to begin in the family; it has to begin also when people have what they used to call quite euphemistically the "blended family" (it was usually more like an explosion). It has to move to communities in terms of the workers, the women, the aged, and the diversity of cultures; but it has to move even beyond that also, to the dialogue between nations.

The community of otherness is not where people are alike but where they have a common concern. The common concern to move forward is possible only if we overcome nuclear weapons. Then we could have a hardheaded coming together that would enable us to distinguish between the propaganda we put out for home consumption, and which keeps people in power by obscuring the economic depression that is upon us, and the real needs and possibilities. All of this is not easy but it is a direction of movement. If instead of spending our billions on nuclear arms, we put energy in the direction of building a community of otherness among the nations, we would discover what the possibilities are. Again, this is not an ideal; there are tragic situations, but we don't know the possibilities until we find them. The great Protestant theologian Reinhold Niebuhr told Martin Buber that it was not possible to have justice in society, only between persons. "I can't accept that these are two different things," Buber replied. "I can't know how much justice is possible in this situation until I go out and my head hits the wall and hurts, and then I know I've reached the limit. But if I hadn't gone on until my head hit the wall, I wouldn't know."

The confirmation of otherness offers us a new approach to the peace movement and the task of reconciliation. Reconciliation depends upon each of us doing his share to build the "community of otherness." Reality is not given in me alone or in some part of reality with which I identify myself. Among primitive peoples, the members of other tribes were often not even considered as human. Even the civilized Greeks saw the rest of the non-Greek world as "barbarians," and since by nature unequal to them, could therefore be forced into permanent slavery when conquered. The ravaging of the American frontier and the ravages of the whaling industry similarly show that a good deal of what has characterized modern man, long before the Nazi exterminations, has been a lack of respect for the otherness of creation, including the nonhuman.

The respect for the otherness of the other does not mean that I love everyone, or even that I have the resources to meet everyone in genuine dialogue. But it does mean that everything that confronts me demands my attention and response—whether of love or hate, agreement or opposition, confirmation or merely letting be. There is a growing tendency today on both sides of the generation gap, on both extremes of the political spectrum, and on both sides of every militant social and racial confrontation to regard people as totally irrelevant if their views are not considered to be viable. The "community of otherness" stands in uncompromising opposition to this tendency. I have freedom, but I am not the whole of reality and I find my existence in going out to meet what is not myself.

The greatest task of contemporary man is not to build "enlightened" utopias but to build peace in the context in which he finds himself. The true peacemakers are those who take upon themselves, in the most concrete manner conceivable, the task of discovering what can be done in each situation of tension and struggle by way of facing the real conflicts and working toward genuine reconciliation.

"A peace without truth is a false peace," said Rabbi Menahem Mendel of Kotsk. What "truth" means here is made clear by the talmudic statement that Hasidic master partly quoted: "Controversies for the sake of heaven endure." This is completely contrary to the assumption in Aristotelian logic that a statement and its opposite cannot both be true. If controversies take place for the sake of heaven, then both sides will endure. It does not mean that eventually one will be proved right and the other wrong. The knowledge that the other also witnesses for his "touchstone of reality" from where he stands can enable us to confirm the other in his truth, even while opposing him. We do not have to liberate the world from those who have different witnesses from ours. The converse of this also holds: that each must hold his ground and witness for his truth even while affirming the ground and the truth of the other. This imaginative task of comprehending a relationship from the other side as well as one's own is essential to the goal of overcoming war, for every war justifies itself by turning the enemy into a Manichaean figure of pure evil.

If the present crises lead us to succumb to the merely political, we shall have reinforced the mistrust between nations that makes them deal with each other not in social or human terms but in political abstractions and catchwords. "Our work is for education," one of the leaders of an organized protest against atomic bombs said to me. If this is so, then this work cannot afford to be purely political and external. It must start from some organic base. It must build on social reality and find its roots in the community already there. It must be concerned about real communication with the people whom it approaches. For the distinction between propaganda and education does not lie in whether one is a Communist or a pacifist but in whether one cares enough for the other to enter into dialogue with him, see the situation form his point of view, and communicate what truth one has to communicate to him within that dialogue. Sometimes that dialogue can only mean standing one's ground in opposition to him, witnessing for what one believes in the face of his hostile rejection of it. Yet it can never mean being unconcerned for how he sees it or denial of the validity of his stance. We must confirm him even in our opposition—not in his "error" but in his right to oppose us, in his existence as a human being whom we value even in opposing.

We must nurture that trust—through which the "other voice" is elicited—of the person who will speak only in an atmosphere that weighs every voice equally, no matter how hesitant or how much in the minority it may be. From 1931 until his death in 1965, Martin Buber continued to insist that Jews live with the Arabs in the Land of Israel and not just next to them, and that the way must be like the goal. The humanity of our existence begins just where we become responsible to the concrete situation by saying: "We shall do no more injustice than we must to live," and by drawing the "demarcation line" in each hour anew in fear and trembling. The covenant of peace—between person and person, between community and community, and between nation and nation—means dialogue.

DIALOGUE AND THE SEARCH FOR PEACE

Dialogue means meeting with the other person, the other group, the other people, in a manner that confirms the other yet does not deny oneself and the ground on which one stands. The choice is not between oneself and the other, nor is there some objective ground to which one can rise above the opposing sides and the conflicting claims. Genuine dialogue is at once a confirmation of community and of otherness and the acceptance of the fact that one cannot rise above that situation. "In a genuine dialogue," writes Buber, "each of the partners, even when he stands in opposition to the other, heeds, affirms, and confirms his opponent as an existing other. Only so can conflict certainly not be eliminated from the world but be humanly arbitrated and led towards its overcoming."

The covenant of peace is neither technique nor formula, and still less is it a universal principle which need only be applied by deduction to the particular situation. Such a covenant starts from the concrete situation, including all of its tensions which we can never hope or even desire to remove entirely, since they belong to the very heart of the community of otherness. The covenant of peace is not an ideal that one holds above the situation, but a patient and never-finished working toward some points of mutual contact, mutual understanding, and mutual trust. It builds community by way of mutual confirmation of otherness, and when this community shipwrecks, as it again and again tends to do, it takes up the task anew. The covenant of peace means a movement in the direction of the community of otherness, such movement as each new hour allows.

In bedrock situations, even a negative protest may be a positive step toward dialogue if it is done in the spirit of dialogue. The covenant of peace implies a "fellowship of reconciliation"; yet it is precisely here that we have fallen short. We have tended to turn "reconciliation" into a platform to expound, a program to put over, and have not recognized the cruel opposition and the real otherness that underlie conflict. We have been loath to admit that there are tragic conflicts in which no way toward reconciliation is at present possible. We have been insufficiently tough-minded in our attitude toward love—turning it into abstract love for mankind or a feeling within ourselves rather than a meeting between us and others. We cannot really love unless we first know the other, and we cannot know her until we have entered into relationship with her.

Only a real listening—a listening witness—can plumb the abyss of that universal existential mistrust that stands in the way of genuine dialogue and peace. The peace movement has not adequately recognized the power of violence in our day, nor that its roots are not only in human nature in general or in the stupidity of individuals, but in the special malaise of modern man—his lack of a meaningful personal and social direction; his lack of an image of the human; his loss of community; his basic loss of trust in himself and others and in the world in which he lives; his fear of real confrontation with otherness; his tendency to cling to the shores of institutionalized injustice and discrimination rather than set out upon the open seas of creating new and more meaningful structures within which the "wretched of the earth," the dispossessed and the systematically ignored, can find their voices too.

The true heart of the covenant of peace is the community of otherness.

Rollo May[5] sees violence as the response, provoked by the sense of powerlessness and apathy, to a situation that is felt to block off all other ways of response. Thus, deeds of violence, despite their negative form, are potentially constructive in that they are a way in which people who feel impotent try "to establish their self-esteem, to defend their self-image, and to demonstrate that they too, are significant." Curiously enough, even when as in America there actually is power, the denial of power in the name of a pseudoinnocence may lead to a feeling of powerlessness. Violence also arises from mutual mistrust, including the mistrust of language: "When the bond between human beings is destroyed—when the possibilities for communication break down—aggression and violence occur." Violence unites the self on a level below the human one, says May. It may also be the only way to wrench social reforms from the dominant group.

Simone Weil defined violence as reducing a person to a thing, the ultimate of which is killing—reducing a person to a corpse. If that is so, then we can no more avoid in our culture or in any culture what Martin Buber calls the "I–It relation," that is, the relation in which we use, know, classify, and categorize one another; for this is an enormous part of our culture and becomes more so every day. It is these very categories which lead us in the first place to prejudice, racism, and violence. But if violence means converting the human Thou into an It, then violence is no more inevitable than the domination of the It. We live in an age in which the machine, the corporation, and the technocrat dominate to an incredible degree. Yet a real possibility remains, through fighting and standing one's ground, of bringing these back into human dialogue. It remains with us and cannot be removed by the fists of any number of economic, psychological, social, military, or political realists who say, "This is the way it is." But if we are going to take this possibility seriously, then in each concrete situation we have to discover the hard way what the resources are for dialogue and for creating something human, and of returning the I and the Thou back into human dialogue, the I and Thou remains.

OTHERNESS AND THE HOPE FOR THE FUTURE

Our recognition that the true heart of the covenant of peace is the community of otherness is similar to the link which Martin Buber pointed out exists between genuine dialogue and the possibilities of peace. In his famous "Letter to Gandhi," Buber rejected Gandhi's suggestion that the Jews in Germany could use *satyagraha* (soul-force) effectively against the Nazis, since death in the concentration camps was anonymous martyrdom, not political witness. But he did see nonviolent civil disobedience as something that was more and more likely to be the demand of the particular situation upon those contemporary persons who are concerned not only for justice but for man as man.[6] He also knew the meaning of tragedy where "each is as he is" and oppositeness crystallizes into unbridgeable opposition.

CLOSING COMMENTS

What we need for our time is an openness, a flexibility, a willingness to resist and to withstand the concrete situation. If dialogue means the recognition of real limits and real tragedy, it also means hope, because it does not assume that what was true this moment will necessarily be true the moment after. Hope is not meant as an idealism, therefore, but rather as a readiness to assess the moment in its concreteness. This also means, of course, the readiness to know the needs of the other. Dialogue, therefore, has to include not just hope of something happening, but hope that will enable you to enter again, both actively and imaginatively, into the concrete situation of the other—to witness and to risk yourself.

Buber stressed that war has always had an adversary that does its work in the stillness: fulfilled speech, the speech of genuine conversation in which persons understand one another and come to a mutual understanding. When the word "soundlessly bears into the hearts of men the intelligence that no human conflict can really be resolved through killing, not even through mass killing, then the human word has already begun to silence the cannonade." In the modern crisis, however, persons and nations no longer entrust their cause to dialogue because its presupposition—trust—is lacking. In every earlier period of peace the living word passed time after time between person and person, drawing the poison from the antagonism of interests and convictions so that these antagonisms did not degenerate into the madness of "must-wage-war."

Through our faithful dialogue in and with the crisis created by omnicide, we may discover a way of remaining true to our humanity in the midst of its hiddenness. Indeed, a revealing of the human image can take place in response to Omnicide. It is perhaps the *only* way in which we can hope to overcome that threat.

NOTES

1. Martin Buber, *The Knowledge of Man: A Philosophy of the Interhuman*, ed. with an introductory essay (Chapter 1) by Maurice Friedman, trans. by Maurice Friedman and Ronald Gregor Smith (New York: Harper Torchbooks, 1966).

2. Maurice Friedman, *Problematic Rebel: Melville, Dostoevsky, Kafka, Camus*, enlarged and radically reorganized 2nd ed. (Chicago: University of Chicago Press and Phoenix Books, 1970); Maurice Friedman, *To Deny Our Nothingness: Contemporary Images of Man*, 3rd rev. ed. with new appendices (Chicago: University of Chicago Press, Phoenix Books, 1978); Maurice Friedman, *The Hidden Human Image* (New York: Delacorte Press and Delta Books, 1974); Maurice Friedman, *Contemporary Psychology: Revealing and Obscuring the Human* (Pittsburgh: Duquesne University Press, 1984).

3. Elie Wiesel, *One Generation After*, trans. by Lily Edelman and the author (New York: Random House, 1970).

4. Maurice Friedman, *The Confirmation of Otherness: In Family, Community, and Society* (New York: Pilgrim Press, 1983).

5. Rollo May, *Power and Innocence: A Search for the Sources of Violence* (New York: W. W. Norton, 1972).

6. Martin Buber, *Pointing the Way: Collected Essays*, ed. and trans. with an introduction by Maurice Friedman (New York: Harper & Row, 1963).

8

A Theology of Fear: The Search for a Liberal Jewish Paradigm

David Ellenson

The dilemma confronting humanity on the issue of weapons of mass destruction is monstrous. We face possible extinction of the planet if disarmament does not occur. Simultaneously, there is an understandable reluctance—given the lessons of aggression and destruction in human history—on the part of present-day super and regional powers to surrender their arsenals for fear that the "other side" will not do so. Solutions to this quandary are not simple, or easily discovered. Guidelines for resolving this dilemma must be forthcoming, for the "fate of the earth," in Jonathan Schell's felicitous phrase, hangs in the balance.

In the light of harsh reality this essay will explore representative writings of liberal Jewish thought during the last century. The goal is to extrapolate positions that are illustrative of the spectrum of possible liberal Jewish opinion on the issue of Omnicide. The effort, however, will be more than descriptive. Instead, through critical evaluation of the various postures, the goal will be to cull insights that might provide hope and guidance for humanity in the midst of our plight.

FRANZ ROSENZWEIG

At one end of the continuum of liberal Jewish opinion stand those thinkers whose views on war and peace can be said to lead to a position approximating the pacifistic. Foremost among these men is Franz Rosenzweig (1886–1929), the famed German-Jewish theologian whose thought has had a profound impact upon the American rabbinate. Rosenzweig, in his theology, saw the calendrical cycle of Sabbaths and holidays with their attendant liturgies as embodying the "essence" of Judaism, and the Jewish people as celebrating the existence of eternity within historical time. On the Sabbath, for example, the Jew, through the recitation of a liturgy which centers on the themes of Creation, Revelation, and Redemption, lives *sub-specie aeternitatis*, in the realm of eternity, and not *sub-specie temporis*, in the mundane sphere of the temporal. Similarly, the Jew steps beyond the constraints of time imposed upon him as a human being and encounters the eternal God through the yearly observance and repetition of the holidays. In short, Judaism requires the Jew to participate in an "eternal present," and, as such, allows the Jew to be part of an eternal people that transcend history. The Jewish people, forever basking in the rays of God's eternal presence, are removed, in Rosenzweig's opinion, from the passages of flux and succession that constitute the life of other nations. Situated beyond time, the Jewish people "must forget the world's growth, must cease to think thereon."[1]

The implications that this theological posture held for Rosenzweig's views on war and peace were immense. For while such a stance need not necessarily evolve into political quiescence, in Rosenzweig's case it did mean that the Jewish people needed to retreat from the political concerns of this world and focus instead upon preserving itself spiritually. "Because the Jewish people," Rosenzweig wrote, "is beyond the contradiction that constitutes the vital drive in the life of nations, . . . it knows nothing of

war. . . ." The Jew, he continued, "in the whole Christian world
. . . is practically the only human being who cannot take war
seriously, and this makes him the only genuine pacifist. For this
reason, and because he experiences perfect community in his
spiritual year, he remains remote from the chronology of the rest
of the world. . . ." Judaism and the Jew are "outside of time
agitated by wars."[2] Rosenzweig's view of war and peace, and that
of Jewish non-involvement in—one could almost say indifference
to—this struggle, is understandable, stemming as it does from a
pre-Holocaust and pre-State of Israel Jewish thinker. However,
his view is widely separated from the intense political concerns of
contemporary proponents of a unilateral and total elimination of
nuclear, chemical, and biological weapons and is obviously open
to modern Jewish charges of irrelevancy and danger in an era
when Jews, out of moral necessity, have entered into the realm of
power politics. Indeed, Emil Fackenheim, commenting upon this
aspect of Rosenzweig's thought, has critically noted that "an
absolute transcendence of time, that is, a Judaism of liturgical and
holiday cycles which refuses to participate in the political and
moral questions of this world is not attainable in our time."[3] At a
moment in history when nuclear apocalypse threatens, a Rosen-
zweigian type of pacifism that both ignores and retreats from the
demands of the day is a luxury whose price Judaism cannot afford
to pay.

ABRAHAM JOSHUA HESCHEL
AND HERMANN COHEN

Rosenzweig's vision of Judaism as a religion unconcerned with the
burdens of this world and history was opposed by Abraham
Joshua Heschel (1905-1972), Professor of Jewish Mysticism and
Ethics at the Jewish Theological Seminary of America for over
two decades. To be sure, Heschel, like Rosenzweig, focused upon
Judaism as a religion of "timelessness." Jewish tradition, he
taught, instructs humanity on "how to experience the taste of
eternity or eternal life in time."[4] For, "to men with God time is
eternity in disguise."[5] Even when he dealt with the concrete phe-

nomenon of the rebirth of the State of Israel and attempted to find a place for it in his theology, Heschel viewed it, as Rosenzweig did the calendar and liturgy of Judaism, through the lens of eternity. Thus, when he authored his work on the State and its significance to religious Judaism, he entitled it *Israel*, with the subtitle, *An Echo of Eternity*. Nevertheless, drawing upon his own roots as a scion of a Hasidic rabbinic dynasty, Heschel emphasized that the traditional Jewish belief in *tikkun olam* (the restoration of the world) obligated each Jew to participate in this world's affairs through what he labeled, in an inspired phrase paraphrasing Kierkegaard, a "leap of action."[6] In opposition to Rosenzweig, Heschel regarded Judaism as being very much involved in politics and saw that arena as one wherein the Jew could fulfill his duties as a member of the Jewish people. This undoubtedly accounts for a great deal of Heschel's own political activism.

Heschel lived in an era unlike that of Rosenzweig's. He knew the Holocaust firsthand, and in his own lifetime he experienced the exhilaration and rebirth of the State of Israel. As an American, he participated in the struggle for civil rights for blacks and other minority groups in the United States during the 1960s, and he witnessed and protested American entry into Vietnam. Most significantly for this chapter, Heschel also lived at the time of Hiroshima and Nagasaki, as well as the proliferation of nuclear weaponry. Writing with a Heideggerian sense of facticity, Heschel knew that the challenge of the nuclear age could not be avoided. In one essay he wrote:

> When Israel approached Sinai, God lifted up the mountain and held it over their heads, saying: "Either you accept the Torah or be crushed beneath the mountain."
>
> The mountain of history is over our heads again. . . . Men all over the world have a dreadful sense in common, the fear of total annihilation. An apocalyptic monster has descended upon the world, and there is nowhere to go, nowhere to hide.[7]

Humanity, in its freedom, was compelled to meet this test successfully. Yet, aware of the finite nature of the human species, Heschel warned that humanity might not be up to the task. In an

146   A THEOLOGY OF FEAR

autobiographical fragment, Heschel recalled the experience he
had as a child of 7 when reading the biblical story relating the
sacrifice of Isaac by his father Abraham:

> Isaac was on his way to Mount Moriah with his father; then he lay
> on the altar, bound, waiting to be sacrificed. My heart began to
> beat even faster; it actually sobbed with pity for Isaac. Behold,
> Abraham now lifted the knife. And now my heart froze within me
> with fright. Suddenly the voice of the angel was heard: "Abraham,
> lay not thy hand upon the lad, for now I know that thou fearest
> God." And here I, crying, broke out in tears. "Why are you cry-
> ing?" asked the rabbi. "You know that Isaac was not killed."
>   And I said to him, still weeping, "But, Rabbi, supposing the
> angel had come a second too late?" The rabbi comforted me and
> calmed me, saying that an angel cannot come late.

Heschel then concluded with the following observation: "An angel
cannot be late, but man, made of flesh and blood, may be."[8] Despite
such caution, Heschel would not surrender to despair, and he
refused to acknowledge that humanity was incapable of forging
peace. Deeply religious, Heschel was convinced that God was
benevolent and that persons created in God's image were co-
partners with God in the work of creation. This meant that humanity not only had the freedom but possessed the ability to establish
peace and break with millennia-old habits of enmity and bloodshed.
Thus, Heschel was not despondent about prospects for making
peace. "Fundamentally," he wrote, "I am an optimist about all of us,
against my better judgment. This is because we have a Father who
cares. Our task is to be deserving of His care."[9] So blessed by God,
humanity's ability to attain peace—despite centuries of proof to the
contrary—was not, in Heschel's view, illusory. In these sentiments,
Heschel echoed Hermann Cohen (1842–1919), the great German-
Jewish philosopher of neo-Kantianism whose thought was prominent in the Berlin intellectual and religious circles of Heschel's
student years.[10]

    Cohen, like Heschel later, recognized that humanity was far
removed from the ideal of peace and wrote of the reality of conflict
between persons and nations throughout history. However, he

postulated that one "should not despair" on account of this, for "the style of the prophets avoids such pessimism." To be sure, "War . . . marks the historical cycle of any nation's existence." Nevertheless, Cohen believed that humanity was capable of "sloughing off" this form of existence and "arising," instead, to a "new life . . . of morality," one in which war would "disappear" and life would be "lived in harmony and justice."[11] As the idea of God gave Cohen "the confidence that morality will become reality on earth,"[12] Cohen optimistically posited that humanity could transform the world of "is," a world of war, tensions, and conflicts, into a realm of "ought," a reality of tranquility and peace.

The seminal influence Cohen had on Heschel in this matter is clear. Heschel, too, claimed that the prophets taught that a world wherein all persons lived in "a relationship of reverence for each other" was possible.[13] They foresaw the day when all would acknowledge that "might is not supreme, . . . the sword is an abomination, . . . violence is obscene."[14] War, from the perspective of the prophets, was not simply immoral. It was also futile and absurd, destined to be repeated until nations came to recognize the basic truth that the "other," as a being created in God's likeness, was endowed with infinite worth and dignity. The task of Judaism was to spread this teaching and, in so doing, help to establish conditions that would cause others to believe in the possibility of peace. Without such faith, Heschel believed that conflict between nations could not be avoided. "Worse than war is the belief in the inevitability of war," Heschel wrote,[15] for such despair would only be self-fulfilling and lead to a tragic denouncement. Instead, humanity had to be convinced of the truth of prophetic teaching and accept the fact that release from the quagmire of seemingly never-ending wars was not a utopian hope. Peace could reign, if humanity only willed it, among nations.

Heschel's faith that peace, albeit difficult, was attainable is embodied in a story he told of Rabbi Ben Zion Uziel, a leading Sephardic rabbi in Tel Aviv. In 1921, in the midst of an Arab-Jewish riot in the Tel Aviv–Jaffa area, Rabbi Uziel positioned himself between Arabs and Jews and asked each side to cease fire. He then addressed himself to the Arabs in a sympathetic manner and concluded by saying, "Our common father, Abraham, the father of Isaac and Ishmael, when he saw his nephew Lot was causing him trouble, claiming that there was not enough room for both his flocks and Abraham's flocks to live together, said to him: 'Let there be no quarrel between you and me, and between your shepherds and my shepherds, for we are people like brothers.' We also say to you, the land can sustain all of us and provide for us in plenty. Let us, then, stop fighting each other, for we, too, are people like brothers." The Arabs, after hearing Rabbi Uziel's words, dispersed quietly. Heschel then ended the tale with the following statement: "Men of goodwill will never cease to pray that the logic of peace may prevail over the epidemic of suspicion."[16]

As this story suggests, the real enemy humanity confronts in its efforts to eradicate war is not another people. It is the distrust and hatred, the evil, that seem to adhere in the nature of existence and foster conditions of tension that transcend national boundaries and particularistic groupings. Heschel nonetheless asserted that as co-partners with God in the work of creation, humanity possesses the ability to overcome all this strife and establish, in its stead, tranquility and understanding. His rendition of a wise and gentle rabbi resolving disputes between two bitter enemies simply reflects his belief in the eventual positive evolution of human interaction. In extrapolating a position on nuclear weapons from Heschel's writings, it thus seems obvious that he would have condemned their employment in any capacity as being not only idiotic and immoral, but sinful. For even the threatened use of nuclear arms would inexorably move humanity on towards renewed conflict and would hasten the destruction of creation itself. It would retard humanity's obligation to participate in a healing process that our situation so desparately requires.

Heschel's commitment to the Jewish religious tradition, it would seem, leads to a type of "pacifism" on the nuclear question similar to that of Rosenzweig's. However, this should not obscure the fact that the sense of activism that animates it is radically distinct from that of the older German thinker. Consequently, Heschel's position is essentially impervious to the kind of criticism Fackenheim hurled at Rosenzweig. Instead, it is the absolute fideism of Heschel's posture—the belief that humanity can refrain from traditional forms of aggressive behavior and establish prophetic visions of peace—that leaves his thought, however inspirational, vulnerable to criticism. For the story of Rabbi Uziel and the Arabs can hardly be regarded as anything other than exceptional. Heschel's account of war and peace thus does not fail because of its perception of what ought to be. Rather, his approach is to be faulted for not fully confronting what is, for ignoring the realities of history and psychology. To base nuclear policy on the assumption that discord can be resolved and harmony established through goodness and reason is to act recklessly in a premessianic world that empirically accords more respect to power than to kindness. Indeed, it is precisely on these grounds that a Richard Rubenstein would adopt a policy position on the nuclear arms race diametrically opposed to that of a Heschel, and his voice, something of a lone one in the liberal Jewish camp, deserves a hearing.

RICHARD RUBENSTEIN

Richard Rubenstein (b. 1924), currently a professor at Florida State University in Tallahassee, received his rabbinical ordination at the Jewish Theological Seminary and completed his doctorate at Harvard in religious thought and psychology. He first gained widespread public attention as a Jewish "Death-of-God" theologian in the 1960s, and his *After Auschwitz* has continued to command a following in religious studies circles. Rubenstein has published extensively and a revised version of his Harvard dissertation, "The Religious Imagination," offers a Freudian interpretation of rabbinic literature. Indeed, it is obvious, when reading Rubenstein's analysis of the nuclear issue, that Sigmund Freud's view of humanity has had a considerable impact upon Rubenstein's thought and that Rubenstein's position on this matter cannot be understood without recourse to him. Consequently, it is vital to take note of a correspondence Freud had in 1932 with Albert Einstein. In that correspondence Freud revealed his own attitude, one which Rubenstein obviously shares, about the prospects for the attainment of peace in this world. On July 30 of that year, Einstein asked Freud, "Is it possible to control man's mental evolution so as to make him proof against the psychosis of hate and destructiveness?" Freud, in response, stated that "there is no likelihood of our being able to suppress humanity's aggressive tendencies. . . . The ideal conditions would obviously be found in a community where every man subordinated his instinctive life to the dictates of reason. Nothing less than this could bring about so thorough and durable a union between men. . . . But surely such a hope is utopian. . . ."[17]

Rubenstein, grounding his argument upon these Freudian views, dismisses as futile any attempt to forge peace on the basis of notions such as mutual respect and goodwill among nations. These efforts, however well-intentioned, ignore the psychological realities of human existence. For persons, by nature, are aggressive and the strongest instinct they possess is that of survival. "Rights do not belong to men by nature," Rubenstein writes. "All that men possess by nature is the necessity to participate in the incessant life and death struggle for existence of any animal."[18] To gloss over this and to establish a nuclear policy in the hope that humans will somehow suppress their aggressive impulses is, from Rubenstein's perspective, just so much wishful thinking. Instead, Rubenstein advises policy-makers to recognize aggression as an ineradicable part of human behavior and to acknowledge that only the instinct for survival can possibly keep it in check. To do otherwise is to desire what never was and never will be. To formulate policy on any other basis is, in the contemporary situation, to act irresponsibly and suicidally. Rather, in full cognizance of humanity's capacity for violence, one should create policy in accordance with the insight that "the power to injure remains the most important credible deterrent to a would-be aggressor's violence."[19] Only if there is sufficient fear on one party's part that its own existence will be threatened should it use violence against a second party—assuming there is a fear that the second party possesses enough power to retaliate in kind—would the first party refrain from doing so. The instinct for survival is the only force more powerful than the drive for dominance.

Applying these arguments to the nuclear arms situation, Rubenstein initially notes the novelty of the present setting in human history. He observes:

In warfare and weapon making, practical reason may have reached its limits. Mass destruction only makes sense to a warring power if it can survive as a viable society. Nuclear warfare renders such an outcome uncertain. . . . For any large-scale war now entails the possibility that nuclear weapons could terminate all life on earth, if not as a direct result of the initial assaults on population centers then as a result of the predictable aftereffects.[20]

The specter of total destruction does not lead Rubenstein to conclude that nuclear weapons should therefore be destroyed. While humanity's capacity for total destruction of the planet might supply a new ingredient in the modern situation, the realities of human aggression nevertheless remain constant. The only prophylactic against them is a policy of deterrence. Disarmament is useless, for no nation would ever trust another nation to fulfill its commitment truthfully. In the Hobbesian universe of Richard Rubenstein, where each side of a nuclear power struggle could assume that only an instinct for survival would outweigh visions of aggrandizement, the threat of total nuclear retaliation would be the one course sufficient to dissuade a would-be attacker from attempting to launch a nuclear attack on its opponent. Given the nature of the world, the existence of nuclear weapons—in that they make victory in war virtually impossible to attain—ironically heightens the prospects for peace. The nature of Rubenstein's position in this regard is seen in the concluding pages of his autobiography, *Power Struggle*. Standing at the top of Masada with his son Jeremy, Rubenstein muses:

As I stood there, I wondered about the future. Was Israel's return after two thousand years of wandering and misery but the prelude to a final nuclear holocaust? After Auschwitz, it is inconceivable that the Israelis would consent to their own annihilation. . . .

For years there have been persistent rumors of Israeli nuclear weapons. I have no hard facts, but it is inconceivable that the Israelis could have listened to threats of annihilation for twenty-five years without producing their own doomsday weapon.[21] Faced with the destruction of the only political entity they can trust to defend their existence and dignity, the State of Israel, they would unleash their bombs on Cairo, Alexandria, Amman, and Damascus in certain knowledge that the extinction of Haifa, Tel Aviv, and Jerusalem would swiftly follow. *There is a limit to the pressure the Arabs can exert.* . . .

Yet, as I thought of Israel's deadly peril, I was mildly optimistic. *Nuclear terror may offer the only credible guarantee of peace.* For twenty centuries it has been possible to slaughter Jews at will. *More often than not there was gain in the bloody venture for the slaughterers.* In the century par excellence of broken promises and broken trust, the dearer it becomes to eliminate Jews, the greater the likelihood that peace will someday come to the Holy Land and all of its peoples.[22]

Rubenstein's position thus turns out to be a simple one. Remove the incentive for war, that is, "gain"—through the prospect of total destruction—and a "credible guarantee of peace" will be achieved.

Rubenstein's solution to the nuclear predicament is open to question on two major grounds. The first is that Rubenstein's stratagem for peace, predicated as it is on the assumption that the only thing unique about the modern era is the increased ability of humanity to unleash destruction, assumes that human instincts and behaviors have not changed. If this is true, why should it then be assumed that opposing sides in a nuclear age will surrender the belief that nuclear wars, like other wars in the past, can be won? After all, with proper technological advancements, it is conceivable that one nation's scientific knowledge and capabilities could so far outstrip a rival's that victory, even in the case of a nuclear war, could be envisioned as attainable by a nation's leadership. Indeed, given pronouncements made by leaders, such a scenario hardly appears fantastical. Thus, there is no reason to assume, along with Rubenstein, that humanity's instinct for survival will suddenly allow it to develop the imagination that nuclear attacks cannot be withstood. The possibility of war, therefore, is not lessened by the ever-escalating manufacture and development of nuclear weapons, which a policy of deterrence would inevitably dictate. Instead, the risks such wars would entail are only heightened.[23]

An even more telling negative response to Rubenstein's posture is a development of relatively recent vintage on the world
scene. Rubenstein's reliance on deterrence as an adequate means
for insuring peace is based upon the contention that the human
desire for survival is so great that no one would knowingly prefer a
total nuclear conflagration to the continued existence of this
planet. However, in a time when thousands of young Shiite Muslims willingly sacrificed their lives at the behest of an Ayatollah
Khomeini in order to earn a martyr's death in the landmines of a
Middle Eastern desert, no such confident pronouncement can be
easily made. Deterrence, in short, is effective so long as one's
opponents fear death for themselves, their families, their nations,
or the world. In the case of religious fanatics who possess no such
fear—in fact, who are convinced that such destruction would lead
to a place in Paradise—the prospect of global annihilation hardly
provides an obstacle to nuclear war. Moreover, given the reality of
nuclear proliferation, the prospects of regional powers fed by
bullyboy dictators for obtaining a nuclear arsenal are great. Rubenstein's contention that deterrence offers the "only credible
guarantee of peace" is suspect. It presupposes that the world is
and will be ruled exclusively by rational persons, who will maintain
total control over nuclear weapons forever. In a world of madmen,
this posture cannot be maintained with absolute certainty. In light
of the nature of our world, an unwillingness to work towards
disarmament is insane.

It seems that we have returned to our original dilemma and
that the positions of Heschel at one end and Rubenstein at the
other both contain serious flaws. It is imperative to move beyond
the Scylla of an unwarranted faith in humanity's capacity to
subdue its instincts and pursue peace and the Charybdis of an
exclusive policy of deterrence which, without any real basis, in-
sists that humanity, in its quest for survival, will not commit a
suicidal act. The issue is certainly not easily resolved. However, by
taking elements from each of these approaches as reflected in the
writings of other modern Jewish thinkers, some directions for
navigating humanity's way out of this complex and hellish maze
may yet emerge.

HANS JONAS

Hans Jonas (1903–1989) for many years enjoyed a worldwide reputation as one of the foremost scholars of Gnosticism and early Christianity. A former student of both Rudolf Bultmann and Martin Heidegger, Jonas also attended the Hochschule für die Wissenschaft des Judentums (the Liberal Rabbinic Seminary) in Berlin. Forced to flee from his German homeland as a result of Nazi persecution, Jonas served in the Jewish Brigade of the British Army during World War II and ultimately came to the United States, where he renewed his academic career and gained prominence not only as a student of the early centuries of the Common Era but as a philosopher as well.

In a seminal essay, "The Concept of Responsibility: An Inquiry into the Foundations of an Ethics for our Age," Jonas argues that the rise of modern technology, with its unprecedented capacity for power and destruction, has changed "the nature and scope of human action . . . decisively."[24] While past systems of morality centered on concepts such as love and reverence, Jonas contends that it is insufficient to ground systems of morality in such sentiments any longer. Instead, "responsibility" must now lie at the heart of a mature and just ethics for the nuclear age. And this "responsibility," he asserts, is nothing less than the preservation of human existence now and in the future. This is the transcendent moral obligation imposed upon humanity at a time when the whole human enterprise is jeopardized by nuclear weaponry. Unlike Rubenstein, Jonas sees the obligation to live as a moral one, and rejects the notion that it is simply a psychological instinct. However, like Rubenstein, Jonas claims that humanity can no longer depend upon the Good, the *bonum*, to motivate it to behave in a proper and responsible moral manner. Moreover, he stated this despite the fact that he recognized that rare individuals will be led to do the morally proper thing by such a motive. Indeed, in an autobiographical reminiscence akin to the story Heschel told of Rabbi Uziel, Jonas stated:

When in 1945 I reentered a vanquished Germany as a member of the Jewish Brigade in the British Army, I had to decide whom of my former teachers in philosophy I could in good conscience visit, and whom not. It turned out that the "no" fell on my main teacher . . . who by the criteria which then had to govern my choice had failed the human test of time: whereas the "yes" included the much lesser figure of a rather narrow traditionalist Kantian persuasion, who meant little to me philosophically but of whose record in those dark years I heard admirable things. When I did visit him and congratulated him on the courage of his principled stand, he said a memorable thing. "Jonas," he said, "I tell you this; without Kant's teaching I couldn't have done it."[25]

Jonas conceded that some human beings are capable of heroic deeds. He acknowledged that there are individuals, who, recognizing the *bonum* (the good), act in accordance with the categorical imperative that a situation reveals. Thus, Jonas did not display the cynicism of Rubenstein. Nevertheless, such deeds are all too rare. Previous systems of morality are outmoded, Jonas argued, not only for this reason but because they did not have to accept the full weight of responsibility that a system of ethics has to bear today. As he phrased it, "*Responsibility* with a never-known burden has moved into the center of political morality," for the complete annihilation of the planet is now possible.[26] An ethic for a nuclear age must confront the possibility that there will be no future. Since the *bonum* as a motivating force has been shown historically to be insufficient to assure that future, then perhaps, Jonas reasoned, fear of the *malum* (the bad) will do so.

Jonas, in an essay entitled "Responsibility Today: The Ethics of an Endangered Future,"[27] argued that at present "we need the discovery of our duties. . . ." It is "the threat" to the continued existence of humanity that marks the modern setting and provides the starting point for contemporary ethical reflection. Unfortunately, "the perception of the *malum* is infinitely easier to us than the perception of the *bonum*; it is more direct, more compelling, less given to differences of opinion. . . . It is forced upon us by the . . . presence of evil. . . ." Jonas concluded, "Therefore moral philosophy must consult our fears prior to our wishes. . . . And although the heuristics of fear is not the last word in the search for goodness, it is at least an extremely useful first word. . . ."

Nuclear weapons have introduced a *novum* into history. Every political leader must now consider the possibility that a wrong decision could signal the end of the planet. This however, gave Jonas cause for hope. He observed:

> Let us return once again to the heuristics of fear I am suggesting. For many the apocalyptic potential of our technology is concentrated in the atom bomb. . . . But it has one consolation: It lies in the realm of choice. Certain acts of certain actors can bring about catastrophe—but they can also remain undone. Nuclear weapons can even be abolished. . . . (The prospect is admittedly small.) Anyway, decisions still play a role—and in those fear. Not that this can be trusted; but we *can*, in principle, be *lucky* because the use is not *necessary* in principle, that is, not impelled by the production of the thing as such (which rather aims at obviating the necessity of its use).[28]

Jonas, like Rubenstein, did not trust, as Heschel did, in the power of goodness to move humanity. His own experience of Nazi Germany—above all, the performance of his teacher Martin Heidegger—undoubtedly prevented him from sharing Heschel's moral optimism. It is his moral pessimism—one could almost say his Gnostic-like vision that morality can emerge from the dark places of the soul—that gave him cause for hope.

Humanity has one primary moral obligation—the preservation of the planet and the life that dwells in it. The destruction of the earth is not "an inevitable *fatum*."[29] This is a moral statement, because it recognizes that humanity possesses the ability to choose between life and death. Jonas, like Rubenstein, was able to advocate deterrence, though he did not do so on the basis of assuming that humanity's psychological desire for survival was stronger than its impulse towards aggression. Rather, he did so because he believed that humanity was sufficiently fearful—had the requisite moral imagination—to conjure up the image of a world destroyed by nuclear attacks and to know that such destruction would be a moral abomination. Mutually assured destruction allows humanity to refuse to empty its weapons. Simultaneously, Jonas's writings permit humanity to consider attempts at disarmament as more than pious wishes. While he conceded that it is unlikely that nuclear powers will pursue this option, it is possible, for humans do possess both moral choice and vision. It is this posture which distinguishes Jonas from Rubenstein and identifies him with the cardinal thrust of the Jewish religious tradition.

MARTIN BUBER

Lest this middle path mapped out by Jonas appear inconsistent, it will be instructive to turn to themes on war and peace in the work of Martin Buber (1878–1965), for Buber, more than any other modern Jewish thinker, uses the metaphor of the "narrow ridge" to symbolize the precarious nature of human decision-making. Buber, who earned worldwide prominence for his most famous book, *I and Thou*, as well as countless other publications, was an active Zionist throughout his life. Consequently, after the Nazis rose to power in Germany, Buber immigrated in 1938 to Palestine, where he served as Professor of Social Philosophy at the Hebrew University. In addition, he was active in numerous social and political causes both in Israel and abroad until his death, and his stances on issues such as Arab-Jewish relations and the Eichmann trial (which he opposed) generated tremendous controversies. His work serves to clarify and amplify the nature of the positions as staked out by Jonas, and his thought provides a fitting conclusion to the positions surveyed in this essay.

For Buber, the meaning and purpose of human existence is found in the fundamentally social nature of reality. The individual is "human" primarily because he is capable of entering into dialogic relationship both with other persons and with God. In a word, the individual is able to communicate. Authentic being consists in being known and knowing that one is being known. One is permitted to say "I" only because there are "Thous." As Buber wrote:

> I become through my relatives to the *Thou*; as I become *I*, I say *Thou*. All real living is meeting.[30]

A person makes his appearance by entering into relation with other persons. . . . He who takes his stand in relation shares in reality, that is, in a being, that neither merely belongs to him nor merely lies outside him. All reality is an activity in which I share without being able to appropriate it for myself. *Where there is not sharing there is no reality. Where there is self-appropriation there is no reality.* The more direct the contact with the *Thou*, the fuller is the sharing.[31]

One is made fully human through others—in a reciprocal dependent independence. Our unique characters, which make each of us individuals, make us essentially other. Yet, our uniqueness, our being for ourselves, constitutively leads us to be for others. Neither the solitary individual nor the social aggregate is the irreducible datum of human existence. Instead, the fundamental reality is the individual person acting in relation to other persons or God. We are persons because we can claim and respond, address and be addressed. We are persons because we are responsible to others. We are persons because we live in community.

True community, where persons both retain their individuality and realize their responsibility for others, forms the backdrop for Buber's views on war and peace. For such a community leads the way to peace and freedom. The decisive test for community, however, was not, Buber believed, life within the community alone. Rather, it was at the edge of the community, at the boundaries that separated one group from another. As "righteousness itself can only become wholly visible in the structures of the life of a people," it is incumbent upon a people to make peace wherever "we are destined to do so: in the active life of our own community and in that aspect of it which can actively help to determine its relationship to another community."[32] The practical application of this for Buber was the nature of the relationship he attempted to forge with his Arab neighbors in the Middle East. He felt it imperative that Jew and Arab not only live next to, but with each other. In describing his role and membership in *Ihud* (Unity), a group which strove for rapprochement between Arab and Jew, Buber said to Mahatma Gandhi, "I belong to a group of people who . . .

have not ceased to strive for the conclusion of a genuine peace
between Jew and Arab. By a genuine peace we . . . infer that both
peoples should develop the land without one imposing its will on the
other. . . . This appeared to us to be very difficult, but not impossible."[33] Like both Heschel and Jonas, Buber posited that humanity
had the ability to transform visions of peace into a reality. However,
as his writings indicate, he recognized that the contingencies of the
human situation provided parameters for this goal that sometimes
made the attainment of peace an impossibility.

   Humanity, Buber observed, had a violent side to its nature.
Thus, when Gandhi, in a 1938 letter to Buber, claimed, "India is by
nature non-violent," Buber refused to grant credibility to Gandhi's
assertion.[34] Contemporary events only support the wisdom of
Buber's refusal. Instead, Buber countered by pointing out to
Gandhi that the world humanity inhabits is an imperfect one.
Violence, evil, destruction exist; and they are not endemic to a
single individual or nation. Consequently, Buber felt compelled to
reject Gandhi's suggestion that the Jews employ *satayagraha*
(soul-force) as a form of nonviolent resistence to Nazi persecutions of the Jews. Instead, he maintained that the Jews, of course,
"do not want force. . . . From time immemorial we have proclaimed the teaching of justice and peace. . . . Thus we cannot
desire to use force. No one who counts himself in the ranks of
Israel can desire to use force." Despite this, the Jews "have not
proclaimed, as did Jesus, the son of our people, and as you do,
the teaching of non-violence, because *we believe that sometimes
a man must use force to save himself or even more his children.*"[35] Judaism does not abjure force, the use of violence, to
combat wrong. While hardly desirable, or even the first recourse
in a confrontation with evil, it must still remain available as a final
option in our dealings in a world where aggression against the
innocent exists. Of course, one employs such force with a great
deal of hesitancy. Nevertheless, its use, real or perceived, may be
the only just course a community can adopt when confronting a
particular situation. Buber's position can be summarized by:

> For I cannot help withstanding evil when I see that it is about to
> destroy the good. I am forced to withstand the evil in the world just

as the evil within myself. I can only strive not to have to do so by force. . . . But if there is no other way of preventing the evil destroying the good, I trust I shall use force and give myself into God's hands.[36]

The purpose of ethics, and the guidance ethical reflection provides, is herein revealed. Ethics must guide the relationships between persons and nations amidst the demands of life. They can neither retreat behind the garb of a pious optimism nor cloak themselves in the vestments of an ostensibly realistic psychological reductionism. Instead, they must provide direction for the world as it is—with all of its complexities and inconsistencies. This is why ethical decisions, in the final analysis, have to be made by persons addressing and caring for others in real situations. They cannot be left to computers, nor can they be preprogrammed and packaged. Thus, in extrapolating a position on the nuclear issue from Buber's writings, it is clear that one cannot simply glorify humanity, optimistically ignore the persistence of human evil, and thereby advocate a policy of disarmament as the answer to the nuclear dilemma. Nor can one posit that humanity is guided by instincts of survival and aggression alone, thereby arriving at the conclusion that only a policy of deterrence will be sufficient to resolve the nuclear issue. Ethical decisions, in facing hard matters such as this, do not have the luxury of dealing in black and white. Violence, or its implied threat, cannot responsibly be forsworn. As Buber observed:

> In order to preserve the community of men, we are often compelled to accept wrongs. . . . But what matters is that in every hour of decision we are aware of our responsibility and summon our conscience to weigh exactly how much is necessary to preserve the community, and accept just so much and no more; . . . that we . . . struggle with destiny in fear and trembling. . . .[37]

Buber's thought, when applied to the question of Omnicide, can be interpreted as having the same themes contained in Jonas's writings. The writings of Jonas and Buber have the virtue of sensitizing humanity to the multilayered nature of this problem.

The paradigm they provide indicates that liberal Jewish thought in the current setting has moved beyond the unbridled faith in humanity that marked liberal Jewish thinkers in the pre-Holocaust Jewish world.[38] Theirs is a paradigm that acknowledges the reality of evil in the world while, at the same time, refusing to surrender a cautious optimism about the possibility of human goodness. Monovalent decisions regarding weapons of mass destruction cannot be made. Peace must be pursued on the levels of both disarmament and deterrence. Policy has to be subtle, polyvocal, and flexible, sensitive to all the nuances involved and outlined in this chapter. This is certainly frightening. The chance that this planet could be destroyed and the inability, in the face of that fact, to derive a single response to this crisis of unparalleled proportions has to strike fear into the hearts and minds of every human being. A theology of fear is unavoidable in our day.

NOTES

1. Franz Rosenzweig, *The Star of Redemption*, trans. by W. W. Hallo (New York: Holt, Rinehart and Winston, 1971), p. 328.

2. *Ibid.*, p. 332.

3. Emil L. Fackenheim, *To Mend the World: Foundation of Post-Holocaust Thought* (New York: Schocken, 1982), p. 324.

4. Abraham Joshua Heschel, *The Sabbath: Its Meaning for Modern Man* (New York: Farrar, Straus & Young, 1951), p. 74.

5. *Ibid.*, p. 100.

6. Abraham Joshua Heschel, *God in Search of Man* (Northvale, NJ: Jason Aronson, 1955/1987), p. 282.

7. Abraham Joshua Heschel, *The Insecurity of Freedom: Essays on Human Existence* (New York: Farrar, Straus & Giroux, 1966), p. 179.

8. Abraham Joshua Heschel, "The Moral Outrage of Vietnam," in Robert McAfee Brown et al., *Vietnam: Crisis of Conscience* (New York: Associated Press, 1967), pp. 51–52. Much of this discussion on Heschel is based on Morton C. Fierman, "Ideas on Peace in the Theology of Abraham Joshua Heschel," California State University Seminar Papers Series (Fullerton, CA: November, 1974), no. 8.

9. Interview in the *Los Angeles Times* (October 4, 1970).

10. During the same period when Heschel was a student at the University of Berlin, Rabbi Joseph Soloveitchek was writing his doctoral dissertation there on the writings of Cohen. This is indicative of the influence of Cohen's thought on those who were within the ambit of German Judaism during those years. Heschel was certainly included among those numbers.

11. Hermann Cohen, *Reason and Hope: Selections from the Jewish Writings of Hermann Cohen*, trans. and ed. by Eva Jospe (New York: Norton, 1971), pp. 110–121.

12. Abraham Joshua Heschel, *The Insecurity of Freedom*, p. 182.

13. Abraham Joshua Heschel, *The Prophets* (New York: Harper & Row, 1962/1967), p. 160.

14. Abraham Joshua Heschel, "The Moral Outrage of Vietnam," p. 60.

15. Abraham Joshua Heschel, *Israel: An Echo of Eternity* (New York: Farrar, Straus & Giroux, 1969), pp. 175–178.

16. *Ibid.*

17. Quoted in Otto Nathan and Heinz Norden, *Einstein on Peace* (New York: Simon & Schuster, 1968). Einstein's quote is found on p. 190 and Freud's statement on pp. 199–200.

18. Richard L. Rubenstein, *The Cunning of History: Holocaust and the American Future* (New York: Harper & Row, 1975), p. 89.

19. *Ibid.*

20. Richard L. Rubenstein, *The Age of Triage: Fear and Hope in Our Overcrowded World* (Boston: Beacon Press, 1968), p. 33.

21. *Time*, in a June 1985 issue, stated uncategorically that Israel does possess such a nuclear weapon. In addition, Shai Feldman, *Israeli Nuclear Deterrence: A Strategy for the 1980's* (New York: Columbia University Press, 1982), argues that Israeli possession of nuclear arms and a concomitant policy of deterrence that accompanies it is the surest safeguard for peace in the Middle East. Abba Eban, *The New Diplomacy: International Affairs in the Modern Age* (New York: Random House, 1983), makes the same argument concerning the efficacy of the policy of deterrence in insuring peace between the superpowers.

22. Richard Rubenstein, *Power Struggle* (New York: Scribner's, 1974), pp. 192–193.

23. I would like to thank my colleague Norman Mirsky, at Hebrew Union College—Jewish Institute of Religion at Los Angeles for this insight.

24. Hans Jonas, *On Faith, Reason, and Responsibility* (Claremont, CA.: Institute for Antiquity and Christianity, 1981), p. 81.

25. As quoted by Fackenheim in *To Mend the World* (New York: Schocken), p. 269.

26. Jonas, *On Faith, Reason, and Responsibility*, p. 99.

27. *Ibid.*, p. 73.

28. *Ibid.*, p. 78.

29. *Ibid.*, p. 79.

30. Martin Buber, *I-Thou*, trans. by Ronald G. Smith (New York: Scribners, 1958), p. 11.

31. *Ibid.*, p. 63.

32. As cited by Maurice Friedman, in *Martin Buber: The Life of Dialogue* (New York: Harper, 1960), p. 144.

33. *Ibid.*, pp. 144–145.

34. Martin Buber and Judah Leon Magnes, *Two Letters to Gandhi* (Jerusalem: Reuben Mass, April 1939), p. 20.

35. *Ibid.*, pp. 19–20.

36. *Ibid.*, p. 21.

37. As cited by Friedman in *Martin Buber*, p. 145.

38. The most cogent statement of this reversal is found in Eugene Borowitz, "Rethinking the Reform Jewish Theory of Social Action, *The Journal of Reform Judaism* (Fall 1980), pp. 1–19.

9

Bishops, Rabbis, and Bombs

Elliot N. Dorff

In an attempt to define and meet the responsibilities of the nuclear age, the United States National Conference of Catholic Bishops issued an extensive Pastoral Letter on War and Peace on May 3, 1983, entitled, "The Challenge of Peace: God's Promise and Our Response."[1] Its impact extended probably further than the fondest hopes of its writers. A national, religious body had taken the time and effort to produce a clear, thoughtful statement on the issue we all try to avoid but which we know we must confront. The very act of doing so brought the issue to national attention—to the point that the Reagan Administration tried to have the final draft modified to fit its policies more closely. Other religious bodies could well be jealous; the Catholics had taken the initiative of addressing the issue and propounding a careful position paper. And indeed, the United Methodist bishops, "inspired by their Roman Catholic counterparts," took up the process of writing a statement of their own.[2]

Jews do not have an organized way of articulating positions on current issues. Many individual Jews and a variety of Jewish organizations speak out from their particular vantage points and in their particular modes (responsa, editorials, articles, books, sermons, etc.), but no one person or body speaks for American or

World Jewry. As Jews we may well regret that, especially when the topic is as crucial as Omnicide, for we are thereby prevented from taking a position as authoritatively and publicly as the Catholics did. We can take some small comfort, though, from the fact that the Catholics are not nearly as well organized as they seem; significant opposition has been voiced in the Catholic community to the bishops' statement, bishops though they be.[3] More importantly, even though the method of obtaining a Jewish response may be somewhat chaotic, there is a coherence in Jewish views on this issue stemming from a shared set of relevant Jewish values, such that even when Jews disagree, their disagreement is more a matter of how to apply those values than it is a dispute about the values themselves.

This chapter, then, is the response of at least one Jew to the bishops' pastoral letter, beginning with the topic of nuclear war itself, and then turning to armament, deterrence, and other proposals for peace. Discussed in this progression are particular areas in which Jews have taken significantly disparate positions, and their reasons for so doing. The chapter concludes with a return to the question of the purpose and status of the moral claims made by both the Catholic and Jewish traditions.

NUCLEAR WAR

Catholic Just-War Doctrine

Catholicism has a long history of thought focused on the subject of war. Pacifism dominated the early centuries of Christian teachings and has resurfaced in a variety of Catholic forms over the centuries[4]; Jesus, after all, taught that one should love one's enemies and not resist evil.[5] In accordance with this, the bishops' statement several times acknowledges the legitimacy of the pacifist option for individual Catholics.[6]

The mainstream Catholic position, however, has not been pacifist. Some of Jesus' disciples were armed, and Jesus even suggested that his disciples purchase swords.[7] While this may seem inconsistent with Jesus' command not to resist evil, some modern New Testament scholars point out that if his remark is translated into Hebrew, "we see that Jesus was not creating a new saying, but quoting a proverb" (Psalms 37:1,8 and Proverbs 24:19). "In modern English we would translate this maxim: Don't compete with evil doers"[8]—or, as the new Jewish Publication Society translation renders it, "Do not be vexed by evil men, do not be incensed by wrongdoers." In other words, do not do to them as they have done to you, but do defend yourself. And indeed, while the Hebrew Bible clearly condones war (Deuteronomy 20), it nevertheless expresses similar sentiments about the wisdom of not responding to the militant acts of enemies in kind.[9]

The dominant Catholic view, then, has been the "just-war theory," first associated with St. Augustine, but developed primarily by his successors in the Catholic Church.[10] In that view, Christian love demands the presumption that we should do no harm to our neighbors. Only when someone attacks an innocent party does that presumption yield to permit violent action to prevent or mitigate the attack, and then only to the extent necessary. Catholic doctrine spells out in some detail the conditions under which going to war is justifiable in the first place (*jus ad bellum*) and the restrictions on the conduct of a justifiable war (*jus in bello*). Together the presumption and the two sets of conditions constitute Catholic "just-war theory."[11]

Briefly, the seven conditions under which recourse to war is permitted (*jus ad bellum*) are as follows:

1. *Just Cause.* War is permissible only to confront "a real and certain danger," namely, to protect innocent life, to preserve conditions necessary for decent human existence, and to secure basic human rights.

2. *Competent Authority.* War must be declared by those with responsibility for public order. This criterion is complicated by the Catholic recognition of a "just revolution" against an oppressive government, with implications for revolts, conscientious objection, and selective conscientious objection.

3. *Comparative Justice.* The rights and values involved must justify killing. "In essence: which side is sufficiently 'right' in

a dispute, and are the values at stake critical enough to override the presumption against war?"[12]

4. *Right Intention.* War can legitimately be intended only for the reasons set forth above as a just cause. During war, right intention requires pursuit of peace, including avoiding unnecessarily destructive acts and imposing only reasonable conditions for cessation of hostility.

5. *Last Resort.* All peaceful alternatives must have been exhausted.

6. *Probability of Success.* "This is a difficult criterion to apply, but its purpose is to prevent irrational resort to force or hopeless resistance when the outcome of either will clearly be disproportionate or futile. The determination includes a recognition that at times defense of key values, even against great odds, may be a 'proportionate' witness."[13]

7. *Proportionality.* The damage to be inflicted and the costs incurred by war must be proportionate to the good expected by taking up arms. The judgments of costs and gains must include not only the physical and economic dimensions but the moral, psychological, and spiritual.

The two conditions for just behavior in war (*jus in bello*) are *proportionality*—meaning that a response to aggression must not exceed the nature of the aggression—and *discrimination*—meaning that a just response to aggression must be directed against unjust aggressors, not against innocent people caught up in a war not of their making. As the bishops note:

> Mobilization of forces in modern war includes not only the military, but to a significant degree the political, economic, and social sectors. It is not always easy to determine who is directly involved in a "war effort" or to what degree. Plainly, though, not even by the broadest definition can one rationally consider combatants entire classes of human beings such as school-children, hospital patients, the elderly, the ill, the average industrial worker producing goods not directly related to military purposes, farmers, and many others. They may never be directly attacked.[14]

The Bishops' Application of the Just-War Doctrine to Nuclear War

In applying these principles, the American bishops arrived at the following conclusions on the use of nuclear weapons in war:

1. *Counter Population Use:* Under no circumstances may nuclear weapons or other instruments of mass slaughter be used for the purpose of destroying population centers or other predominantly civilian targets. Retaliatory action which would indiscriminately and disproportionately take many wholly innocent lives, lives of people who are in no way responsible for reckless actions of their government, must also be condemned.

2. *The Initiation of Nuclear War:* We do not perceive any situation in which the deliberate initiation of nuclear war, on however restricted a scale, can be morally justified. Nonnuclear attacks by another state must be resisted by other than nuclear means. Therefore, a serious moral obligation exists to develop non-nuclear defensive strategies as rapidly as possible. In this letter we urge NATO to move rapidly toward the adoption of a "no first use" policy, but we recognize this will take time to implement and will require the development of an adequate alternative defense posture.

3. *Limited Nuclear War:* Our examination of the various arguments on this question makes us highly skeptical about the real meaning of "limited." One of the criteria of the just-war teaching is that there must be a reasonable hope of success in bringing about justice and peace. We must ask whether such a reasonable hope can exist once nuclear weapons have been exchanged. The burden of proof remains on those who assert that meaningful limitation is possible. In our view the first imperative is to prevent any use of nuclear weapons and we hope that leaders will resist the notion that nuclear conflict can be limited, contained or won in any traditional sense.[15]

Catholic and Other Critiques of the Bishops' Position

The bishops themselves state that "not all statements in this letter have the same moral authority. At times we state universally binding moral principles found in the teaching of the Church; at other times the pastoral letter makes specific applications, observations and recommendations which allow for diversity of opinion on the part of those who assess the factual data of a situation differently."[16] The principles of just-war theory are the "universally binding moral principles" of the Church; the conclusions cited above are some of the applications to which Catholics are expected to give serious consideration, but with which they may differ. And indeed, Catholics have written in opposition to the bishops' statement.

Probably the most thoughtful and articulate Catholic critique of the pastoral letter is Michael Novak's article, "Moral Clarity in the Nuclear Age,"[17] which was publicly endorsed by several dozen prominent conservatives. Although written in response to the second draft of the pastoral letter and published a month before the final draft appeared in print, it speaks to many of the salient points of the bishops' statement. Most of Novak's criticisms center around the bishops' position on armament and deterrence, which is discussed later in the chapter; but he does delineate a number of "gaps in just-war theory today." These include some that deal with the questions of the waging of war itself. In the context of modern guerrilla warfare and terrorism, who constitutes a competent authority to launch a war, even in the name of a "just cause?" Under what circumstances, if any, are the tactics of terrorism justified? Is a war of espionage and counterespionage to be preferred over a war of conventional weapons, or as a means of defense, and, if so, according to what standards of behavior? And finally, is it ever the case that nations acquire moral responsibilities, in the name of justice, to intervene in other countries to preserve human rights? Nazi Germany is the obvious case in point, but the same question arises in regard to many Third World countries.

In another critique, David A. Hoekema points out that the bishops' understanding of noncombatant immunity is not a necessary result of the just-war theory.[18] The bishops object to nuclear war in part because it would not discriminate between combatants and noncombatants, which, they claim, is never justifiable. Hoekema, however, cites two alternative theories of noncombatant immunity. George Mavrodes has argued that noncombatant immunity is morally binding only if the parties to a particular war have agreed to accept this principle by mutual agreement.[19] Michael Walzer thinks the prohibition of direct killing of noncombatants draws its force from our abhorrence of wanton killing, even if it occurs in the heat of battle; and he argues that that principle should be waived in situations of "supreme emergency," when all that we value in our society and way of life are under threat.[20] "All three approaches are rooted in the just war tradition," Hoekema notes, "but they diverge in their conception of the nature of its requirements."[21] Therefore, the failure of nuclear war to discriminate between combatants and noncombatants is not as clearly rooted in just-war theory as the bishops make it seem.

Novak probes the bishops' other primary argument against the use of nuclear weapons, the proportionality doctrine. He does not claim outright that nuclear war can itself be justified on that ground; in fact, after demonstrating that nuclear defense is less expensive than a buildup of conventional arms, he nevertheless recognizes "that moral means may be more costly than less moral means, as conventional deterrence may be more costly than nuclear deterrence, but we accept this as the price of moral behavior."[22] Having said that, however, he argues strongly for nuclear deterrence which would include the reluctant intention to use it if necessary. "To abandon deterrence occasions the greatest evil, for it entails endangering that liberty which is more precious than life itself. Free societies are an indispensable social condition of free moral life and the preservation of human rights."[23]

Along similar lines, Novak objects to the bishops' acceptance of pacifism:

[I]f love demands the defense of others (such that a failure to defend them can be a sin), both love and justice also command self-defense. Peace is sometimes unjust; war is sometimes morally imperative. . . . Moreover, sufficiency to deter aggression is a

moral imperative of the right to self-defense and the duty to defend
the innocent from unjust aggression.[24]

As David A. Hoekema points out, however, the two major formu-
lators of the just-war tradition in Christian social ethics, Augustine
and Aquinas, both deny the moral propriety of the use of lethal
force in self-defense; that may be consistent with justice, but not
with Christian love. War is consonant with Christian love only
when the sovereign launches it to protect innocent lives. Under
such circumstances Jesus' prescription to love one's enemy is
understood as an inward disposition which one must have, even if
one must use outward means of violence to protect the innocent.
The bishops were correctly careful not to base the legitimacy of
war on the moral right or obligation of violent self-defense, because for Catholicism neither exists.[25]

Jewish Justifications for War

Jews have not focused on the subject of war to the extent that
Catholics have. As Rabbi Louis Jacobs has pointed out, "There
has been no systematic treatment in the Jewish sources on 'just
war,' and this for a very good reason. For 2,000 years Jews had no
state of their own, so that the whole question was academic."[26]
The Torah and the Talmud discuss the rules of war, but the
classical Jewish source closest to a thorough treatment of the
subject is Maimonides' code.[27]

Several principles emerge from the sources that can serve as
a basis for comparison to the bishops' statement. Like Catholicism, Judaism begins with the premise that peace is to be sought
as vigorously as possible. Again, like Catholicism, though, war is
sometimes countenanced and sometimes actually commanded.

Specifically, the Mishnah speaks of three categories of war:
commanded wars (*milhamot mitzvah*); obligatory wars (*milhamot
hovah*); and discretionary wars (*milhamot reshut*). The Babylonian Talmud in *Sotah* defines the difference between the first two
types of war in terms of whether God specifically commanded
engaging in the war or only indirectly commanded it. God specifically commanded the wars against the seven Canaanite nations to

conquer the land for the Israelites[28] and the war against Amalek.[29] Another talmudic passage specifically mentions and sanctions defensive wars—to the point of permitting them on the Sabbath if the enemy intends to take lives as well as property.[30] According to Rabbi Judah in the Talmud, God indirectly commanded wars "to diminish the heathens so that they shall not march against them" through the general biblical obligation of self-defense based on Exodus 22:1. Most of the later commentaries, however, treated such preemptive wars as discretionary wars.[31] All agree that the wars of kings to expand the territory of the Land of Israel are discretionary wars. Discretionary wars could be waged only under a number of restrictions which cannot be satisfied today (except under the broadest of interpretations), and so in practice the only kinds of wars which Jews are currently permitted to fight, according to Jewish law, are the three categories of commanded wars.

Self-Defense versus Protecting the Innocent

These principles make a number of contrasts clear. Contrary to Catholic doctrine, each individual Jew is required to defend himself or herself; the rabbis of the Talmud established that duty on the basis of Exodus 21:1, saying, "If someone comes to kill you, get up early in the morning to kill him first."[32] Moreover, in contrast to the Catholic just-war teaching, Jewish law specifically permits—nay, commands—the community to fight a defensive war.[33] The rationale for such wars is *not* to defend other innocent victims against aggression, as it is for Catholicism; it is to defend onself and one's own nation.

Indeed, there is a real question in Jewish law whether one would be permitted to engage in a war declared to defend other people if there were not an element of self-defense in it as well. An *individual* is required to intervene to stop a pursuer (*rodef*) from killing another person,[34] but that obligation does not apply when one's own life would be endangered.[35] Maimonides even says that anyone who chooses to give up his life in performing a commandment when the law does not require him to do so is culpable of suicide.[36] Moreover, the intended victim, and even more so a third party, may stop a pursuer only if he will not simultaneously kill innocent bystanders, for, as the Talmud says, "One life may not be taken for another."[37] Since wars inevitably involve casualties among noncombatants, engaging in a war to defend a group of innocent people may well not be justified. There are rabbinic authorities who permit and even demand acting on behalf of innocent victims, whether individuals or groups, despite the danger to oneself and others;[38] but the legitimacy of such action (or the demand for it) is at best a matter of dispute in Jewish law whereas for Catholics it is the prime justification for waging war. Thus, the Jewish and Catholic traditions went in exactly opposite directions on this issue: Judaism emphasizing self-defense; Catholicism, the aid of others in according legitimacy to war.

This is not to say that Judaism ignored the demands of love of others. "Love your neighbor as yourself," after all, appears in the Torah long before Jesus enunciates it as one of his fundamental principles.[39] Moreover, Judaism delineated numerous specific ways in which that love was to be expressed in many areas of life, including, for example, providing hospitality, visiting the sick, comforting mourners, burying the dead, redeeming captives, and helping newlyweds rejoice at their wedding.[40] This was not only to be a matter of sentiment or lip service; Jews had to express their love in concrete ways. God, however, requires not only that you love your neighbor as yourself, but that "your neighbor live *with you*," which means, according to the Talmud, that your life takes precedence over your neighbor's.[41] Hence, the demand for self-defense. But the specificity with which Judaism delineates the command to love someone else indicates the seriousness Judaism has attached to it.[42]

The Principle of Discrimination

Discrimination between combatants and noncombatants is an important principle in Catholic doctrine both in the decision to wage a war and in the conduct of the war. A similar principle appears in Jewish practice, but it does not have the same scope.

The Bible demands that the Israelites "not let a soul remain alive" among the Canaanite nations that they were to conquer "lest they mislead you into doing all the abhorrent things that they have done for their gods and you stand guilty before the Lord your

God"; but when the Israelites fought other distant towns, they were to "put all its males to the sword" but were allowed to take the women and children as booty.[43] Even that partial distinction between combatants and noncombatants, however, was *permission* extended to them for purposes of affording them booty; it was not a moral imperative. According to the plain meaning of the biblical text, they could, presumably, kill all of the women and children in distant wars, too, if they did not want to take spoils. Maimonides, however, restricts the biblical command to kill everyone to the seven Canaanite nations and Amalek, and the biblical permission to preserve conquered women and children of all other nations as slaves he understands as a command.[44] This, then, would constitute one form of discrimination between combatants and noncombatants in the conduct of war.

Another manifestation of the same principle occurs in one of the early rabbinic interpretations of the Torah, the *Sifre*. It requires that Jews besiege a city only from three sides so that anyone who wants to flee may, and Maimonides includes that ruling in his law code.[45] That would seem to be a clear basis for discrimination between combatants and noncombatants.

Nahmanides interprets the law that way, but he also suggests that its rationale is at least partially tactical—specifically, to encourage desertion from the enemy's troops, thereby weakening their fighting potential.[46] Moreover, he and others claim that this rule applies only to a discretionary war[47]; this would make it inapplicable to commanded wars of self-defense, the only type of war to which Jewish law is clearly applicable today. Although others insist on this procedure for commanded wars too,[48] even for their leaving a direction for civilians to flee is a requirement affecting the conduct of war and not a condition on the permissibility of waging war in the first place.

There are a few sources that would indicate a concern for avoiding wars in which many innocents would suffer or die. For example, although God commanded Moses to wage war against Sihon the Amorite, the king of Heshbon, the Midrash notes that Moses (Deuteronomy 2:24,26) instead sent messengers to sue for peace:

God said to him: "I commanded you to make war against him, but instead you made peace. By your life, I will affirm your decision. Every time the people of Israel shall enter into war, they shall begin with a declaration of peace, as stipulated in the verse, "When you draw near to a city to fight against it, proclaim peace to it" (Deuteronomy 20:10).

Who fulfilled this passage? Joshua, the son of Nun. Rabbi Samuel, son of Nahman, said: "What did Joshua do? In every place he came to conquer, he first published an edict to the following effect: 'Whoever desires to go, let him go; whoever desires to make peace, let him make peace; and whoever desires to make war, let him make war.' What did the Girgashites do? They departed to make way for the Israelites, and God gave them another land in Africa as beautiful as their original land. As for the Gibeonites, who sought to make peace, Joshua made peace with them. But when thirty-one kings made war against Joshua, God made them fall by his hand."[49]

Similarly, King David, despite a distinct biblical directive to the contrary, attempted to establish peaceful relations with the Ammonites, and that was commended by some later sages.[50] Joshua's three letters are mentioned not only in midrashic passages but also in a legal section of the Jerusalem Talmud; and it is probably on that basis that Maimonides includes them in his code. He claims, in fact, that such an effort for peace must be made in all wars, even the commanded wars against the Canaanites and Amalekites. If the conditions of peace are accepted, war must not be waged.[51] It is not clear, however, whether the demand to sue for peace is simply a manifestation of the desire to avoid war altogether, or whether it derives from a concern to protect noncombatants in particular.

The situation is yet more complex. According to the *Sifre*, Israelites may besiege a city only to make war on it, "not to make (its inhabitants die of) starvation, thirst, or disease."[52] One modern commentator understands that passage to forbid subjecting a city to a blockade of hunger, thirst, or disease before beginning negotiations for peace.[53] Interpreted in that way, this rule would prohibit inflicting suffering on those who are not clearly combatants. On the other hand, if the city does not make peace, that same passage permits the Israelites to wage war on it "and even to make (its inhabitants die of) hunger, thirst, or disease."[54] Even though the *Sifre* requires a direction to be left open for those who want to flee, presumably most of the noncombatant women, children, and old men would remain in their city. The fact that the *Sifre* openly permits starving a city in this way, then, indicates that in some circumstances discrimination between combatants and noncombatants is not required even in the conduct of war. The later codes do not mention this early source, either to affirm it or deny it; but since it is the only passage in rabbinic literature that deals specifically with our question, it raises doubts about whether Judaism requires a distinction between combatants and noncombatants even in the conduct of war.

In any case, Jewish law does not include the criterion of discrimination between combatants and noncombatants as a condition for waging war, even though some sources seem to prescribe that principle regarding the conduct of war. Since the lack of discrimination is one of the two major reasons why the bishops think that the intent to use nuclear deterrent force is illegitimate, the absence of such a criterion for engaging in war in Jewish law would mark a major difference between the two religions.

One can understand the ambivalence of Jewish sources on this issue; in war it is often difficult, if not impossible, to determine who is and who is not a combatant. On the contrary, one has to assume that the enemy's entire population is mobilized in fighting against you, contributing to the war effort in whatever way it can. The only exceptions would be those who openly help you, as Rahab helped the two spies whom Joshua sent to Jericho. In such cases, you certainly have a moral obligation to repay the favor, as Joshua did in saving her and her family.[55]

Although discrimination between combatants and noncombatants is a crucial part of modern Catholic just-war theory, it is a relatively recent moral concern. It began during the fourteenth or fifteenth century as part of the rules of chivalrous conduct among knights. By the seventeenth century the principle had been so well established that Shakespeare has Fluellen say in *Henry V*: "Kill the poys and the luggage! 'tis expressly against the law of arms."[56] From the fifteenth to the twentieth centuries numerous codes of the rules of war in Western countries included the principle, but the most important for contemporary law are the Hague Conventions of 1907 and the Geneva Conventions of 1949, as amended by the two Additional Protocols of 1977.[57]

The founders of the State of Israel made this modern concern to distinguish between combatants and noncombatants a sacred principle—often with fatal consequences for the Israelis. These were largely nonreligious or even antireligious people, and so their commitment to this principle is clearly not based on religious sources—although it undoubtedly was shaped by a general Jewish sense of the ethical and the experience of hundreds of years of persecution in addition to an appreciation of modern sensitivities.

For close to twenty years after World War I, the Zionist political leadership insisted that Jews engage in defensive action only. Specifically, they could build fortifications and defend settlements from behind the fences, but they were not permitted to take the initiative against the Arabs despite the riots of 1920, 1921, 1929, and 1936 in which many Jews were killed. These rules of *havlagah*, "self-restraint," were an attempt to prevent the spread of military conflict.

When it became clear that this policy was not working, a British officer, Captain Charles Orde Wingate, convinced the Israelis to engage in offensive measures to prevent further massacres.[58] Even so, their actions were restricted by the principle of *tohar ha-neshek*, "purity of arms"—that is, the requirement to fight combatants exclusively. Jewish leaders insisted on that for both moral and tactical reasons; they knew that wholesale counterattack would arouse further Arab hostility, and they hoped that selective action against combatants would discourage the Arab masses from following those who incited them to military action.[59]

The ethic of purity of arms has informed Israeli policy from the 1930s, but incidents in which that ethic caused the death of Israeli soldiers have raised questions about it from the very beginning. One of the stories coming out of Israel's War of Independence was that the group of thirty-five Jewish soldiers killed on the way to relieve embattled Gush Ezion on January 16, 1948 were betrayed by an old Arab shepherd whom they came across and let go as a noncombatant.[60] The same ethic—and the same problem in differentiating combatants from noncombatants—arises in

some of the conversations of Israeli soldiers recorded after the Six
Day War (1967).[61] Similarly, Yigal Lev describes an incident during the years of "the war of attrition" after 1967 in which an Arab
woman hid three terrorists by standing in front of the opening of a
cave. Two of the Israeli soldiers pursuing the marauders lost their
lives because they did not treat the woman as a combatant.[62]

In the last several years, with the transformation of most
military action against Israel to terrorist activities, major questions
have been raised about continuing this ethic. Meir Pa'il has argued
strongly for maintaining the ethic on four grounds: (1) "Two
wrongs do not make a right." Even if Arabs have little concern for
"purity of arms" and operate on the basis of crude retribution,
that "does not justify our acting the way they do." (2) "Maintaining
purity of arms does not detract from any unit's fighting ability,
from the soldiers' courage, or from the units' accomplishments."
(3) Since military superiority will not buy peace, purity of arms is a
good political tool for making it possible ultimately to reach a
position of mutual respect and coexistence with Israel's present
enemies. (4) "This is the most important point of all; it asserts that
the maintenance of purity of arms is one of the most important
ways in which the decency of the nation, as a whole, can be
preserved" because Israel's army involves almost all of its male
citizens between the ages of 18 and 55 and all its women from 18
to 25. The moral standards maintained by the military therefore
have a direct impact on the nation's morality as a whole.[63]

On the other hand, Harold Fisch has argued that special
concern for women and children is a vestige of medieval notions of
chivalry and is hardly sensible under the conditions of modern
warfare. "When one throws a hand grenade or drops a bomb, the
explosion which follows makes no distinctions among its victims
between men, women, and children"—and, presumably, it makes
no difference whether the thrower is a man, woman, or child,
either.[64]

Despite these misgivings, purity of arms continues to be the
policy of the Israel Defense Force. In the 1983 incursion into
Lebanon, for example, the Israelis specifically resisted bombing
purely civilian targets even though saturation bombing would have
been much easier than carefully selecting targets. In one impor-

tant way Israeli behavior along these lines is more significant than the sources of Jewish law: the latter are only theoretical guidelines while the former is actual practice. Even so, Israelis have adopted the rule of discriminating between combatants and noncombatants as a mode of operation within war, not as a condition for determining whether it is just to wage a war in the first place. Judaism, then, would not share the bishops' concern about the nondiscriminatory nature of nuclear war or for that matter, biological or chemical weapons in deciding whether waging such war is moral. Judaism would, however, try to discriminate between combatants and noncombatants in the nature of the war.

The Principle of Proportionality

Would a defensive *nuclear* war be commanded? Consideration of that question brings us close to the Catholic criteria of likelihood of success and proportionality.

The question was debated by two prominent Orthodox rabbis in the early 1960s under the rubric of "Red or Dead." Rabbi Maurice Lamm claimed that *individuals* may not risk their lives in order to avoid domination by the Soviet Union because, however difficult it would be to live as a Jew under a Soviet government, it would be possible to maintain one's "Basic Moral Life," that is, refrain from murder, idolatry, and adultery. The Western *nations*, however, would not be able to sustain basic moral life under Russian rule, and consequently they must maintain deterrent nuclear power, even though it entails a risk of possible death for all humanity.[65]

Lord (Rabbi) Immanuel Jakobovits, on the other hand, points out that for Maimonides the obligation to surrender to death rather than violate the prohibitions against murder, incest, and idolatry stems from the duty to sanctify the Name of God, and so "if the alternative to surrender is the destruction of the whole Jewish people, the sacrifice lacks all meaning, since God can no longer 'be sanctified in the midst of the children of Israel' . . . It is absurd to defend Judaism by risking the liquidation of the last Jew to uphold it." Thus the vastness of destruction in a nuclear war would, for Jakobovits, effectively nullify the command to defend onself—similar to the Catholic doctrine of proportionality. "The Jew has ever preferred life with indignity and servitude to death with glory."[66]

The possibility of such a debate among Orthodox rabbis demonstrates convincingly that the principle of proportionality is not nearly as clear and authoritative a tenet in Judaism as it is in Catholicism. In the extreme case of nuclear war, Lord Jakobovits suggests that considerations of proportionality would demand a pacifistic response. Pacifism has been only an undercurrent in Judaism[67]—as it has been in Catholicism—but that, of course, is based on sources that do not contemplate the immensity of nuclear destruction. This debate indicates that it is not clear for Judaism whether that stance would change in a nuclear age.

What is clear is that the mainstream Jewish position legitimated and indeed commanded war as a means of self-defense, but only if there is no other way to accomplish that end. In a later replay of the "Red or Dead" debate—this time by Rabbi Maurice Lamm again on one side and Arthur Waskow, founder and director of the Shalom Center, on the other—Waskow takes up precisely that qualification. Aside from the many dangers involved in nuclear armament—including especially the lure of striking first and losing control in retaliation—nuclear armament, Waskow argues, simply does not provide an effective means of self-defense. Moreover, it does not even increase either side's ability to exert political pressure on other nations, because everyone knows that both superpowers are afraid to use their full nuclear military potential. Consequently, if either superpower just maintained its current nuclear ability to blow up the world and ran the arms race in reverse by *not* building the next system, it would maintain military deterrence and be able to use its energies and resources more effectively to change the world according to its own ideology. There would then be enough money to sell, loan, or give away enough food, energy, housing, and other goods to bribe other nations to do almost anything, and there would also be enough to hire people to serve as peace corps personnel or, if necessary, even guerillas to change another nation according to the superpower's will. Ultimately, the other superpower would be forced to adopt the same policy or see its political influence erode entirely. "This is not unilateral disarmament. No nation that has enough weapons to blow up the world has been disarmed. It *is* aggressive 'transarmament'—choosing weapons that will really work."[68]

Whatever one thinks of Waskow's suggestion, it does continue the Jewish tradition of seeking peaceful ways to accomplish one's ends while yet maintaining both the right and the potential to defend oneself with violent means if necessary. Waskow recoils from the sheer destructiveness and the lack of proportionality involved in a nuclear confrontation, but he is not content to leave the argument against nuclear armament at that. Perhaps that is because he realizes that the Jewish tradition spoke clearly about the need to defend oneself but not so clearly about proportionality.[69] Even if considerations of proportionality do not override the command to defend oneself, however, they certainly do underscore the traditional Jewish demand that we actively seek peace.

ARMAMENT, DETERRENCE, AND OTHER PROPOSALS FOR PEACE

The Bishops' Position

Probably the most controversial section of the bishops' pastoral letter is their view of deterrence. Diplomatically quoting statements by both the dovish Pope John XXIII and the relatively hawkish Pope John Paul II, they assert that deterrence based on a balance of nuclear weapons, "certainly not as an end in itself but as a step on the way toward a progressive disarmament, may still be judged morally acceptable." That, however, is a minimal form of peace always subject to explosion, and therefore ultimately "the fundamental principle on which our present peace depends must be replaced by another, which declares that the true and solid peace of nations consists not in equality of arms but in mutual trust alone."[70]

Few would disagree with that. But the bishops go further:

No *use* of nuclear weapons which would violate the principles of discrimination or proportionality may be *intended* in a strategy of

deterrence. The moral demands of Catholic teaching require reso-
lute willingness not to intend or to do moral evil even to save our
own lives or the lives of those we love.[71]

On the basis of policy statements and clarifications of U.S. government officials, the bishops determined that it is not the intention of American strategic policy to target the Soviet civilian
population as such, but "attack on military targets or militarily
significant industrial targets could involve 'indirect' (unintended)
but massive civilian casualties"—to the point that "the number of
deaths in a substantial exchange would be almost indistinguishable from what might occur if civilian centers had been deliberately and directly struck. . . . The problem is not one of producing
highly accurate weapons . . . [because] those civilian deaths
would occur both immediately and from the long-term effects of
social and economic devastation" as well as radioactive fallout.
Therefore, "in our judgment, such a strike would be deemed
morally disproportionate, even though not intentionally indiscriminate."[72]

The bishops save their harshest words for the arms race:
"The arms race is one of the greatest curses on the human race; it
is to be condemned as a danger, an act of aggression against the
poor, and folly which does not provide the security it promises."[73]

Part of this antipathy to the arms race stems from moral
aspects of the nuclear military situation. Based upon the principle
of proportionality, the bishops conclude that "if nuclear deterrence exists only to prevent the use of nuclear weapons by others,
then proposals to go beyond this to planning for prolonged periods of repeated nuclear strikes and counter-strikes, or 'prevailing'
in nuclear war, are not acceptable."[74]

But the bulk of the bishops' objections to the arms race is
based on economic considerations. In their view, increasing nuclear weapons means that morally necessary programs for the
welfare of the poor cannot be funded. Moreover, the money spent
on nuclear arms does not bring the security it promises: in an
interdependent world the security of one nation is related to the
security of all and is not afforded by military might alone.[75] On the
contrary, only solving the social and economic problems of hu-

manity, and especially of the Third World, will bring the security we seek:

> Public attention, riveted on the big powers, often misses the plight of scores of countries and millions of people simply trying to survive. The interdependence of the world means a set of inter-related human questions. Important as keeping the peace in the nuclear age is, it does not solve or dissolve the other major prob-lems of the day. Among these problems the pre-eminent issue is the continuing chasm in living standards between the industrialized world (East and West) and the developing world. . . . The East–West competition, central as it is to world order and important as it is in foreign policy debate, does not address this moral question which rivals the nuclear issue in its human significance.[76]

Those who share the bishops' sentiment often quote the words of President Dwight D. Eisenhower along the same lines:

> Every gun that is made, every warship launched, every rocket fired signifies, in the final sense, a theft from those who hunger and are not fed, those who are cold and are not clothed. This world in arms is not spending money alone. It is spending the sweat of its labor-ers, the genius of its scientists, the hopes of its children. . . . This is not a way of life at all in any true sense. Under the cloud of threatening war, it is humanity hanging from a cross of iron.[77]

For all these reasons, then, the bishops conclude that a significant effort must be made to reduce arms. This includes attention to the economic difficulties of converting defense industries to other purposes; nuclear arms that are maintained must be held on the basis of sufficiency to deter, not for nuclear superiority.

The bishops go further: We must take energetic, positive steps to promote peace. The third part of their letter is a thought-ful, often eloquent program for promoting peace. The bishops support immediate, bilateral, verifiable agreements to halt the testing, production, and deployment of new nuclear weapons systems; deep cuts in the arsenals of both superpowers, especially their retaliatory forces; a comprehensive test-ban treaty; new efforts to prevent the spread of nuclear weapons in the world and to control the conventional arms race, particularly the trade in weaponry; and the establishment of some form of global authority adequate to the needs of promoting the international good. Regarding the last of these points, the bishops point out that the modern nation state developed in response to new economic conditions in modern times, but the nuclear potential now makes the individual sovereignty of each state obsolete.

In this way and others, what is required is a complete "moral about-face," including a comprehensive program to deter violence in all of its forms. In their view, this includes prohibiting abortion, and at one point they make it seem as if the solution to our nuclear problems is directly dependent on banning abortion. The pastoral letter concludes with sensitive addresses to separate groups of people whom they charge with special responsibilities in promoting peace—religious professionals, educators, parents, youth, military personnel, the staff of defense industries, scientists, media personalities, and public officials:

> In the words of the Holy Father [Pope John Paul II], we need a "moral about-face." The whole world must summon the moral courage and technical means to say no to nuclear conflict; no to weapons of mass destruction, no to an arms race which robs the poor and the vulnerable; and no to the moral danger of a nuclear age which places before humankind indefensible choices of constant terror or surrender. Peace-making is not an optional commitment. It is a requirement of our faith.[78]

Catholic Critiques of the Bishops' Position

Novak and his conservative confreres vehemently objected to the bishops' recommendations on political, military, and economic grounds. Reflecting a hardline, coldwar posture, they found the bishops to be politically and morally naive in their misunderstanding of the Soviet Union's threat to impose Communism upon the world. The bishops claimed that militarily the principle of proportionality requires that there be no intention to use nuclear weapons, even if a country like the United States has them for purposes of deterrence. Novak pointed out that militarily that was an untenable position. There simply was no deterrent value in having nuclear weapons if your known intention was never to use them.

Beyond that, Novak attacked the moral premise of the bishops' claim. He distinguished between fundamental, secondary, and architectonic intentions in the use of weapons. The fundamental moral intention in nuclear deterrence was never to have to use deterrent force. This intention can be realized, however, only if a country has/had a secondary intention to use them, if necessary. Even that was not enough; there had to be an "architectonic," or "objective" intention, that is, a concrete plan of action for creating and maintaining the deterrent force. Citizens or their representatives must vote funds for research, development, and maintenance of the deterrent weapons; elaborate systems of communication and command must be established and maintained.

> The position that a nation may possess a deterrent, but may not intend to use it, is fulfilled by the fundamental intention but not by the objective intention and the secondary intention. To condemn the latter is to frustrate the former and to invite a host of greater evils.[79]

In addition to these political and military claims, Novak criticized the economic sections of the bishops' letter. Writing in the days before Gorbachev, Novak did agree that "lower spending on defense would be advantageous to all," and that "we favor the minimum amount of defense spending consistent with moral obligations to defend the innocent with just means." Nonetheless, maintaining nuclear defense is definitely cheaper than switching to a totally conventional defense. Therefore, on purely economic grounds, the bishops' arguments on behalf of the poor should have swayed them to endorse a nuclear deterrent rather than object to it.[80]

These combined political, military, and economic considerations led Novak to a position significantly different from the bishops', even though both began with the "just war" theory. Novak agreed that, despite the additional cost, it is "both morally good and morally required" to supplant our reliance on tactical nuclear weapons with a sufficient conventional deterrent; but "prudence dictates that the nuclear deterrent be held in reserve," presumably even after that replacement is accomplished.

Novak wrote this with special reference to the arms race between the United States and the Soviet Union. Even after the demise of the cold war, Novak's salient point is that in a contentious world, military requirements as well as economic wisdom and moral concern for the poor dictate that the West maintain and update its nuclear deterrent—and intend to use it if necessary. Indeed, a few years later, Novak credited Ronald Reagan's "decisive military buildup," with the Soviet Union's subsequent decision to move towards a nuclear arms builddown.[81]

Jewish Approaches to Armament and Deterrence

Jews argue the specific issues of nuclear armament and deterrence in much the way that Catholics do. Paramount is the concern to avoid human annihilation, but that is balanced by the imperative of self-defense and the prohibition against suicide. Military, economic, and social concerns also play an important role, and the complexity of the issue requires difficult judgment calls on all sides.

The interesting thing is that people who often differ markedly on other issues find themselves on the same side on nuclear armament. So, for example, Reform Rabbis David Saperstein and Alexander Schindler, Reconstructionist spokesman Arthur Waskow, Conservative Rabbis Samuel Dresner, Louis Jacobs, and David Novak, and Orthodox Rabbis Immanuel Jakobovits and Walter Wurzburger have all written against nuclear armament. Similarly, resolutions voted by the organizations of all four religious groups and a variety of secular Jewish organizations have opposed nuclear armament.[82]

Moreover, the rationales against nuclear armament are repeated across denominational lines. So, for example, one would expect Reform spokesmen to think that the welfare of the poor should take precedence over military spending in light of the strong representation of the Reform Movement in civil rights activities of the 1960s, but Conservative and Orthodox representatives have stressed the same economic argument.[83]

The differences among Jews on nuclear armament are thus not aligned along religious lines; they rather stem from individual Jews' views on the nature of mankind. Those who trust Human beings to desire what is good for all and make binding agreements on that basis, argue for nuclear reductions or freezes; those who fear the selfishness, malevolence, and deceitfulness of people support nuclear armament. Of course, both positions are true: Human beings are both good and evil, caring and destructive, trustworthy and fickle. Some human beings are more generally of one character than of another. The difficulty is determining what will motivate governments to avoid aggression and work for everyone's mutual benefit. Is it the force of arms or the sweet voice of reason? Or some combination of them? Or something else?

As in the Catholic case, policy disagreements among Jews in the past decades have been more a matter of differing judgments about how values should be applied to the contemporary situation than they are debates about the values themselves. And ultimately the clash in how to apply the values reduces to a dispute about the nature of mankind. Everyone would prefer to have a world in which there was no need for armament of any kind, certainly including nuclear arms; but both traditions recognize that that is a messianic hope, not a present reality. The spokesmen of the two religions then respond to the current situation in ways which emphasize either the need for nuclear self-defense and its effectiveness in assuring peace, or the dangers of nuclear arms and the need to pursue peace in other ways. People of both inclinations are convinced of the horror of nuclear war; they differ in how to prevent it. That, in turn, stems from a dispute about the nature of human beings and what motivates them.

THE PURPOSE AND STATUS OF RELIGIOUS POSITIONS ON NUCLEAR ISSUES

Since Catholics and Jews can be found in all camps on matters of nuclear war and armament, why bother articulating a religious stance at all? In other words, what does either religion add to the general political debate if it does not affirm a clear position on these issues and rule out other views? And even if a religion does propound its own statement of principle, what authority does such a document have?

While liberals and conservatives can equally find roots in the Catholic and Jewish traditions, that does not mean that the religions are useless. They provide, first, important *conceptual frameworks* in which to posit the problems of our age of Omnicide. A theory which, for example, claims that it makes no difference whether many people will be killed in a nuclear holocaust is effectively ruled out by doctrines which both Judaism and Christianity share concerning the sanctity of human life. Nobody who believes that God created the world and that human beings have responsibilities to preserve it can talk about the destruction of humanity or nature in a cavalier fashion.

Second, both religions provide *ethical guidelines* for judging proposed solutions to a moral problem even if they do not mandate a specific solution. This article has concentrated on the differences and similarities between Jewish and Catholic moral principles regarding war. The moral doctrines of each religion call attention to the aspects of a particular situation which the Jew or Catholic should consider, including those which are ethically desirable and those which are not. They also offer some help in weighing conflicting values. Is a particular result of a plan of action totally unacceptable or simply a regrettable result which must be pursued for some other, morally important goal? For example, does the lack of proportionality in a nuclear conflict make nuclear defense unacceptable, or is it rather a factor which should impede the use of nuclear weapons and motivate us all the more strongly to work for peace, but which does not preclude a defense system based on nuclear arms? As already discussed, Judaism and Catholicism probably disagree on that one.

And finally, religions are often effective reservoirs of *motivation* to act ethically. For the religious person moral rules are not just pragmatic maxims or communal conventions; they are commands of God. They carry with them not only historical, communal, and practical incentives, but also moral and theological promptings. These include the desire to gain reward and avoid punishment, but that is only a small part of religious motivation to act morally. At least as important are the desires to fulfill one's covenantal promises to God; to repay God's favors to us through obedience to Him; to act in the exemplary way that He through His wisdom has prescribed; and to enhance one's relationship with God by fulfilling His will in love. Since moral action is often difficult, these additional motivations to act morally are important contributions of religions to the ethical enterprise.

Therefore, even if there is not unanimity among adherents of a given religion as to how to handle a particular moral problem, there are clear advantages to dealing with the problem in a religious context.[84] But what is the authority of any directives that issue out of such a religious discussion?

For the adherent of a given religion, of course, the authority may be considerable. Depending upon the person and the religion, moral prescriptions couched in religious terms may be more authoritative than any governmental law. Knowing that, the bishops openly distinguished the authority they intended to ascribe to the various sections of their pastoral letter so as to provide room for discussion and debate where they thought it was appropriate.[85] The bishops hope for the establishment of a truly effective international authority to enforce moral behavior, and they suggest ways to work toward creating it. Then such moral discussions would have international governmental authority.[86] Even if they lack that degree of authority, though, they minimally carry with them the demand to take the issue and the adopted viewpoint seriously. Catholics may not obey the Pope's directives on contraception, but they cannot help thinking about them. Similarly, politically conservative Catholics like Michael Novak may disagree with the bishops, but they cannot be blithely ignored.

The bishops openly recognized, however, that many of their readers would not be Catholics. For such people, of course, the bishops' words would not carry religious authority. Knowing this, the bishops expressed the hope that the thoroughness of their argumentation and the passion of their moral concern would persuade non-Catholics of their position and that other Christians, Jews, and Muslims would work with them in achieving their goals.[87]

For such is the nature of moral argumentation: its persuasive power is ultimately its only power for those outside the community in which the discussion takes place. But if the reasoning is careful and sensitive, that may be all that is needed. In the case of nuclear war and armament, the Jewish and Catholic analyses cannot but help people of the contemporary world think and act more thoughtfully and morally in the face of Omnicide. For religious Jews and Catholics, of course, these discussions have special meaning. The fact that religious, informed people cannot agree on proper strategies to deal with nuclear destructiveness is simply a manifestation of the complexity of the problem. For both the liberal and conservative sides to these issues are right: The means of self-defense *and* the methods of promoting peace must be both more sophisticated and more energetically pursued in our own day in light of the nuclear cloud hanging over us. May God help us succeed in both tasks:

> Depart from evil and do good; seek peace and pursue it (Psalms 34:15). The Torah did not demand that you go out of your way in pursuit of fulfilling the commandments; . . . it is only if specific situations should come your way that you are commanded to perform the concomitant duties. You need not, however, search for opportunities to fulfill them. But in the case of peace, you must "seek peace" wherever you happen to be, and "pursue it" if it is elsewhere.[88]

Acknowledgment: I would like to thank Dr. David Lieber and Dr. Elieser Slomovic for their helpful comments on an earlier draft of this chapter.

NOTES

1. The National Conference of Catholic Bishops, *The Challenge of Peace: God's Promise and Our Response* (Washington, DC: 1983). Hereinafter called "*Challenge.*"

2. *Los Angeles Times*, August 3, 1985, Part II, p. 4.

3. *Time*, July 29, 1985, p. 58.

4. *Cf.* Roland Herbert Bainton, *Christian Attitudes toward War and Peace* (Abingdon: 1960), chs. 4, 5, 10; J. Yoder, *Nevertheless: Varieties of Religious Pacifism* (Scottsdale, AR: 1971); Thomas Merton, *Faith and Violence: Christian Teaching and Christian Practice.* (Notre Dame, IN: University of Notre Dame Press, 1968); G. Zahn, *War, Conscience, and Dissent* (New York: 1967).

5. Matthew 5:43–44; 26:51–54; Luke 6:27–36; *cf.* Romans 12:14–21.

6. *Challenge*, pp. iv–v, 23–24, 34–36.

7. Luke 22:36, 38, 49–50.

8. David Bivin and Roy Blizzard, *Understanding the Difficult Words of Jesus* (Arcadia, CA: Makor Foundation, 1983), p. 108. I would like to thank my friend and student, David Hershey, for pointing this out to me.

9. Exodus 23:4–5; 1 Samuel 24:17–20; Proverbs 24:17; Job 31:29.

10. Augustine, *City of God*, IV, 15; XIX, 7; etc. *Cf.* Paul Ramsey, *War and the Christian Conscience* (Durham: Duke University Press, 1961), pp. 34–36, for the relevant texts. *Cf.* also Frederick H. Russell, *The Just War in the Middle Ages* (Cambridge: Cambridge University Press, 1975); Arthur Holmes, ed., *War and Christian Ethics* (Grand Rapids, MI: Baker Book House, 1975).

11. *Cf.* Aquinas, *Summa Theologica*, II–IIae, q. 40, 64; Paul Ramsey, *The Just War: Force and Political Responsibility* (New York: Scribners, 1968); James Johnson, *Just War Tradition and the Restraint of War: A Moral and Historical Inquiry* (Princeton, NJ: Princeton University Press, 1981).

12. *Challenge*, p. 29.

13. *Ibid.*, p. 30.

14. *Ibid.*, p. 34.

15. *Challenge*, pp. v–vi.

16. *Ibid.*, p. i.

17. Michael Novak, "Moral Clarity in the Nuclear Age," *National Review* 35:6 (April 1, 1983), pp. 354 *ff.*

18. David A. Hoekema, "Morality, Just War, and Nuclear Weapons," *Soundings* 67:4 (Winter 1984), pp. 360–361.

19. George Mavrodes, "Conventions and the Morality of War," *Philosophy and Public Affairs* 4:2 (Winter 1975), pp. 117–131.

20. Michael Walzer, *Just and Unjust Wars* (New York: Basic Books, 1977), Chapter 16.

21. Hoekema, "Morality," p. 373.

22. Novak, "Moral Clarity," p. 367.

23. *Ibid.*, p. 383; *cf.* pp. 383–386.

24. Novak, *ibid.*, pp. 364, 382.

25. Hoekema, "Morality," pp. 360–361. The relevant texts in Augustine and Aquinas can be found in Paul Ramsey, *War and Christian Conscience* (Durham, NC: Duke University Press, 1961), pp. 34–46.

26. Louis Jacobs, *What Does Judaism Say About . . . ?* (New York: Quadrangle, 1973), p. 228.

27. *Cf.* Deuteronomy 20; *Sotah* 8:7 (44b) and the *Gemara* there; *Mishneh Torah, Laws of Kings*, chs. 5–8.

28. Numbers 31:7, 15*ff*; 33:55; Deuteronomy 7:2; 20:16*ff.*, etc.

29. Exodus 17:14–16; Deuteronomy 25:17–19.

30. *Eruvin* 45a; *cf. Mishnah Eruvin* 4:3; *Tosefta Eruvin* 3:5, 8; *Yerushalmi Eruvin* 4:3 (21d); and Saul Lieberman, *Tosefta Kifshutah* (New York: Jewish Theological Seminary, 1962), pp. 342–344.

31. *Sotah* 44b. *Cf.* J. David Bleich, "Preemptive War in Jewish Law," *Tradition* 21:1 (Spring 1983), pp. 3–41, for a thorough discussion of this topic.

32. *Berakhot* 58a; *Yoma* 85b; *Sanhedrin* 72a; Genesis *Rabbah* 21:5; etc.

33. Although one might be tempted to infer the community's duty of self-defense from that of each of its citizens individually, there are difficulties in that and special sanction is necessary for the community; *cf.* Bleich, "Preemptive War," pp. 18–19.

34. *Sanhedrin* 72b–73a; *Mishneh Torah Laws of Murder* 1:6–7, 9; *Shulhan Arukh, Hoshen Mishpat* 425:1.

35. *Teshuvot Radbaz*, III, No. 1052; *Pri Megadim, Orah Hayyim, Mishbetzot Zahav* 328:7; *Arukh Ha-Shulhan, Hoshen Mishpat* 426:4; and *Pithei Teshuvah, Hoshen Mishpat* 426:2.

36. *Mishneh Torah, Fundamental Principles of the Torah* 4:4.

37. *Sanhedrin* 72b. *Cf.* Rashi, *ibid.*, s.v. *yatza rosho; Shulhan Arukh, Hoshen Mishpat* 425:2, and *Pithei Teshuvah* there.

38. *Kesef Mishneh, Hilkhot Rotzeah* 1:14 and *Bet Yosef, Hoshen Mishpat* 426. On this issue, cf. Solomon Joseph Zevin, *Le'or Ha-Halakhah*, (Tel Aviv: Abraham Zioni Books, 1957), pp. 13–18.

39. Leviticus 19:18; Mark 12:30–31; Matthew 19:19.

40. Cf., for example, Louis Jacobs, *The Book of Jewish Belief* (New York: Behrman House, 1984), chapter 19; *Encyclopaedia Judaica* 11:529–530; *Enziklopedia Talmudit* 1:210–215 (Hebrew).

41. Leviticus 25:36; *Bava Mezia* 62a. Cf. Jakob J. Petuchowski, "The Limits of Self-Sacrifice," in Marvin Fox, ed., *Modern Jewish Ethics* (Columbus, OH: Ohio State University Press, 1975), pp. 103–118.

42. Cf. Warren Zev Harvey, "Love: The Beginning and the End of Torah," *Tradition* 15:4 (Spring 1976), pp. 5–22, for a good demonstration of the centrality of love in Judaism.

43. Deuteronomy 20:10–18.

44. *Mishneh Torah, Laws of Kings* 6:4. Cf. Zevin, *Le'or Ha-Halakhah*, pp. 44–45.

45. *Sifre, Mattot* no. 157; *Midrash Tannaim*, Deuteronomy 20:12; *Mishneh Torah, Laws of Kings* 6:7. Cf. also *Sifre* on Numbers 31:7.

46. Nahmanides' commentary on Maimonides' *Book of the Commandments*, Commandment no. 5.

47. Nahmanides, *ibid.*; Rabbi David ben Solomon ibn Abi Zimra (Radbaz) (1479–1573), on *Mishneh Torah, Laws of Kings* 6:7; *Sefer ha-Hinnukh* (ascribed to Aaron ha-Levi of Barcelona, end of thirteenth century) (Jerusalem: Mossad, 1968), no. 503 (*Shofetim* no. 13), pp. 523–524.

48. Joseph ben Moses Badad, *Minhat Hinnukh*, on *Sefer ha-Hinnukh* 503 (*Shofetim* no. 13).

49. Deuteronomy *Rabbah, Seder Shoftim*, Part 5, Sec. 13–14. Cf. *Leviticus Rabbah* 17:6.

50. Deuteronomy 23:7; 2 Samuel 10:1 *ff.*; *Kesef Mishneh* to *Mishneh Torah, Books of Kings* 6:6; *Sefer Hasidim* (ed. Vistinetsky), p. 252 (1002). Cf., however, Numbers *Rabbah* 21:5.

51. *Yerushalmi Shevi'it* 6:1 (36c). *Mishneh Torah, Laws of Kings* 6:1–5. Others restrict the demand for a suit for peace to permitted wars.

52. *Sifre* to Deuteronomy 20:10.

53. David S. Shapiro, *Studies in Jewish Thought* (New York: Yeshiva University Press, 1975), Vol. I, p. 345; reprinted in *Violence and the Value of Life in Jewish Tradition*, Yehezkel Landau, ed. (Jerusalem: Oz veShalom Publications, 1984), p. 85.

54. *Sifre* on Deuteronomy 20:12.

55. Joshua 2; 6:21–25.

56. William Shakespeare, *Henry V*, Act 4, Scene 7.

57. Leslie C. Green, "Human Rights and the Law of Armed Conflict," *Israel Yearbook on Human Rights*, Vol. 10 (Jerusalem: Alpha Press, 1980), pp. 10-11. *Cf.* also the 14 articles on human rights in warfare in *ibid.*, Vol. 1 (1971), especially those by Levie and Gottlieb regarding civilians.

58. Dan Kurzman, *Genesis 1948: The First Arab-Israeli War* (New York: World, 1970), p. 105.

59. Netanel Lorch, *The Edge of the Sword: Israel's War of Independence, 1947-1949* (New York: G. P. Putman's Sons, 1961, and Jerusalem: Massada, 1968), p. 58.

60. David Ben Gurion, *B'Helahem Yisrael* (*When Israel Fought in Battle*) (Tel Aviv: Am Oved, 1975), p. 46 (Hebrew). *Cf.* also Dov Knohl, *Siege in the Hills of Hebron* (New York: Thomas Yoseloff, 1958), p. 103; Ada Paldor, *Milhemet Ha-Shihrur* (Jerusalem: R. Portnoy, 1978), pp. 38, 40 (Hebrew).

61. Avraham Shapira, ed., *The Seventh Day: Soldiers Talk about the Six-Day War*, Henry Near, trans. (London: Deutsch, 1970), pp. 141-142; *cf.* also pp. 116-117.

62. Yigal Lev, *Ha-Milhamah Ohevet Gevirim Tzeirim* (*War Likes Young Men*) (Tel Aviv: Bitan, 1972), trans. by Meir Pa'il in *Modern Jewish Ethics*, ed. Marvin Fox (Columbus, OH: Ohio State University Press, 1975), pp. 205-206.

63. Meir Pa'il, "The Dynamics of Power: Morality in Armed Conflict after the Six Day War," in *Modern Jewish Ethics*, pp. 193-195. *Cf.* note 2 for the original lecture in which he developed these points.

64. *Ibid.*, p. 227.

65. Maurice Lamm, "Red or Dead," *Tradition* 4:2 (Spring 1962), pp. 165-197; reprinted in David Saperstein, ed., *Preventing the Nuclear Holocaust: A Jewish Response* (New York: Union of American Hebrew Congregations, 1983), pp. 15-18, 21-23.

66. Immanuel Jakobovits, "Rejoinders," *ibid.*, p. 204; in Saperstein, *Preventing*, p. 19.

67. *Cf.* Reuven Kimelman, "Non-Violence in the Talmud," *Judaism* 17:3 (Summer 1968), pp. 316-334.

68. Arthur Waskow, "Transarmament: A Jewish Nuclear Strategy," *Sh'ma* 15/297 (September 20, 1985), pp. 134-135. *Cf.* Maurice Lamm, "As Our Community Confronts Nuclear War," *ibid.*, pp. 129-132.

69. Remember that the context here is *communal* responses to aggression. An individual *is* bound by considerations of proportionality; cf. *Sanhedrin* 72b and note 31 above.

70. *Challenge*, pp. iii–iv, 30–34.

71. *Ibid.*

72. *Ibid.*, pp. 57–58.

73. *Ibid.*, p. iv.

74. *Ibid.*, p. 59.

75. *Ibid.*, p. 83.

76. *Ibid.*, p. 80.

77. President Dwight D. Eisenhower, from a speech before the American Society of Newspaper Editors, April 16, 1953.

78. *Challenge*, p. vii; *cf.* pp. vi–viii and 63–103.

79. Michael Novak, p. 385.

80. *Ibid.*, pp. 381, 366–368.

81. *Ibid.*, pp. 388, 390, 370.

82. Saperstein, Schindler, Jacobs, Kovak, Jakobovits, Wurzburger, and the organizations' resolutions are all quoted in David Saperstein, ed., *Preventing the Nuclear Holocaust* (New York: Union of American Hebrew Congregations, 1983), pp. 13–47; Waskow, "Transarmament," pp. 132–135; Dresner, *God, Man and Atomic War* with a preface by Lewis L. Strauss (New York: Living Books, 1966).

83. Cf. David Novak, *Halakhah in a Theological Dimension* (Chico, CA: Scholars Press, 1985) (Brown Judaic Studies 68), pp. 111–112; Walter Wurzburger and resolution of Rabbinical Council of America in Saperstein, *ibid.*, pp. 43, 59.

84. For more on this, *cf.* my "The Interaction of Jewish Law with Morality," *Judaism* 26:4 (Fall 1977), pp. 455–466. There are also disadvantages; *cf.*, for example, Morris Cohen, "The Dark Side of Religion," *The Faith of Liberal* (New York: Henry Holt & Company, 1944), pp. 337–361.

85. *Challenge*, pp. i, 4, etc.

86. *Ibid.*, pp. 97*ff.*; 102.

87. *Ibid.*, pp. ii, 97*ff.*

88. Numbers *Rabbah, Seder Hukkat*, Part 19, Section 27.

JEWISH LAW

10

Confronting Omnicide

Lord Immanuel Jakobovits

WAR AND THE MORAL ORDER

While peace is Judaism's greatest blessing (*Mishnah Uk-tzin*, end), and in its absence nothing else is worthwhile (Rashi, Leviticus 26:6), Jews have by no means embraced pacifism as a teaching of their faith. Only a cursory look at the Bible and biblical history is needed to be convinced that from time to time, and only too frequently, ancient Israel engaged in warfare. The very entry into the Promised Land under Joshua called for major and continuous battles, enjoined as a religious precept.

The regulations on warfare in the Halakhah (Jewish Law) likewise oscillate between encouraging and restraining the pursuit of battle against enemies. On the one hand, there are obligatory wars—those fought against the original inhabitants of Israel's land or in self-defense. Calling the people to arms were "Priests anointed for war," and the fighting units were to be aroused to show valor and blessed with *Shema Yisrael* as they entered into battle (Deuteronomy 20:2 ff.). Even optional wars for the greater glory of Israel's kings and country were sanctioned, provided the justice of the cause was approved by the supreme court (Sanhedrin).

On the other hand, whatever their justification, the prosecution of all wars was severely restricted by numerous regulations to ensure that peace was always the first option and that, if the offer of an accommodation was rejected, the enemy would be treated humanely. For instance, the law required that one side of a city be left open during a siege to allow the inhabitants to escape, and any wanton destruction of property or plants was altogether prohibited (Maimonides, *Hilkhot Melakhim*, 5 and 6).

Moreover, there was always a distinctly moral dimension to the pursuit of any war in compliance with Jewish directives. Thus, any peace agreement with the enemy had to include their submission to the basic moral order as defined in the Seven Noachide Laws (that is, against idolatry, murder, adultery, and incest, etc.). At another level, the supremacy of the moral aspect found expression (Deuteronomy 20:7; 24:5), as if to show that the consolidation of a Jewish home was regarded as contributing more to national security than military service. Conversely, the association in the Torah of going out to war with marriages to non-Jewish women captives, leading to broken homes, juvenile delinquency, and the most heinous crimes generally, was taken to warn against the danger of war undermining the values sustaining the moral fabric of society (Deuteronomy 21:10–23 and Rashi).

Altogether, the prosecution of even the most righteous wars was incompatible with the noblest ideals of holiness. David, King of Israel and conqueror of Jerusalem, yearning to consummate his establishment of Israel's capital and the unification of the Jewish people by building the First Temple there was told, "You shall not build a house for My Name, for you are a man of war and have shed blood" (1 Chronicles 22:8; 28:3). In the building of the Temple and the altar, metal implements were not to be used, since objects from which swords are made profane the sanctuary (Exodus 20:22). The ultimate striving for messianic fulfillment lies in universal peace, when "They shall beat their swords into ploughshares, and their spears into pruning hooks; nation shall not lift up sword against nation, neither shall they learn war any more" (Isaiah 2:4). In the Jewish view, the whole vision of the eventual moral order presupposes as a prime condition the elimination of war. There can be no perfect world, no redemption of man, without the destruction of war itself as the first and ultimate prerequisite.

NUCLEAR PARADOXES

Alas, the time-honored reflections and regulations on war and peace are of little relevance to considerations which far transcend victory or defeat, the horror of bloodshed or the triumph of human harmony. With human existence itself now at stake, the atomic age has posed altogether new challenges for which it is hard to find precedents in the Jewish or any other tradition. The dilemma is rendered even more intractable by the unrealism, if not irrelevance, of the arguments that have swept many millions into fierce agitation against the policies of their governments, whether democratic or totalitarian.

The complexities and perplexities of the nuclear debate can be illustrated by just a few propositions, each of them consisting of two parts which appear mutually contradictory and yet are equally true:

1. Nuclear weapons pose the greatest menace to human survival in history; yet they have ensured the longest spell of peace between the great powers in modern times.
2. Enough nuclear arms exist to kill every human being twenty times over; yet not a single life has been lost through them since the Second World War, while over 10 million have died in some 150 conventional wars in these forty-five years.
3. The agitation for nuclear disarmament is the most universally supported campaign in history; yet even if it were to succeed, the world would hardly be safer, since enough weapons would still be left to wipe out all human life many times over.
4. Nuclear arms are the largest nonproductive drain on the world's economy; yet starvation faces hundreds of millions because of expenditure not on nuclear but on conventional arms, particularly in the Third World.

5. The betrayal of secrets which enabled the Soviet Union to become the second nuclear power was regarded by many as the crime of the century; yet the only occasion on which nuclear weapons were used in earnest was when they were possessed by only one power.

These apparent pradoxes are all based on facts which will hardly be disputed. They are meant to indicate how difficult it is to apply rational criteria to a debate which evidently defies reason and transcends the ordinary norms of logic. The entire argument is charged with highly emotive feelings, indeed with passions super-charged by the very enormity of the issues and consequences at stake.

Difficult as it is, therefore, to subject these momentous arguments to the dispassionate scrutiny of purely rational thought, it is even harder to inject into such a discussion the absolutes of ethical or halakhic imperatives, even if the requisite precedents and principles could be established with a reasonable degree of certainty. A debate founded on such unreasoned conflicts of factual data—depending on the perspective from which they are viewed—does not easily lend itself to resolution by philosophical or religious *obiter dicta*.

PRECEDENTS FOR DIFFICULT CHOICES

The debate itself, though greatly intensified in recent years, is of course not new. The semantics of the argument, and perhaps also its urgency, may have changed. But the essentials of the same dilemma were just as heatedly discussed in the past and especially in the early 1960s, then under the heading "Red or Dead." How identical the fundamental issues then and now are, is itself an issue of some importance, since there would be at least some comfort and reassurance in the discovery, if it can be confirmed, that exceedingly acute fears at the time have been overcome by a measure of stability. After all, we have passed since then through highly volatile decades; they witnessed several explosive flash-points, from the Cuban missile crisis to the invasion of Afghanistan, any of which in the *absence* of a nuclear threat might have led to open East-West warfare. The nuclear danger *prevented* these inflammable situations from igniting.

That the basic predicament has scarcely changed since 1962 becomes apparent in an examination of the central issues of that time. The underlying question in the "Red or Dead" issue, as it confronted us at the moment, was *not* whether we would choose the one or the other. Naturally, we preferred neither. The actual question was whether (1) the free world should continue its atomic buildup—both as a deterrent to prevent an attack and as a means to "massive retaliation" in the event of an attack—even at the risk of universal destruction ("Dead"); or (b) it should disarm unilaterally to avoid the alternative of global annihilation even at the risk of eventual enslavement ("Red").

The principal antecedents in Jewish thought and law discussed with regard to the issue were acts and wars of self-defense, martyrdom in the cause of ideals worth more than life itself, and the distinctions, if any, between Jewish national and human universal considerations which may have a bearing on the moral concerns involved. These three categories continue to provide a structure for our examination of the nuclear debate.

In the face of atomic annihilation, even the self-defense argument, however firmly upheld in Jewish law, may not be very conclusive: In moral terms the problem is reduced primarily, I believe, to the question of whether the unquestioned right of self-defense (surely the only justification for war or its preparation) includes the threat (deterrent) or act (retaliation) of destroying one's own life together with that of the aggressor. So long as wars were limited, and it was likely that the belligerents would survive, and one would emerge victorious, the basic right to arm and to wage war was clearly asserted by the law of self-defense, whether what was to be defended were lives or moral values. But if both the lives and the values to be defended may, as now appears possible, themselves be destroyed together with the aggressor in the exercise of self-defense, the right to resort to it is questionable.

Halakhically this question may be defined in relatively simple terms. A major source in the Torah for the law of self-defense is the provision exonerating from guilt a potential victim of robbery, with possible violence, if in self-defense he struck down and, if necessary, even killed the attacker before he committed the crime (Exodus 22:1). Hence, in the words of the rabbis, "If a man comes to slay you, forestall by slaying him!" Now this law confers the right of self-defense only if the victim will thereby *forestall* the anticipated attack and save his own life at the expense of the aggressor's. But the defender would certainly not be entitled to frustrate the attack if this could be done only at the cost of both lives; for instance, by blowing up the house in which he and the robber encounter each other. Presumably, the victim would then have to submit to the robbery and even to death by violence at the hands of the attacker rather than take "preventive" action, which would be sure to cause two deaths.

In view of this vital limitation of the law of self-defense, it would appear that a defensive war likely to endanger the survival of the attacking and defending nations alike, if not indeed of the entire human race, can never be justified. On the assumption, then, that the choice posed by a threatened nuclear attack would be either complete mutual destruction or surrender, only the second alternative may be morally vindicated.

Next to be considered was the martyrdom theme: whether for example, the moral values to be preserved transcend the worth of life itself, so that we are required to defend them to the death. The laws of martyrdom have, of course, a specifically Jewish dimension. They are postulated within the rubric of "the Sanctification of the Divine Name," and as such mandated in the words, "And I shall be sanctified in the midst of the Children of Israel" (Leviticus 22:32). This very context evidently negates the relevance of the martyrdom theme to the issue at hand, for the verse implies that the martyrs will be survived by other Jews who will be inspired to similar heroism by such a test of faith, or who will at least continue to uphold the sanctity of the Name. But if the alternative to surrender is the destruction of the whole Jewish people, the sacrifice lacks all meaning, since God can no longer "be sanctified in the midst of the Children of Israel."

This explains, no doubt, why—the regulations on obligatory wars notwithstanding—Rabbi Johanan ben Zakkai and his party opposed the Zealots' plan to fight the Roman aggressors to the finish, choosing instead to surrender to their godless conquerors rather than to risk the extinction of the Jewish people. And the Romans after all were at least as "Red"—in terms of the enslavement and moral degradation inflicted by their conquest—as the Communists at the height of their former power ever were. Yet rabbinic Judaism never censured Rabbi Johanan ben Zakkai for his fateful decision against "Dead." It is absurd to defend Judaism by risking the liquidation of the last Jew to uphold it. History has triumphantly vindicated the profound wisdom and justice of this historic decision. It would likewise be utter folly to fight for the preservation of our Western ideals at the expense of the human element able to transmit them to future generations.

The attempt to resolve our problem by direct reference to whatever Jewish sources could be found thus proved inconclusive, if not altogether questionable.

Over the ensuing years, the sources have remained the same and the reasoning based on them has not changed. Even the facts have not been substantially altered. The pile-up and the ever-increasing sophistication of nuclear weapons have changed the situation only in degree, not in kind. What has radically changed in the intervening period is the lesson we have learned from living with such awesome power of destruction.

The options to be weighed today are no longer "Red or Dead." The balance of terror and its proven deterrent effect are now such that, short of a catastrophic miscalculation or some mechanical fault, recourse to nuclear aggression is simply no longer a feasible factor in modern statecraft on the part of any superpower. Each side knows there can be no survival for either side. Hence, nuclear blackmail, too, must now be ruled out as a practical instrument of politics, among the superpowers.

To return to the above analogy with the potential victim of a robbery: True, even the right of self-defense does not entitle him to blow up the house at the cost of the robber's as well as his own life, and he would have to surrender. But the past decades have shown that, still using the analogy, robberies do not take place if the criminal knows that the house is boobytrapped against any intruder, liable to kill him together with the owner on any forced entry. The owner would then be quite in order to protect his life in this manner, deterring the aggressor by the certain knowledge that both lives would be lost if a robbery were attempted.

If nuclear war has ceased to be an option, so has total nuclear disarmament. In realistic terms, that choice, too, is no longer open to us. With nuclear warheads by the tens of thousands now existing, no disarmament program can be expected to lead to their complete elimination on either side. Atomic weaponry simply cannot be uninvented, and once it exists neither side will or can dispose of it completely without leaving a minimal margin of national defense. And each side knows that even following a preemptive strike the other will have enough weapons left to ensure that there can be no victors in an atomic conflict.

The only circumstances in which atomic blackmail would become feasible would be if the potential victim were left without the power of retaliation. For that reason alone, complete unilateral disarmament, far from reducing the risk of an atomic strike would only increase it.

This argument applies with equal force to minor nuclear powers, such as Britain and France in Europe. Their unilateral renunciation of nuclear defense could only envisage one of two alternatives: either a readiness to capitulate to nuclear blackmail should it ever be threatened, or else a reliance on America's nuclear umbrella without contributing anything towards it. Either choice would be immoral. To contemplate surrender without even being forced to consider the possibility of a nuclear conflagration is just as unjustified as to purchase one's freedom and survival at the sole cost of others'. This comment is clearly only a marginal footnote to the central issue facing the superpowers.

This leaves only one valid conclusion on the nuclear arms race forty-five years after the first and only atom bombs were used. Having reached and passed the saturation point of mutual annihilation long ago, the more the knowledge that there can be no survival sinks in, the less useful can these weapons be for either threatening or waging war. Their sole value thus lies in serving as an effective deterrence against military encounters of any kind, as proved by the absence of any hot war between East and West over the past decades.

CONVENTIONAL PERILS AND NUCLEAR COSTS

Two new factors have emerged to provide moral challenges and to call for intense public attention so far almost completely denied to them. The more important of these two factors is that the nuclear debate has totally obscured the immorality of the trade in conventional arms. Since the Second World War, different parts of our planet have been ravaged by some 150 wars with well over 10 million casualties. All these wars were fought with conventional arms, virtually all of them supplied by one or another industrial power for commercial or political gain. Added to this huge toll of death and suffering are the thousands of victims of terrorist outrages, again all perpetrated with conventional weapons peddled by arms manufacturers and dealers for financial gain or political intrigue.

For the victim, there is little difference between being killed by a bullet or hand-grenade and being incinerated twenty times over in a series of atomic explosions. The only actual difference is that the former is real and happening every day, while the latter is hypothetical; it neither has occurred nor is likely to occur since atomic retaliation became a certainty. Yet, there is no public outcry, no sense of outrage, not even any agitation for international negotiations on this evil trade in the export of death for profit on a massive scale. If such exports were banned by international agreement, there would be no wars anywhere in the world. Aggressors or terrorists would be starved of weapons instead of millions dying by violence and starvation because scores of nations divert their limited resources to giving their people little but bullets to bite.

Greed for making a lucrative living out of Esau's assignment "By your sword shall you live" is so blind and irrational that, for instance, Israel became an arms-supplier to oppressive dictatorships, avowed enemies included, and that British servicemen were killed by weapons the British themselves had sold to the Argentines—only to be used in the Falklands War. The rationalization that such exports are required to sustain the supply-nations' own arms industry for self-defense lacks every moral basis, at least in Jewish teaching. You can never save your own life at the cost of threatening or taking another.

Next to the nuclear debate completely overshadowing the real danger to peace through the trade in conventional arms is the crippling economic cost of the nuclear arms race. Now that the overkill capacity has long been exceeded, whether for offensive or defensive purposes, the continued investment of huge financial resources into an utterly futile competition is as unconscionable as it would be to invest billions into the manufacture of bullets or bombs made out of gold or other precious metals. Superpowers would be neither more safe nor less safe if a complete moratorium were called on any new nuclear arms production or research.

Never in history has the prohibition of *bal tash'hit* (Deuteronomy 20:19)—rabbinically interpreted to include any wasting of resources—been transgressed on such a gigantic scale. The United States alone, it is estimated, provides the Third World with 10 billion dollars worth of arms—to give only one example of the huge number of lives that could be saved if, literally, swords were turned into ploughshares by the industrial nations. The diversion of these astronomical sums to constructive ends would be sufficient to provide every human being on earth with all the food, education, and health services they require to overcome the scourge of starvation, ignorance, and widespread disease, not to mention the threat of war and terrorism.

11

Nuclear War through the Prism of Jewish Law: The Nature of Man and War

J. David Bleich

The prophet Habakkuk asks plaintively, "Why . . . art Thou silent when the wicked swallows up the man more righteous than he? for Thou makest men as the fish of the sea" (Habakkuk 1:13–14). Among the myriad species of the animal kingdom there is virtually none which preys upon its own kind. Carnivorous animals will devour other animals but not members of the same species. Preying upon one's own species is a phenomenon found only among the fish of the sea. Even a fish will swallow only a fellow creature smaller than itself. Man is unique among land animals in his propensity for attacking and destroying not only others smaller and weaker than himself, but also in attempting to swallow up others equal to and better than himself.

"Pray for the welfare of the government, for without fear of (the government) men would swallow one another alive," advises the Mishnah.[1] The base instincts of man are curbed only by fear.

Individuals have reason to fear the power of the state. States, however, are subject to no higher temporal authority and hence have no reason for fear. Nations, as human institutions, give collective expression to the selfsame base instincts which are inherent in the individuals of whom they are comprised. As a result, nations, in their relationships with one another, behave precisely in the manner which the Mishnah putatively ascribes to individuals: they "swallow one another alive."

The nations of the world have indeed attempted to regulate warfare, but its elimination remains a utopian ideal which eludes mankind. The Geneva Convention, the United Nations Charter, and international treaties of friendship have certainly not effected a metamorphosis in the basic nature of man. There is a well-known anecdote concerning a missionary who was sent to the wilds of Africa. When asked by his superiors to submit a report there was little of a positive nature for which he could claim credit. "Well," he was asked, "did you at least succeed in eradicating cannibalism in your area? "No," he replied, "the natives are still cannibals, but at least they now eat with knives and forks." Renunciation of chemical and biological warfare, humane treatment for prisoners of war, and so on, are certainly marks of "civilized" peoples. But on a more fundamental level such matters are little different from a convention requiring cannibals to eat with knives and forks. "Civilized warfare" is inherently a self-contradiction.

It is entirely understandable that Jewish teaching with regard to nuclear warfare cannot be examined other than in the context of its attitude toward war in general. To be sure, nuclear war poses a threat to the very survival of the human race. But Judaism has long recognized that "he who destroys a single life is accounted as if he has destroyed the entire world; and one who preserves a single life is accounted as if he has preserved the entire world."[2] Every person is a small world, a microcosm in himself, and of infinite value in the eyes of the Creator. Thus, the moral problems posed both by conventional and nuclear warfare are essentially alike; in nuclear warfare the problem becomes magnified simply because of the sheer magnitude of the number of potential victims.

THE SANCTIONING OF WAR

Halakhah, as it applies to Jews, recognizes that man has no right to make war against his fellow. Standard translations of the Bible render Exodus 15:3 as "The Lord is a man [Ish] of war; the Lord is His name." Rashi, citing similar usages having the same connotation, renders the Hebrew Ish as "master." Thus the translation should read, "The Lord is the master of war; the Lord His name." God is described as the master of war because only He may grant dispensation to engage in warfare. The very name of the Lord signifies that He alone exercises dominion over the universe. Only God, as the Creator of mankind and proprietor of all life, may grant permission for the taking of the lives of His creatures.

War is sanctioned only when commanded by God, for example, when divine wisdom dictates that such a course of action is necessary to the fulfillment of human destiny. Even a *milhemet reshut*, a permitted or "discretionary war" is discretionary only in the sense that it is initiated by man and does not serve to fulfill a divine commandment. But even a *milhemet reshut* requires the acquiescence of the *urim ve-tumin*. The message transmitted via the breastplate of the High Priest is a form of revelation granting divine authority for an act of aggression. Judaism sanctions violence only at the specific behest of the Deity. Human reason is far too prone to error to be entrusted with a determination that war is justified in the service of a higher cause. Such a determination can be made solely by God.

SELF-DEFENSE

The teachings of Judaism with regard to non-Jews are somewhat more complex. Non-Jews are not held to the same standards of behavior as Jews. Although the Noachide Code, which embodies divine law as it is binding upon non-Jews, prohibits murder, it does not necessarily describe as murder the taking of human life under any and all circumstances. It is quite clear that when confronted by a situation in which an individual's life is threatened, all persons, non-Jews as well as Jews, have an absolute right to eliminate the aggressor in self-defense.[3] "*Ha-ba le-hargekha hashkem le-hargo*—If [a person] comes to slay you, arise and slay him first"[4] is a principle which applies to Noachides (that is, Gentiles who are bound by the basic laws of morality), as well as to Jews. Accordingly, a defensive war would appear to require no further justification. Such action could be justified as simple self-defense.

However, war quite frequently results in situations in which a person is called upon to take the life of an enemy, not to save his own life, but in order to preserve the lives of fellow countrymen. In situations in which an individual's own life is not directly threatened, but a threat exists with regard to the life of another human being, Jews are bound by the Law of the "pursuer" (*rodef*). Jewish law not only permits, but demands, that anyone finding himself in the position of being able to save the life of an intended victim must do so, even if such rescue necessitates sacrificing the life of the pursuer.

The question which requires examination is whether the law of pursuit, which mandates intervention by a third party in order to save the life of an intended victim, extends to Noachides as well. Rabbi Joseph Ben Moses Babad concludes that Noachides have discretionary authority to intervene in such situations but do not have an absolute obligation to do so.[5]

The Talmud attempts to derive the "law of the pursuer" from the commandment "You shalt not stand idly by the blood of your neighbor" (Leviticus 19:16).[6] This commandment establishes a general obligation to come to the aid of a person whose life is endangered. Ultimately, the Talmud derives an obligation to preserve the life of the victim, even if it is necessary to sacrifice the life of the pursuer in order to accomplish this end, from the verse "For . . . the betrothed damsel cried and there was none to save her" (Deuteronomy 22:27). From this statement the Talmud infers that, were a bystander to be present, he would be obligated to preserve the betrothed damsel from isolation by any means possible, including summary execution of the would-be rapist. By virtue of the juxtaposition (*hekesh*) of homicide and rape of a "betrothed damsel" in the immediately prior verse, the Talmud derives a binding obligation requiring any and all bystanders to intervene and to preserve the life of the intended homicide victim by any means possible.

Rabbi Babad cogently argues that the commandments expressed in Leviticus 19:16 and Deuteronomy 22:27 are incumbent only upon Jews and hence cannot establish obligations upon non-Jews, who are bound only by the provisions of the Noachide Code. Rabbi Babad does, however, adduce another source which serves as a basis for derivation of the "law of the pursuer" and which is applicable to Noachides as well.

The Talmud[7] cites the verse "Whosoever sheddeth the blood of man, by man shall his blood be shed" (Genesis 9:6) as granting dispensation to preserve the intended victim by eliminating the pursuer. The phrase "by man" is understood as calling for the shedding of blood "by any man," that is, by persons witnessing the act, rather than as a reference to punitive measures to be undertaken subsequent to the act. Thus the Talmud understands the verse as referring not to an act of homicide that has already been committed, but to the prevention of a would-be homicide. The verse, which was addressed to Noah, establishes a law not only for Jews but for Noachides as well. The general principle is that any commandment given prior to Sinai is binding upon Noachides even subsequent to the Sinaitic revelation, provided it has been reiterated at Sinai. The law of the pursuer is indeed repeated in Exodus 22:1. In the course of the same discussion, the Talmud[8] states that the statute formulated in this passage, which provides that a thief who breaks into a dwelling during the night may be smitten without penalty, is based upon the assumption that the thief is intent not only upon larceny but will commit homicide as well if he meets resistance. Hence the thief is, in effect, a pursuer and may be put to death if necessary by virtue of the "law of pursuit." Tosafot,[9] commenting on the redundancy of the multiple scriptural sources for the "law of pursuit," states that Exodus 22:1 serves only to establish license for execution of the pursuer but does not make such a course of action obligatory. The obligation, according to Tosafot, is expressed solely in Deuteronomy 22:27. Rabbi Babad assumes that Tosafot intends this comment to apply as well to the interpretation of Genesis 9:6, which presents the same difficulty. The phrase "ba-adam damo yishafekh," according to this understanding, should thus be translated "by man *may* his blood be shed," and serves to grant permission to put the aggressor to death when necessary to preserve the life of the victim, but does not mandate such action.[10] Accordingly, concludes Rabbi Babad, Noachides are justified not only in acting in self-defense but may eliminate a threat to the lives of others as well, even though, in contradistinction to Jews who are bound by Sinaitic revelation, they are under no obligation to do so.

Rabbi Meir Dan Plocki[11] argues that a non-Jew is not only permitted but, according to Maimonides, is obligated to kill an aggressor in order to preserve the life of the intended victim. Rabbi Plocki bases his argument upon Maimonides' understanding of the *mitzvah* of *dinin*, the last of the seven commandments which constitute the Noachide Code. According to Maimonides, the commandment of *dinin* establishes an obligation binding upon non-Jews to enforce the provisions of the Noachide Code and to punish Noachide transgressors. Accordingly, argues Rabbi Plocki, a non-Jew must kill the aggressor, not by virtue of the "law of the pursuer," but because of the *mitzvah* of *dinin* which obliges every Noachide to enforce the provisions of the Noachide Code. That code provides, *inter alia*, for the execution of murderers. Rabbi Plocki expresses some reservation with regard to this argument. He expresses uncertainty with regard to whether the commandment of *dinin* mandates only execution of transgressors after the fact, or whether it requires intervention in the sense of "prior restraint" as well, in order to prevent an infraction of the Noachide Code. However, examination of a ruling by Maimonides[12] should dispel any doubt with regard to this point. Maimonides rules that Noachides are required, by virtue of the *mitzvah* of *dinin*, to establish a judiciary system. The courts are required both to execute judgment and "to admonish the populace." The obligation "to admonish the populace" certainly establishes an obligation with regard to prior restraint in enforcing the Noachide Code. Although Maimonides does not explicitly state that Noachides are empowered to use lethal force in preventing such infractions, it may well be argued that the Noachide court may use whatever coercive measures the situation may require in order to accomplish this end. Since the *mitzvah* of *dinin* is incumbent not only upon an established judiciary but also upon every individual Noachide, it then follows that any Noachide may use lethal force, if necessary, in order to prevent commission of a capital transgression by another Noachide.

Three other authorities, Rabbi Isaac Schorr,[13] Rabbi Isaac Schmelkes,[14] and Rabbi Chaim Soloveitchik,[15] clearly state that Noachides no less than Jews are obligated to eliminate an aggressor in order to preserve the life of an intended victim. These authorities maintain that the law of pursuit constitutes an obligation binding upon Jew and Gentile alike.

It may be inferred from Maimonides' ruling[16] that a Noachide may execute a pursuer in order to preserve the victim. Jewish law specifies that if it is possible to preserve the life of the intended victim by merely maiming the pursuer, it is forbidden to take the life of the latter. However, should a Jew take the life of the pursuer when, in fact, it is not absolutely necessary to do so, Maimonides elsewhere rules[17] that he is culpable only at the hands of Heaven but is not to be executed by a human court. Maimonides[18] draws a distinction between a Jew and a Noachide with regard to this provision and rules that a Noachide who might have preserved the life of the intended victim by merely maiming the aggressor is to be put to death for having taken a human life. The clear inference of this statement is that when it is necessary to take the life of the pursuer in order to preserve the victim, it is permissible, and perhaps even obligatory, for a Noachide to do so.[19]

The "law of pursuit" is certainly no less applicable when it is an entire community or nation, rather than an individual, which is pursued. Thus, military action is certainly justifiable when undertaken either in self-defense or on behalf of a victim of aggression.

CIVILIAN CASUALTIES

Acceptance of the premise that the principle of self-defense applies to Noachides as well as to Jews does not serve to justify any and all military action even if limited to wars of defense. War almost inevitably results in civilian casualties as well as the loss of combatants. Yet, the taking of innocent lives certainly cannot be justified on the basis of the law of pursuit. The life of the pursuer is forfeit in order that the life of the intended victim be preserved. However, should it be impossible to eliminate the pursuer other than by also causing the death of an innocent bystander, the law of pursuit could not be invoked even by the intended victim, much less so by a third party who is himself not personally endangered. Since the law of pursuit is designed to preserve the life of the innocent victim, it is only logical that it is forbidden to cause the death of a bystander in the process, since to do so would only entail the loss of another innocent life. In such situations the talmudic principle "How do you know that your blood is sweeter than the blood of your fellow?"[20] is fully applicable.

If war on the part of non-Jews is sanctioned solely on the basis of the law of pursuit, military action must perforce be restricted to situations in which the loss of life is inflicted only upon armed aggressors or upon active participants in the war effort; military action resulting in casualties among the civilian populace would constitute homicide, pure and simple. Following this line of reasoning there could certainly be no justification for military action intentionally designed to claim civilian lives. Thus, despite the resultant diminution of casualties among the armed forces, the nuclear bombing of Hiroshima and Nagasaki—or saturation bombing using conventional munitions—could not be justified on the basis of the law of pursuit. Justification of the use of atomic weapons simply as an act of war is contingent upon resolution of the question of whether or not non-Jews have been granted the right to engage in war.

There is one other avenue which should be explored as possible justification of military action which results in casualties among noncombatants. Jewish law, to be sure, recognizes a distinction between willful transgression (*mazid*) and inadvertent transgression (*shogeg*). The latter occasions no punishment at the hands of a human court but, in terms of heavenly law, requires penance and expiation. In the case of certain serious infractions, a sacrifice is required as atonement. Inadvertent transgression, or *shogeg*, is defined as ignorance of the prohibition itself or ignorance that the act performed is proscribed because of confusion with regard to a factual detail (for example, knowledge that a certain act is forbidden on the Sabbath but ignorance of the fact that it is the Sabbath day). Even minimal culpability as a *shogeg* requires that the act itself and its consequences be fully intended. Performance of an act with intention to achieve an innocuous result, even when that act is performed in a manner which may well result in an unintended infraction, engenders no culpability even if the actual result is one which, were it intended, would be a forbidden act. Since the resultant act is unintended (*davar she-eino mitkhaven*), no expiation is required. The source for this provision of halakhah is the Mishnah,[21] which records a dispute between Rabbi Judah and Rabbi Simon with regard to culpability for such acts. The halakhah is in accordance with the permissive opinion of Rabbi Simon. Thus, for example, a bed, chair, or couch may be dragged along a dirt floor, provided that there is no intention to gouge a hole in the floor. The act is entirely permissible and the person acting in such manner incurs no liability even if a hole is dug inadvertently. Accordingly, it might perhaps be argued that a person intent upon killing a pursuer need not be constrained by the concern that his act may possibly cause the death of an innocent bystander, since the result is unintended. A similar concept appears in other theological systems, perhaps as a result of the influence of Jewish law, and is known as the "double effect" theory.

This argument may be rebutted on a number of grounds. Although most authorities make no such distinction, Rabbi Aha'i Ga'on[22] maintains that the concept of a *davar she-eino mitkhaven* is applicable only with regard to possible violation of Sabbath restrictions, but the acts which might result in transgression of other prohibitions are forbidden even if the proscribed effect is unintended. *Tosafot*[23] asserts that acts of such nature are forbidden whenever the possible result is a capital transgression.

Furthermore, an act is permitted even though the unintended effect is forbidden only when it is not a certainty that the proscribed effect will occur. When the forbidden effect will of necessity take place, the act is forbidden even though it is intended solely in order to effect an innocuous result. Thus, for example, a person may not sever the head of an animal on the Sabbath on the plea that he intends only to remove the head in order to feed it to a dog, but not to kill the animal. Such an act is known as a *pesik reisheih*.

The rationale underlying this provision is that a necessary effect cannot be regarded as unintended. Accordingly, military action which of necessity will result in civilian casualties cannot be justified on the contention that the killing of innocent victims is unintended, since the loss of those lives is the inescapable result of such action. According to most authorities, such acts are forbidden even if no benefit is derived from the proscribed effect.

One point requires further clarification. There may be some question with regard to whether circumstances involving a *pesik reisheih* defeat the plea of *davar she-eino mitkhaven* insofar as violation of the provisions of the Noachide Code by non-Jews is concerned. Such a distinction is found with regard to a somewhat related matter. In most circumstances, a Jew may not direct a non-Jew to perform an act which the Jew himself is forbidden to perform. Some authorities, however, permit a Jew to ask a non-Jew to perform an act which entails a *pesik reisheih* that is, the desired result for which the particular act is intended is entirely permissible, but would be forbidden to the Jew only because it necessarily entails a concomitant result which is proscribed.[24] Thus, for example, these authorities permit a Jew, on the Sabbath, to direct a non-Jew to remove a pot from among the burning coals in which it is embedded even though some coals are necessarily extinguished in the process. The rationale underlying this ruling is not entirely clear. If it is understood that this ruling is based on the principle that, for non-Jews, even a *pesik reisheih* is encompassed in the category for an unintended effect (*davar she-eino mitkhaven*), the selfsame provisions would apply to the culpability of non-Jews with regard to the provisions of the Noachide Code. If so, insofar as non-Jews are concerned, any *davar she-eino mitkhaven* would be permissible, including acts which constitute a *pesik reisheih*. It should be noted, however, that many authorities forbid allowing a non-Jew to perform an act on the Sabbath on behalf of a Jew which involves a *pesik reisheih*.[25] Moreover, the permissive ruling formulated by some authorities with regard to performance of an act involving a *pesik reisheih* by a non-Jew may only reflect the view that the rabbinic prohibition against permitting a non-Jew to perform forbidden acts on behalf of a Jew is circumscibed in nature, and is limited only to situations in which the Jew desires the forbidden effect which is accomplished on his behalf by the non-Jew. If so, there is no evidence that non-Jews are relieved of culpability with regard to unintended violations of the Noachide Code when such acts are committed in the form of a *pesik rei-sheih.*

PARTICIPATION IN WAR

More fundamental is the question of whether or not there exists a general exclusion to the prohibition against homicide which justifies the taking of human life under conditions of war. Insofar as the halakhah applicable to Jews is concerned, there are obviously conditions, limited though they may be, under which this is the case. The various categories of obligatory war (*milhemet mitzvah*) and discretionary war (*milhemet reshut*) encompass situations in which there exists no immediate danger to the warring party. War is nevertheless permissible under at least certain restricted conditions even though the taking of human life is inevitable. These categories are, however, limited to Jews. The war against Amalek and war for the conquest of Land of Israel are wars which only Jews may undertake. A discretionary war may be undertaken only upon the initiative of the monarch of the Jewish commonwealth with the approval of the Sanhedrin and the *urim ve-tumim.* No analogous provision is found in Noachide law. It is therefore not surprising that virtually no discussion of whether or not a Noachide may legitimately engage in warfare is to be found in the writings of early authorities.

One latter-day authority does find grounds upon which to rule that non-Jews who engage in war are not guilty of murder. Rabbi Naphtali Zevi Yehudah Berlin finds dispensation for warfare in the very verse which prohibits homicide to the Sons of Noah: "And surely your blood of your lives will I require . . . and at the hand of man, at the hand of every man's brother will I require the life of man" (Genesis 9:5).[26] The phrase "at the hand of every man's brother" appears to be entirely redundant since it adds nothing to the preceding phrase "at the hand of man." Rabbi Berlin understands this phrase as a limiting clause: "When is man punished? [If he commits homicide] when it is proper to behave in a brotherly manner." However, in time of war when animosity reigns among nations, the taking of life in the course of military activity is not punishable. Elsewhere,[27] this authority states that "even" a Jewish monarch may engage in battle, thereby implying that Gentiles are certainly not prohibited from doing so. Earlier, Rabbi Judah Loew Ben Bezalel,[28] commenting upon the action taken by the sons of Jacob against the inhabitants of Schechem, states that the family of Jacob constituted, in effect, a sovereign people and were permitted to do battle against another since war is not forbidden under the Noachide Code. This position is, however, contradicted by a number of other authorities. Rabbi Moses Sofer,[29] cites the talmudic declaration that non-Jews do not enjoy legal prerogatives of conquest (*lav benei kibush ninahu*). Rabbi Sofer demonstrates that the Talmud elsewhere[30] does indeed affirm that non-Jews may acquire title to lands captured in wars by virtue of conquest. The phrase *"lav benei kibush"* must then be understood, argues Rabbi Sofer, as meaning that non-Jews have no right to engage in war for purposes of conquest even though *post factum* they may acquire title in this manner. The identical argument is advanced by Rabbi Abraham Dov Ber Kahane-Shapiro[31] and by Rabbi Menachem Ziemba.[32] These authorities are in agreement with Rabbi Sofer's view that non-Jews may not engage in a war of aggression under any circumstances.

NUCLEAR WARFARE

It must be noted that, even according to the authorities who maintain that non-Jews may engage in wars of aggression, there are strong grounds for arguing that the devastation associated with nuclear warfare renders such warfare illicit. The Talmud[33] declares, "A sovereign power which slays one-sixth [of the populace] of the universe is not culpable." It is to be inferred that the death of one sixth of the inhabitants of the universe entails no culpability, but that slaying more than one sixth of the population of the universe does engender culpability. *Tosafot*, understanding the dictum as referring to the monarch of a Jewish state, indicates that the Talmud here imposes a constraint upon a discretionary war in circumstances such that it may be anticipated that an inordinate number of people will perish as a result of hostilities. According to this analysis, a similar restriction does not apply to wars that are mandated by Scripture.

The various categories of obligatory war certainly do not apply to non-Jews who are not the recipients of any specific scriptural commandments concerning war. According to the most permissive view, non-Jews are merely permitted to engage in military activity but, for non-Jews, warfare cannot be deemed obligatory under any circumstances. Accordingly, limitations upon warfare undertaken as a discretionary war would assuredly apply to wars undertaken by non-Jews. Hence, according to *Tosafot*, non-Jews are not entitled to engage in a war that is likely to result in the annihilation of more than on sixth of the population of the world. This restriction applies even to wars of defense in which not only the aggressors are destroyed but the lives of a large number of innocent victims are claimed as well. The nature of nuclear warfare is such that, in all likelihood, more than one sixth of the world's population would be destroyed in a nuclear holocaust.

A careful distinction must be drawn between abjuration of nuclear warfare and unilateral disarmament. Although nuclear retaliation may not be consistent with halakhic norms, the *threat* of retaliation is an entirely legitimate means of discouraging aggression. A wise man would do well not to resist a mugger and to surrender his wallet without protest. Yet only a fool would carry a placard on his shoulder proclaiming that message and announcing to all and sundry that he may be accosted with impunity. Nuclear arms prudently deployed may well serve as a deterrent even though a moral government would eschew their use.

NOTES

1. *Yerushalmi Avot* 3:2.
2. *Bavli Sanhedrin* 37a.

3. See *Bavli Sanhedrin* 57a; R. Yehudah Rosenbaum, *Teshuvot Ben Yehudah*, no. 21; and *Minhat Hinnukh*, no. 296.

4. *Bavli Sanhedrin* 72a.

5. *Minhat Hinnukh* no. 296.

6. *Bavli Sanhedrin* 73a.

7. *Bavli Sanhedrin* 72b.

8. *Ibid.*

9. *Ibid.* 72a.

10. Rabbi Shlomoh Zevin, *Le-Or ha-Halakhah*, p. 17, argues against *Minhat Hinnukh's* position and maintains that Noachides are not merely permitted but are obligated to execute the pursuer in order to preserve the pursued. He argues that this is evident from the phrase "*damo yishafekh*," which he maintains must be translated, "by man shall his blood be spilled." It would, however, appear that the question raised by *Tosafot, Bavli Sanhedrin* 73a, s.v. *af*, with regard to the earlier cited verse which speaks of the *ba ba-mahteret* applies with equal validity to this verse. It would appear that *Tosafot's* statement that the verse establishes permission rather than an obligation applies to the subsequently cited verse *ba-adam damo yishafekh* as well.

Rabbi Zevin also cites the verses in Obadiah 1:11–13 addressed to Edom:

> In the day that thou didst stand aloof,
> In the day that strangers carried away his substance,
> And foreigners entered into his gates
> And cast lots upon Jerusalem,
> Even thou wast as one of them
> But thou shouldst not have gazed on the day of thy brother,
> In the day of his disaster . . .
> Yea, thou shouldst not have gazed on their affliction
> In the day of their calamity.

The prophet chastises Edom for standing by silently while aggression is committed against Israel. The implication, argues Rabbi Zevin, is that Noachides have an obligation to do battle against an aggressor.

11. *Hemdat Yisrael* by Rabbi Meir Dan Plocki (New York: Grosman, 5725), p. 178, citing the *Zekhuta de-Avraham*.

12. *Mishneh Torah, Hilkhot Melakhim* 9:14.

13. *Teshuvot Tevu'ot Shor*, no. 20, p. 32b.

14. *Teshuvot Bet Yizhak, Yoreh De'ah*, II No. 162, Sec. 4.

15. Hiddushei Rabbenu Hayyim ha-Levi al ha Rambam, *Hilkhot Rotzeah* 1:9.

16. *Hilkhot Melakhim* 9:4.

17. *Hilkhot Rotzeah* 1:13.

18. *Hilkhot Melakhim* 9:4.

19. See, however, Teshuvot ben Yehudah, no. 21, cited by Sedei Hemed, *Klalim, ma'arekhet ha-gimel*, no. 44, who maintains that the "law of pursuit" does not apply to Noachides. Teshuvot Ben Yehudah asserts that Maimonides means to imply that only the pursued Noachide victim may kill his aggressor but that, under the Noachide Code, a third party has no right to intervene.

20. *Bavli Sanhedrin* 74a.

21. *Bavli Beitzah* 23b.

22. *Sh'iltot, She'ilta* 105.

23. Cited by Hiddushei ha-Ran, *Sanhedrin* 84b.

24. See Magen Avraham, *Orah Hayyim*, 277:7 and *Mishnah Berurah* 253:31 and 277:15.

25. See Magen Avraham, *Orah Hayyim* 253:41; *Mishnah Berurah* 253:99–100, 253:51, and 277:30. Cf., R. Benjamin Silber, *Brit Olam* 16:1 and accompanying note.

26. *Ha'amek Davar* (Commentary on the Pentateuch) on this verse.

27. *Ha'amek Davar* on Deuteronomy 20:8.

28. Gur Aryeh, *Parshat Va-Yishlah*, Commentary on the Pentateuch.

29. Teshuvot Hatam Sofer referring to *Sanhedrin* 59a.

30. *Bavli Gittin* 38a.

31. *Dvar Avraham*, I. no. 11.

32. *Zera Avraham* no. 24.

33. *Bavli Shevu'ot* 35b.

12

Nuclear Deterrence and Nuclear War

Walter S. Wurzburger

The development of nuclear weapons has placed us in an absurd position. For our "security" we rely upon the possession of nuclear weapons, which we perceive to be completely unusable because their use would precipitate unspeakable catastrophe.

Yet, these utterly "useless" weapons have been extremely useful. They have provided us with the protective shield of a precarious "balance of terror" which, in spite of a cold war and numerous provocations, have for a relatively long time prevented the outbreak of outright hostilities between the superpowers. But for all its success, deterrence is widely regarded as a highly vulnerable policy. It not only poses intolerable risks for the survival of the human species, but the very possession of nuclear weapons in itself is fraught with grave moral dilemmas to which we must address ourselves from the perspective of our religious tradition.

THE LIMITATIONS OF PRECEDENT

It must be stated at the outset that unequivocal definitive rulings concerning the possession or use of nuclear weapons can hardly be expected from our halakhic resources. For close to 2,000 years, the Jewish people lived under conditions where the agonizing moral problems associated with the exercise of power were merely of academic interest. Until the establishment of the State of Israel in 1948, there was little if any incentive to examine questions relating to the legitimacy of the use of force on the part of a sovereign state. It is therefore not surprising that, as opposed to Catholicism which during the Middle Ages developed the highly sophisticated "just-war" doctrine, Jewish political thought (with some notable exceptions such as the views of Maimonides and Abrabanel) remained in limbo during this period. Unlike Maimonides' *Mishneh Torah*, most Jewish legal codes omitted all references to those sections of talmudic law which relate to rights and duties of a sovereign Jewish political entity.

Understandably, with the return of the Jewish people into the arena of power, rabbinic authorities were once again compelled to address themselves to the legitimacy and the limits of the use of power on the part of a sovereign state. In response to newly emerging needs, a number of leading scholars plumbed the halakhic sources to extract guidelines for the operation of a Jewish state in conformity with Jewish Law. Of special interest for our purposes is the systematic treatment of questions relating to the conduct of military operations, in the writing of Rabbis Kook,[1] Goren,[2] Zevin,[3] Israeli,[4] Waldenberg,[5] and Gershuni.[6] But for all their intrinsic merit, those halakhic pronouncements hardly shed light on the unique problems posed by nuclear warfare. If, as is frequently argued, nuclear war is not merely quantitatively but qualitatively so different from previous forms of warfare as to constitute a category *sui generis*, then traditional norms governing warfare cease to be relevant. It must be borne in mind that whatever legitimacy Jewish law confers upon various types of warfare (namely, discretionary, prescribed, and obligatory wars) is contingent upon one important condition: the prospect of victory.[7] But nuclear war between the superpowers, it is widely assumed, would produce no winners—only losers. No one can benefit from a nuclear exchange; it offers only the madness of MAD (Mutually Assured Destruction) and thus for all practical purposes amounts to mutual mass suicide.

Despite our unequivocal opposition to nuclear war, unilateral nuclear pacifism is totally unacceptable. We must be wary of absolutes. Simplistic solutions simply will not do. The complexities of our situation engender moral ambiguities. We must bear in mind that, in spite of its deep-rooted abhorrence of war and love of peace,[8] Judaism enjoins resistance to evil. Failure to resist aggression, either in self-defense or for the protection of the innocent, is condemned as morally reprehensible.

CAN NUCLEAR WAR BE SANCTIONED?

It is one thing to accept as a tragic necessity the sacrifice of human lives in the effort to overcome evil, but it is another to reconcile ourselves to the kind of mass suicide that would result from nuclear warfare. While Jewish sources do not explicitly deal with the element of proportionality which plays such a dominant part in the just-war theory, Tosafot[9] stresses that discretionary wars must not be waged under conditions when they are expected to result in the loss of one sixth of either the total population or perhaps of the fighting forces. Obviously, nobody can accurately predict the unimaginable consequences of a full-scale nuclear war. But we dare not discount the fear of those scientists who warn that a nuclear winter might render the entire globe uninhabitable by human beings. Jewish religious thought stresses man's responsibility for the world. *Yishuv haolam* (concern for the settlement of the world) represents a fundamental religious axiom. Jewish Law goes so far as to disqualify a professional gambler from serving as a witness on the ground that he does not contribute to "the settlement of the world."[10] How then could we condone the waging of a nuclear war that could jeopardize the very survival of the human species?

Even if such fears were groundless, nuclear war could not be sanctioned. There are limits to the amount of destruction that may be unleashed even in pursuit of perfectly legitimate objectives. Significantly, the Torah mandates concern for the environment even in time of war. The biblical injunction against destruction of fruit trees is placed within the context of a host of other regulations governing military operations.[11] It is necessary to guard against the tendency of becoming so obsessed with winning a war as to be totally oblivious of all environmental concerns. Even amidst the exigencies of war, we are not permitted to ignore our responsibilities for the protection of the environment. Jewish Law prohibits a scorched earth policy. How then can one justify the horrendous ecological impact of atmospheric pollution, which, over and above the immediate devastation of the environment, would be the consequences of even a limited nuclear war?

These weighty factors are insignificant by comparison with the staggering cost in human lives. Even if military installations, were the only targets, large numbers of noncombatant casualties would be inevitable in the event of a nuclear attack. To be sure, commitment to the sanctity of life does not necessarily rule out all types of military operations that would involve the loss of noncombatants. In contradistinction to the Catholic Just War doctrine, Jewish religious law does not make an absolute distinction between the loss of combatants and noncombatants. It must be remembered that so-called combatants need not necessarily be actively engaged in aggressive acts. We may therefore maintain that when confronted with a choice between incurring heavy casualties among combatants and lighter casualties among non-combatants, one ought to opt for a strategy that would minimize the loss of human lives, irrespective as to whether combatants or noncombatants would be affected.[12]

The belief that in cases of military necessity the loss of some noncombatants may be morally justifiable rests upon the rather plausible assumption that the norms governing warfare need not necessarily coincide with those applicable to the conduct of individuals engaged in self-defense or in the protection of innocents. When faced with aggression, individuals are only authorized to take the lives of aggressors—but not those of innocent third parties. The Talmud asks the rhetorical question, "How do you know that your blood is sweeter than that of your fellow human being?"[13] Thus, quantitative as well as qualitative factors are dismissed as utterly irrelevant when they impinge upon the sanctity of life. Each life possesses infinite value. Hence the life of one innocent individual must not be taken even for the purpose of saving another life. When it comes to taking life, there are no priorities. Jewish Law operates by the principle "one must not displace one life for the sake of another."[14] Obviously this is a far cry from utilitarianism; in the Jewish view, even if it is deemed necessary to save the lives of large numbers of individuals, a human being never may be deprived of life unless he directly imperils the life of another.

Applying this norm to modern warfare, it would be virtually impossible to conduct military operations. For as a general rule, some loss of life on the part of noncombatants is unavoidable. Such casualties cannot possibly be legitimized on the ground of self-defense against the aggressor. Noncombatants, by definition, are not directly implicated in acts of aggression. Most Jewish authorities, however, concur that the factors which are relevant to individuals need not necessarily apply to political entities such as states. While the former may employ force only against the aggressor himself, the latter, whenever recourse to warfare is legitimate, are authorized to employ force even when noncombatant casualties can be expected.

There are serious disagreements among religious authorities whether under contemporary conditions any nation has the right to engage in warfare except for purely defensive purposes. It is generally accepted, nevertheless, that whenever warfare is regarded as legitimate, it represents a category sui generis and hence need not conform to the standards governing the conduct of individuals whose lives are threatened by aggressors.[15]

We therefore must not categorically rule out the use of nuclear weapons simply on the grounds that noncombatant casualties would be unavoidable. One might be able to adopt Paul Ramsay's[16] position and sanction counterforce nuclear weapons that are directed against military installations rather than population centers, even though the loss of substantial numbers of noncombatants would be inevitable. But the use of nuclear weapons as envisaged in MAD strategy would be an entirely different matter. Direct attack against civilian population centers could not possibly be sanctioned. By no stretch of the imagination could such an attack fall under the rubric of legitimate military operations, especially since it would violate internationally accepted conventions governing warfare. It must also be noted that even the most lenient halakhic opinion with respect to the legitimacy of warfare unequivocally condemns any type of operations that run counter to internationally accepted rules of war.[17]

There are, however, other considerations that preclude the use of nuclear weapons even when directed solely against military targets. Many military experts believe that limited nuclear war is simply not feasible. The logic of events dictates that, once unleashed, limited nuclear war escalates into the unspeakable catastrophe of an all out nuclear confrontation, which might doom all of human life. In view of this peril, one might be persuaded to insist upon a total ban on the possession of nuclear weapons, inasmuch as this would constitute the only reliable guarantee against a nuclear holocaust.

CHOOSING THE LESSER EVIL

For all its simplicity, such a "solution" creates enormous difficulties. We live in an unredeemed world. Evil must be resisted. In contrast to the Christian tradition, Judaism mandates, and not merely condones, the use of violence not only for the protection of the innocent but even for self-defense. For this reason, despite Judaism's yearning for peace and hatred of war, it never advocated pacifism. The legitimization of some wars represented not just a concession to realism but a moral imperative. It does not make moral sense to apply to an unredeemed world the standards appropriate to a world redeemed from sin and injustice.

As long as our adversaries are equipped with nuclear weapons, "nuclear pacifism" is untenable. A one-sided categorical renunciation of the use of nuclear weapons at this stage of history would leave us open to all and sundry forms of nuclear blackmail. Our nuclear arsenal can function as a deterrent against aggression only to the extent that an adversary is persuaded that we will retaliate with nuclear weapons. Were an adversary to believe that moral restraints would prevent us from actually using these dreadful weapons, our entire nuclear arsenal would be treated as a mere bluff. Without the resolve to use nuclear arms, even the most advanced technology would cease to present a credible deterrence. We are therefore caught on the horns of a dilemma. On one hand, the actual use of nuclear weapons must be ruled out, for it is inconceivable to sanction the very extinction of the human species. On the other hand, a total ban on the use of nuclear weapons would be tantamount to unconditional surrender not only of a national self-interest but of our entire value system which gives meaning to our existence. Obviously one-sided renunciation of the use of nuclear weapons would rule out any possibility of defense or deterrence against adversaries who threaten nuclear aggression. Since both alternatives are totally unacceptable, we have no choice but to continue to rely on the threat of nuclear retaliation to deter nuclear aggression. To be sure, such a policy is fraught with enormous moral problems. The mere intent to resort to indiscriminate killing of noncombatants, even in retaliation, strikes us as completely immoral. Can we justify deterrence if it relies upon the intent to respond to aggression by the killing of staggering numbers of innocent individuals who by no stretch of the imagination can be charged with participation in the act of aggression? Would we not unequivocally condemn individuals for seeking to ward off potential aggressors by threatening retaliation involving the killing of the aggressor's family?

Since an effective deterrent presupposes not only the possession of nuclear weapons but the "immoral" intent to use them, we find ourselves in the unenviable predicament where we cannot avoid evil. Under such conditions, our only option is to choose the lesser evil. Perfectionism will not do. Given our predicament it appears that no matter how unpalatable, deterrence with the intent to retaliate with nuclear weapons is preferable to the otherwise unavoidable sacrifice of our value system in the face of nuclear blackmail. We therefore reluctantly conclude that as long as we are confronted with the tragic reality of the existence of nuclear weapons systems, our overriding concern must be the prevention of the actual outbreak of nuclear war itself. We have no alternative but to fall back on provisions in Jewish Law which sanction departures from ordinary norms and procedures under extraordinary circumstances (*raisons d'état*—in modern parlance). Halakhah operates with categories such as *horaat shaah* (temporary suspension of laws enabling society to cope with extraordinary situations) or *lemigdar milta* (recourse to extraordinary measures by communal authorities for the protection of the common good).[18]

HALTING THE INEVITABLE

Because our justification of nuclear deterrence hinges upon such notions as *horaat shaah* and *lemigdar milta*, it can only be invoked for a limited period of time and must be treated as a strictly temporary expedient. Moreover, the vulnerability of nuclear deterrents increases geometrically with the passage of time. It therefore becomes a matter of extreme urgency to remedy the conditions that leave us no choice but to resort to such deterrence.

By far the most serious pitfall of our present strategic policy is the possibility of failure. Nuclear war may be precipitated either by design or by accident. Every effort must be made to diminish the likelihood of such a catastrophe. For this reason the nuclear arms race must be halted immediately. Apart from the enormous strain on human resources that are diverted from constructive purposes into what we hope and pray will be at best merely nonusable weapons, the escalation of the arms race, far from contributing to our security, introduces destabilizing elements into the balance of terror which so far has saved us from the ultimate disaster. With respect to the hazards associated with destabilization, it hardly matters whether defensive or offensive capabilities are involved. Even an increase in our defensive capability (be it Star Wars or civilian defense) will be perceived by an adversary as a threat to his security and thereby increase the risk of a preemptive strike.

Although far from being a perfect solution, a verifiable reduction of the nuclear arsenals would considerably reduce the hazards posed by the arms race. Of even greater value is the universal acceptance of the "no first-use pledge." As President Roosevelt put it so long ago, "We have nothing to fear but fear itself." The fear of attack by a nuclear power is the most probable cause of an unwanted nuclear war which would be precipitated by a preemptive nuclear first strike launched by a nation which perceives itself as threatened. Anything we do to at least partially allay those fears is an important contribution to the security of mankind.

We recognize that the increased risk that the removal of the threat of nuclear retaliation against aggression renders much more likely an attack by conventional weapons. In spite of the acerbation of tensions between the superpowers, the outbreak of hostilities has been prevented until now because both sides are rational enough to be afraid of a nuclear holocaust. We might, therefore, plausibly contend that under present conditions it is preferable to marginally increase the risk of nuclear war rather than create conditions which will dramatically increase the likelihood of a conventional war.

But even if we were to conclude that present conditions compel us to consider nuclear deterrence against all forms of aggression as the only viable alternative, its potential for disaster, especially in the light of Murphy's Law, is so frightening as to render it unacceptable. We dare not wax complacent about the prospect that miscalculation, malfunctioning of equipment, accident, human error, or fanaticism may plunge us into nuclear holocaust leading to Omnicide. Ours is a religious mandate to help ensure the survival of God's creation and especially of those creatures that bear His image. We dare not betray this sacred task.

NOTES

1. Abraham Isaac Kook, *Mishpat Cohen* (Jerusalem: Mossad Rav Kook, 1985), pp. 142–144, 305–348.

2. Shelomoh Goren, *Meshiv Milchamah* (Jerusalem: Adirah Rabbah, 1982).

3. Shelomoh Yoseph Zevin, *Le'or Hahalakhah*, pp. 9–84.

4. Shaul Yisraeli, *Amud Hayemini*, pp. 162–200.

5. Eliezer Waldenberg, *Hilkhot Medinah*.

6. Judah Gershuni, *Mishpat Hamelukhah* (Jerusalem: Moznaim Publishing, 5744), pp. 415–430.

7. See *Sifri* ad Deuteronomy 20:19.

8. For an excellent treatment of this subject, see David S. Shapiro, "The Jewish Attitude Towards Peace and War" in *Studies in Jewish Thought* (New York: Yeshiva University Press, 1975), vol. 1, pp. 316–363.

9. *Bavli, Shavuot* 356.

10. *Bavli Sanhedrin* 24b.

11. Deuteronomy 20:19–20.

12. See George I. Movrodes, "Convention and the Morality of War," *Philosophy and Public Affairs* (Winter 1975), 4:119–131, for a cogent argument that finds the distinction between combatants and noncombatants a pure convention.

13. *Pesachim* 105b.

14. *Mishnah Ohalot* 7:6; *Sanhedrin* 72b.

15. See especially, Zvi Yehudah Berlin, *Haamek Davar* ad Genesis 9:6, and Zevin, *ibid.*

16. Paul Ramsey, *War and the Christian Conscience* (Durham, NC: Duke University Press, 1961).

17. See especially Shaul Yisraeli, *ibid.*

18. Maimonides, *Hilkot Mamrim* 2:4.

WITNESS

13

From Genocide to Omnicide: The Jewish Imperative to Save the Earth

Louis René Beres

Scholars build the structure of peace in the world. (*Berakhot* 64)

If Rabbi Hanina's faith in the power of scholarship is to be justified, there is no time to lose. Dominated by the implements of megadeath, humankind lies in a stupor, ready to receive oblivion. Captivated by glib archaeologists of ruins-in-the-making, our species has allowed its leaders to transform life into unfathomable depths of silence. In the next several years, we must decide whether we shall survive, or whether—like a face drawn in sand at the edge of the sea—we shall be erased.

It should not be a difficult decision. Approached from Jewish tradition and experience, the threat of Omnicide demands one overriding response: a reaffirmation of life. And this reaffirmation must be based upon the incontrovertible understanding that Omnicide is like any other incurable disease. The only hope lies in *prevention*.

THE BALANCE OF TERROR IN DISEQUILIBRIUM

The nuclear arms race cannot last forever. In a world already shaped by some 6,000 years of organized warfare, it is difficult to imagine that nuclear weapons will not be put into use amidst steadily accelerating preparations for nuclear war. Rather, the unprecedented possibilities that now lie latent in these weapons are almost certain to be exploited, either by design or by accident, by misinformation or by miscalculation, by lapse from rational decision or by unauthorized decision.

Nuclear strategy is a game that truly decent world leaders morally may play only as an interim step towards genuine disarmament. The existing balance of terror is destined to fail. Complicated by the spread of nuclear weapons to other states and by renewed preparations for active and passive defense, this balance promises only a temporary reprieve.

Consider the historical record. The balance of power has never been durable; it has never had anything to do with equilibrium. Since it is always a matter of individual and arbitrary perceptions, adversary states are never really confident that strategic conditions are well-balanced. Rather, each side always fears that it may be just a little bit "behind." The net effect of this search for balance, therefore, is inevitably disequilibrium and insecurity.

But what of the argument that nuclear deterrence has worked since 1945? Doesn't this suggest a certain durability, a measure of reasonable optimism about continued success? The answer, of course, is manifestly negative. Since nuclear deterrence is a dynamic process, changing almost daily with modifications of doctrine and with new entrants into the nuclear club, there is no logical basis for faith in nuclearism. The situation is very much like that of the chain smoker who contends that because he has been smoking cigarettes for twenty-five years without ill effects, smoking must be safe. The real question is whether smoking will *ultimately* kill him. If it does, the final assessment of costs and benefits will turn out quite differently.

Significantly, the notion of nuclear deterrence now embraced by the United States (and soon to be embraced by other nuclear powers) is not a notion that has been with us from the start.

Reflecting far more provocative principles of national security, the United States now assumes that successful deterrence requires not only the capacity to assuredly destroy an aggressor after absorbing a nuclear first-strike (Mutually Assured Destruction, or MAD), but also the capacity to fight a "protracted" nuclear war (Nuclear Utilization Theory, or NUT). Based on such assumptions, the United States and other nations now plan to deploy a variety of weapons that are unsuitable for anything but an initial move of war.

None of this should suggest, however, that the danger of nuclear war arises primarily from the possible overlap of irrationality and nuclear capability. Although the portent of such overlaps is significant and must be taken very seriously, it is substantially less ominous than the threat posed by leaders who are entirely sane and rational. This is the case because the very context within which nuclear strategy decisions must be made requires ventures in escalation, risk-taking and committal ventures that, by their very nature, must surely fail.

In the final analysis, the national leaders who would bring down the curtain on human history would actually, even desperately, want peace. Driven by the inexorable momentum of "logic" in the nuclear age, however, their doomsday judgments would be unleashed for perfectly "scientific" reasons.

We must call into question the very idea of sanity and rationality in the present world. Does it make sense to identify these traits with a professed willingness to destroy all of creation? Like Adolph Eichmann, who was pronounced "perfectly sane" by a psychiatrist in Jerusalem, the head of state who gives the order to commence nuclear warfare would, in all likelihood, act in a fashion deemed consistent with the rules of official doctrine. Confronted with such a world—one wherein sanity can be reconciled with both Genocide and Omnicide—there can be no greater insanity than to be totally sane.

THE JEWISH WITNESS

"Everything is possible!" Beginning with Elie Wiesel's sobering intimation of collective fragility in the face of overwhelming evil, we must reject all government-sanctioned delusions of immortality. Trapped in the ambit of what Philippe Aries, in *The Hour of Our Death*, calls "dirty," "obscene," or "invisible" death, we must oppose all government efforts that substitute gibberish for purposeful thought. As we know from studies of the "nuclear winter,"[1] a nuclear war could bring all life to final extinction. Before any semblance of a livable species could be born from the radioactive ash of a nuclear war, a gravedigger would have to wield the forceps.

In a real sense, however, the very concept of a nuclear "war" is a contradiction in terms. Surely the Torah would not place the threat of Omnicide, which imperils all life, in the same category as war.[2] Since the stockpiled nuclear weapons that exist today could kill all life and render any further reproduction of living cells impossible, a nuclear conflict would kill not only life but life-giving death. It would, therefore, destroy not only all of nature but even the natural relation of death to life.[3]

Classical Judaism has a great deal to say about warfare—when and how it is to be conducted, who may or may not participate, the correct treatment of prisoners and noncombatants, and so on. But what possible rationale can be found for an event that would put all the earth in danger? In the absence of any meaningful criteria for victory and justice, nuclear war should elicit only one response—*avoidance*. Acknowledging the universal, life-embracing spirit of the Torah, we must understand the overriding imperative to preserve the earth. As expressed by Isaiah, "God created the earth . . . not a waste. He formed it to be inhabited" (Isaiah 45:18).

Judaism does not teach the pursuit of peace at any price, but the meaning of resistance in the nuclear age presents a new situation. Since a nuclear war could never defend life, but would destroy all parties to the conflict, the dominant evil to be excised is the death-machinery itself. Giving new meaning to the command "Thou shalt remove the evil from the midst of thee" (Deuteronomy 13:6), nations must build the earth into a new ark of renewal. Under no circumstances must they accept Samson's tormented plea: "Let me die with the Philistines" (Judges 16:30).

There is a story by Jorge Luis Borges[4] in which a condemned man, having noticed that expectations never coincide with reality, unceasingly imagines the circumstances of his own death. Since they have become expectations, he reasons, they can never become reality. So it must be with nuclear war. Recognizing that fear and reality go together naturally, we must begin to place ourselves firmly within the arena of morality. Only then can we begin to take the first critical steps back from a future that glows menacingly as a numbing hallucination.

If it is to serve its intended purpose, the fear generated by our straightforward look at nuclear war must lead us away from the idea that such an event can be "just." Although the Jewish tradition acknowledges a proper place for war in certain circumstances, this tradition must be revised in the light of a fundamentally unique species of conflict. This is not to suggest that there can never be a justifiable rationale for nuclear arms and nuclear deterrence, but that such a rationale must be limited to the most extraordinary circumstances.[5]

In this connection, Jews have a special responsibility to prevent nuclear war. Forever touched by the dark memories of the Holocaust, we already have some idea of what a nuclear conflict might inflict on human societies. Indeed, together with the aftermath of atomic destruction in Japan, the Holocaust offers a dark visionary look at what may lie ahead. The total immersion in death; the smell of tens of thousands of burning bodies; the overwhelming imagery of unending terror, disintegration, and loss that were the central features of these events offer us the clearest picture of "life" in a post-apocalypse world.

At the time of their descent, the survivors of Auschwitz and Hiroshima, of Treblinka and Nagasaki, reacted to the otherworldly grotesqueness of their conditions with what Yale psychiatrist Robert J. Lifton describes as a profound sense of "death in life."[6] Witnessing, in the one case, the thrusting of newly delivered babies, *alive*, into ovens, and in the other, the appearance of long lines of severely burned, literally melting ghosts, the survivors found themselves, in Bruno Bettelheim's words, an "anonymous mass,"[7] or in the Japanese term *muga-muchu*, "without self, without a center." Such a total disruption of individual and social order, of one's customary personal and community supports, produced consequences that went far beyond the immediate physical and emotional suffering. Indeed, this understanding is incorporated in the Japanese term for atomic bomb survivors, *Hibakusha*, which delimits four categories of victims, including those who were *in utero* at the time of the blast.

In the case of nuclear war, of course, the precise symbols and images that are needed to interpret the idea of *total extinction* simply do not exist. The absence of such symbols and images makes it impossible for us, in thinking about such a calamity, to follow Martin Buber's injunction to "imagine the real." Nevertheless, even if a world numbed by nuclear apocalypse is not psychologically absorbable at the moment, imaginings of such a world must be encouraged.

Prophetic voices of survivors have already been raised. In writings and public appearances, Elie Wiesel has linked Genocide and Omnicide, the Holocaust and atomic war. Similarly, Samuel Pisar warns that we must understand the fate of the Jews at the hands of the Nazis not only as history's most unpardonable crime, but also as a presentiment of worldwide obliteration. Vitalized by an informed understanding of the link between past and future, he urges us to confront the dying world of the late twentieth century not as victims, but as gifted creators.

In the final chapter of his important book, *Of Blood and Hope*, Pisar speaks of "the storm ahead"—a storm in which all mothers, Jewish and Gentile, "must be warned that new holocausts of all kinds can once again swallow up their daughters and their sons." Addressing Israel's Knesset and the International Holocaust Survivor's Conference in Jerusalem, Pisar challenged the Jewish community to recognize the Holocaust not only as "an indelible memory of horror," but also as "a permanent warning":

> For we have seen the end of creation. In the shadow of permanently flaming gas chambers, where Eichmann's reality eclipsed Dante's vision of hell, we have witnessed a pilot project for the destruction of humanity, the death rattle of an entire species on the

eve of the atomic age, of thermonuclear proliferation—the final solution.[8]

Pisar's message is clear. To celebrate our redemption, Jews must give new meaning to the sacred command *Never Again*. Affirming the primordial importance of Judaism's ethical values, we must oppose—with rage and partisanship—a nuclear threat that can transform an entire planet from radiance to crematorium. From Jerusalem, a torch of hope can be carried to a paralyzed world, offering safety and salvation to all who would rise above the dreadful marriage of technology and barbarism.

There is no alternative. The background of the contemporary world is highlighted by an unprecedented vastness of infamy. Yet humankind now also confronts a new calculus of potentiality, a last opportunity to choose life over death. In seizing this opportunity, the Jewish people can be a light unto all nations, an archetype of survival and rebirth. Redeemed in both its particularity and its universality, the Jewish people can serve as a mentor to the world.

The first section of the Memorial Wall at Yad Vashem represents the Holocaust. At its center stands the furnace (shaped like an industrial plant), and to the left of the furnace we see the "raw material" of extermination—a long line of human beings on the last stretch of their march. For them, the world is about to be consumed in fire; the Holy is utterly profaned.

Today, an entire species stand ready to begin such a march. Anesthetized to both reason and the biblical concept "Do not destroy!" (*bal tash'hit*), it has failed to learn a central lesson of the Holocaust: Everything is possible! We must believe the unbelievable!

In *One Generation After*, Elie Wiesel tells the story of Moshe the Beadle. When Moshe returned to his small village from the killing fields of the *Einsatzcommando*—and he was one of the very few who were able to escape—his warnings fell on deaf ears. It was all too absurd. His audiences, weary and naive, would not and could not believe. Finally he fell silent.

Looking back, perhaps the residents of that small village, Bichkev, did not act unreasonably. How, after all, could they

believe what they were told? Could even the Nazis eliminate
aharit hayamin [the End of Days]? Were they empowered to
cancel the Messiah?

We, however, are another story. Living with both the memory and the expectation of holocaust, we must heed the present
warnings of a global nuclear wasteland. Knowing that the heart of
darkness can exist in the most civilized and technologically advanced societies, we are commanded to resist and to protect the
earth. Should we ignore this commandment, we—unlike our
6 million brethren—will have no satisfactory explanation. We, unlike the 6 million, know that we must believe *because* it is unbelievable.

THE ROAD BACK TO LIFE

"The dust from which the first man was made was gathered from
all the corners of the world" (*Sanhedrin* 38b). Nurtured by this
cosmopolitan field of consciousness, we must acknowledge the
dignity of all humankind and the essential communion of all peoples. Above all else, this means a worldwide effort to counter the
strategic mythmakers of all nations and the militaristic national-
isms that prod people toward everlasting despair. Stripped of false
hopes, and without hatred of his fellows, man may yet stare at the
specter of nuclear war with passionate attention and experience
the planetary responsibility that will bring liberation.

The capacity to prevent nuclear war is inseparable from our
national leaders developing a new consciousness. The essence of
this new consciousness must be the avoidance of self-delusion and
unacceptable risk. It is wrong to "defend" one's nation by taking
steps that hasten total liquidation.

Again, there is an important lesson here from the history of
the Jewish people. As explained by Yehoshafat Harkabi in *The
Bar Kokhba Syndrome*, the rebellion against the Romans in
132 C.E. undermined Jewish life because it was fated to fail.[9]
Spawned by an unwillingness to confront actual political circumstances, the subsequent defeat pushed the Jewish people to the
very margins of history.

For the United States today, the choice is even clearer. Unlike the only choice available to Jews under Roman rule, slavery or death, we are not obliged to surrender. Our only choice is between an accommodation that is consistent with full freedom and prosperity, and annihilation. While the Jewish choice in the second century was between servitude and national suicide, our choice is between good life and unheroic death.

But the "tough-minded" disposition of professional strategists does not imply genuine understanding. As Hannah Arendt noted some time ago, this new priesthood is cold-blooded enough to consider discomforting thoughts, but in such consideration it does not really *think*. In Arendt's words:

> Instead of indulging in such an old-fashioned, uncomputerizable activity, they reckon with the consequences of certain hypothetically assumed constellations without, however, being able to test their hypotheses against actual occurrences. The logical flow in these hypothetical constructions of future events is always the same: what first appears as a hypothesis—with or without its implied alternatives, according to the level of sophistication—turns immediately, usually after a few paragraphs, into a "fact," which then gives birth to a whole string of similar non-facts, with the result that the purely speculative character of the whole enterprise is forgotten. Needless to say, this is not science, but pseudo-science.[10]

With its current strategy, the priesthood of "nuclearism" stands before the world as a spiritual and intellectual void. Embracing neither virtue nor reason, its profane bravado offers little more than a vast emptiness of dogmas. The appointed groups that dissolve thought with such dogma have all of the seriousness of any theological elite, but behind their ritualistic incantations there is only blasphemy.

Ironically, present policies—intertwined with an elaborate canon of nuclear theology—will cause evil by wanting heroically to triumph over it. There is nothing about present preparations for nuclear war that suggests deliberate evil. In contrast to Freud's view, which is focused very specifically on base motives, these preparations may be entirely consistent with good intentions. Searching for a heroic victory over evil, nations now inadvertently create evil—not in pursuit of debased ideals but for purity, goodness, democracy, and righteousness. In a sense, U.S. nuclear strategy bears a strange affinity to certain ancient Hebrew writings that were found in caves near the Dead Sea. In its preparations for an apocalyptic war, it resembles the Qumran text *The War of the Sons of Light and the Sons of Darkness*. While the Scrolls declare that God, with His human and celestial partisans, will do final battle against the forces of Belial, it envisions a conflagration betwen secular superpowers that represent good and evil.

Our government, of course, may not recognize such resemblance. The Brotherhood of Qumran, regarding itself as the true Congregation of Israel, *knew* that it was preparing for the ultimate contest. Our government, however, seems to believe that by preparing for nuclear war it might be able to prevent its occurrence. For the authors of the Scrolls, the task was to bring Man back, in an age of apostasy, to the True Way before the Final Judgment. For the government of the United States the task seems to be to avoid nuclear war by displaying an exaggerated willingness to fight such a war. If, however, nuclear war becomes inevitable, our leaders urge that we learn to recognize the benefits of rational war-waging, that we begin to value the Apocalypse.

In its picture of Last Things, Jewish tradition concerning the final conflict identifies the adversaries of God primarily with the unrighteous elements among Man. To prepare for this conflict, *The War of the Sons of Light and the Sons of Darkness* offers a precise plan, one that conforms to standard Roman patterns of military organizations, procedure, and strategy. American plans for fighting a nuclear war are also specific. This military program for the United States envisions precise cycles of moves and countermoves that might take place over an extended period of time. According to the Scroll, salvation was to come only after victory in the struggle against the iniquitous Sons of Darkness. Although current American nuclear strategy has never consciously *sought* a nuclear Armageddon, several of its principal exponents have fantasized publicly about its near inevitability and even its long-term benefits. And while no government spokesmen have suggested that a post-Apocalypse world order would be anything but catastrophic, there are those who have suggested that we can endure.

Though attached to this world, such suggestions do not really belong to it: there is something nonterrestrial about the policy makers' formulations. Reflecting a desolate "perspicacity" that eludes our perceptions, their invitation to finality is merely a memory projected into the future, a nostalgia for distant imaginations of redemption twisted into public policy. But it is their fate, even as they aspire to happiness, to encourage only death.

It is wrong to cast the Apocalypse as healer. It is not for the nations to decide when to end the world. Rabbi Yanai says: "A man should never put himself in a place of danger and say that a miracle will save him, lest there be no miracle, and if there be a miracle, his being thus saved will diminish his share in the world to come. . . ."[11] Prudence is the true responsibility of nations. If redemption is to come from catastrophe, it is not for the nations to make such catastrophe imminent.

The people of the world must begin to understand that the growing number of formulations of livable post-Apocalypse worlds are both nonsense and dangerous. Pursued by a tangible evil, Americans have begun to spark a confrontation with those who would substitute "gobbledygook" for truth. With these beginnings, there can now be a plausible paradigm of nuclear war that puts an end to false hopes and empty promises. Now we can begin to take the first feeble but critical steps back to life, steps based not on illusions of immortality, but on a summoning-forth and a mastery over visions of total annihilation.

In taking these steps, we must direct special attention to the importance of *language*. The prospect of nuclear war is tied very closely to the vocabulary human beings have adopted for strategic studies. Euphemisms such as "crisis relocation," "limited nuclear war," "collateral damage," "countervalue" and "counterforce" strategies, and "enhanced radiation warfare" (the neutron bomb) are insidious to the cause of peace because they tend to make the currency of nuclear war-fighting valid coin. Just as the barbarisms of the Nazis were made possible through such linguistic disguises as "final solution," "resettlement," "action," "special treatment," and "selections," so do the euphemisms of the nuclear age etherize an unwitting humanity into accepting nuclear war.

REALPOLITIK AND THE LAMED VOV

In taking these steps, we must also transform the underlying system of militaristic nationalism and realpolitik in world affairs, a sinister caress that subordinates all humankind to the imminent needs of the state. Although it has long been observed that states must always search for an improved power position as a practical matter, the *glorification* of the state is a development of modern times. This glorification, representing a break from the traditional political realism of Thucydides, Thrasymachus, and Machiavelli, was fully elaborated in Germany. From Fichte and Hegel through Ranke and Von Treitschke, the predatory advance of realpolitik has sanctified a kingdom of systemwide and systematic murder.

The idea of the state as a sacred phenomenon was formalized by the growth of fascism in the twentieth century. Fascism takes as its motto: "Everything for the state; nothing against the state; nothing outside the state." But it is not only fascism that holds the state to be sacred. The Soviet Union, rejecting the generous cosmopolitanism of the Manifesto—"Working men of all countries, unite!"—has acted precisely as other executioner states do in pursuit of their perceived national interests. And the United States, conceived in the principles of the Enlightenment, seems intent upon sacrificing its ideals at the altar of lethal, purposeless competition.

Today, leaders of the United States often despise the spirit of the Age of Reason, the spirit that gave birth to their country. They also find it necessary to execrate it as a source of impiety. As a result, they have fostered a spirit of realpolitik that goes far beyond the bounds of an earlier ancient pattern of reluctant pragmatism. In this spirit, the perceived interests of the United States *are* the ultimate value, even though their lack of congruence with worldwide interests renders them self-destructive.

The United States must begin to act upon entirely different principles of international relations—principles that are based not on the misdirected ideas of geopolitical competiton, but upon the spirit of cooperation. To make this possible, our leaders will need to understand that realpolitik proves its own insubstantiality, that it is an unrealistic principle whose effects are accentuated by the steady sacrilization of the state.

Today the state assumes its own rationale. Holding its will as preeminent, it has become a sacred phenomenon, intent upon sacrificing private interests and personal life to an omnivorous abstraction. A stand-in for God, the state is now a providence of which everything is accepted and nothing expected. The fact that it is prepared to become an executioner state is not hard to reconcile with its commitment to Goodness, since both the End of Days and progress are expressions of the sacred.

Rationalist philosophy had derived the idea of national sovereignty from the notion of individual liberty, but cast in its modern (after the seventeenth century and the Treaty of Westphalia) expression, the idea has acted to oppose human dignity and human rights. Left to develop on its continuous flight from reason, the legacy of unrestrained nationalism can only be an endless reservoir of subhumanity, extraneous to every purpose save loathing and ritual slaughter.

Worn threadbare, militaristic nationalism must cease to be a principal source of meaning. At the same time, we must not assume that nationalistic feelings are always harmful. The contributions of nationalism as a force against discrimination and exploitation are well known, especially to the Jewish people and to the State of Israel. It is only when this force oversteps its worthy objectives to become an agent of interstate conflict that it must be curbed.

It is all a matter of what are customarily described as "stages of development" in world political life. Up to a point, the forces of nationalism represent a progressive influence, serving to supplant oppressive patterns of control with a legitimate expression of national needs and prerogatives. After a time, however, these forces may become retrograde, no longer serving vital human needs but rather the contrived "interests" of states, interests that no longer bear any relation to those of individual persons. When the forces of nationalism become maladaptive, the requirements of civilization must yield to the more enduring imperatives of planetization.

The problem was brilliantly foreseen by Martin Buber in 1921. Speaking to the Twelfth Zionist Congress as a representative of the *Hitachdut*—a newly formed coalition of non-Marxist socialist Zionist parties—Buber reminded the gathering that there were distinct types of national self-assertion, including a "degenerate" kind of self-righteous, egocentric nationalism. This "hypertrophic" nationalism, as he called it, obscures the humanity of other peoples, thus distorting the higher purpose of nationalism. Instead of healing the afflictions of one's own nation and those of humankind as a whole, such a posture narrows moral consciousness and defiles all who are touched by it. In Buber's words:

A nationalist development can have two possible consequences. Either a healthy reaction will set in that will overcome the danger heralded by nationalism, and also nationalism itself, which has now fulfilled its purpose; or nationalism will establish itself as *the* permanent principle; in other words, it will exceed its function, pass beyond its proper bounds, and—with overemphasized consciousness—displace the spontaneous life of the nation. Unless some force arises to oppose this process, it may well be the beginning of the downfall of the people, a downfall dyed in the colors of nationalism.[12]

The world now exists outside of history, in parentheses. Ever fearful of metamorphoses that represent its only hope for survival, it can no longer abide the seductive virulence of realpolitik. Accepting that right does not arise from wrong, it must now grasp the principles of public and private responsibility, acknowledging them as the only proper and pragmatic standard for planetary life.

During the next several years, humankind must begin to erect durable structures of peace. Spurred on by the irresistible challenge of a vast chaos from which there can be neither escape nor sanctuary, our species must display new forms of understanding. Casting aside the desolate clairvoyance of realpolitik, it must accept a new pattern of thinking, one based on the affirmation of reason and global identity.

In the aftermath of the Holocaust, Karl Jaspers addressed himself to the question of German guilt. His response articulates one of the most fertile and important concepts of modern philosophy, the idea of "metaphysical guilt." In this connection, wrote Jaspers: "There is a solidarity not only among fellow citizens but also among mankind. The responsibility of the inactive bystander ranges from the mutual one of fellow citizens to one that is universally human."[13] Jaspers's doctrine suggests an urgent need to seek peace without further delay.

The mark of contemporary humankind is that it does not really *listen*. Yet, only when one really listens can there be a meeting with others and a progression to the sphere of the "between" that Martin Buber knows to be the "really real." In an age of death, hate, and brutalization, one in which the technology of destruction has finally caught up with our species' most base and terrible inclinations, this suggests a need to "listen" to individuals everywhere. The resultant dialogue and communication would not only be of service to these other individuals, but also to the "self" of all states through authentic feelings of relatedness.

To fulfill the expectations of a new global society, one that would erect effective barriers around humankind's most murderous tendencies, initiatives must be taken *within* states. National leaders can never be expected to initiate the essential changes on their own. Rather, the new evolutionary vanguard must grow out of informed publics throughout the world. And this vanguard can be nurtured by the insights of Jewish tradition and experience.

In *Anti-Semite and Jew*, Jean-Paul Sartre speaks of the importance of Jewish authenticity, of choosing oneself *as Jew*.[14] Although Sartre is concerned with combating the virulence of anti-Semitism ("The authentic Jew *makes himself a Jew*, in the face of all and against all . . . and the anti-Semite is deprived of his weapons"), Jewish authenticity can have another function. Understood as a reaffirmation of humankind's partnership with God to sustain and replenish the Earth, it implies a primary responsibility to prevent extinction—the ultimate form of desecration and profanation. Moreover, as products of a history overstocked with martyrs, Jews know that even the unspeakable is possible, a knowledge that must be shared with all others.

According to ancient Jewish tradition, a tradition that certain talmudists trace back to the time of Isaiah, the world rests upon thirty-six just men—the *Lamed-Vov*. For those who remain unknown to themselves, the spectacle of the world is insufferable beyond description. Inconsolable at the extent of human pain and woe, for them (according to the hasidic story) there is never a moment of tranquility. So from time to time, God himself—in an effort to open their souls to Paradise—sets forward the clock of the Last Judgment by one minute.

There are many meanings to this tradition, one of which offers special hope in our present nearness to global annihilation. *We require a whole world of just men.* We must create the conditions whereby every inhabitant of an endangered planet feels the full pain and portents of the *Lamed-Vov*. Only then can we begin to take the necessary steps from defilement to sanctification. Faced with a choice between life and death, "the blessing and the curse," we will "therefore choose life."[15]

NOTES

1. For information on the concept of a "nuclear winter," see: Richard P. Turco, Owen B. Toon, Thomas P. Ackerman, James B. Pollack and Carl Sagan, "The Climatic Effects of Nuclear War," *Scientific American*, 251(2), August 1984, pp. 33–43; Paul R. Ehrlich et al., *Long-Term Biological Consequences of Nuclear War, Science*, December 23, 1983, pp. 1293–1300; R. P. Turco et al., "Nuclear Winter: Global Consequences of Multiple Nuclear Explosions," *Science*, December 23, 1983, pp. 1283–1292; Carl Sagan, "Nuclear War and Climatic Catastrophe: Some Policy Implications," *Foreign Affairs*, 62:2, Winter 1983/1984, pp. 257–292; Curt Covey et al., "Global Atmospheric Effects of Massive Smoke Injections from a Nuclear War: Results from General Circulations Model Simulations," *Nature*, March 1, 1984, pp. 21–25; and Carl Sagan, "The Nuclear Winter," published by the Council for a Livable World Education Fund, Boston, MA, 1983, 10 pp.

2. On this point, see Arthur Waskow, "The Bomb and the Torah," in David Saperstein, ed., *Preventing the Nuclear Holocaust: A Jewish Response* (New York: Union of American Hebrew Congregations, 1983).

3. John Somerville, "Philosophy of Peace Today: Preventive Eschatology," Wallach Award Essay 1981, *Peace Research*, 12(2), April 1980, p. 63.

4. It is worth noting here that Borges identified as a Jew. Acknowledging that he had dabbled in the kabbalah, he said, "Many a time I think of myself as a Jew, but I wonder whether I have the right to think so. It may be wishful thinking." See Willis Barnstone, ed., *Borges at Eighty: Conversations* (Bloomington, IN: Indiana University Press, 1982), p. 75.

5. In this connection, one thinks of Israel's extraordinary security needs and the implications of nuclear proliferation in the Middle East. For a detailed consideration of this question, see Louis René Beres, ed., *Security of Armageddon: Israel's Nuclear Strategy* (Lexington, MA: Lexington Books, 1985).

6. Robert Jay Lifton, *Death in Life: Survivors of Hiroshima* (New York: Vintage, 1967).

7. Bruno Bettelheim, *Surviving* (New York: Knopf, 1979).

8. Samuel Pisar, "A Warning," in Saperstein, *op. cit.*, p. 32.

9. Yehoshafat Harkabi, *The Bar Kokhba Syndrome: Risk and Realism in International Politics* (Chappaqua: NY: Rossel Books, 1983), p. 206.

10. Hannah Arendt, *On Violence* (New York: Harcourt Brace and World, 1970), p. 7.

11. Talmud (*Sota* 32a) and Codes (*Yoreh De'ah* 116).

12. Martin Buber, "Nationalism," in Paul R. Mendes-Flohr, ed., *A Land of Two Peoples: Martin Buber on Jews and Arabs* (New York: Oxford University Press, 1983), p. 52.

13. Karl Jaspers, *The Question of German Guilt*, trans. by E. B. Ashton (New York: Capricorn Books, 1961), p. 92.

14. Jean-Paul Sartre, *Anti-Semite and Jew* (New York: Schocken, 1948), p. 137.

15. Deuteronomy 30:11–20.

14

Morality and
Nuclear Weapons

Edward Teller

Morality is the basic question of any human society; without it, cooperation between people could not work. That religion is deeply connected with morality is obvious. And most people accept the concept that wars and the weapons of war should be subject to moral judgment.

Having stated the obvious, we can quickly approach the absurd. If moral society renounces nuclear weapons as immoral precisely because they are powerful and destructive, and if the leadership of an immoral society develops, deploys, and is ready to use these weapons, then the immoral can and will impose its will on the moral. The outcome of this simple and logical deduction is a situation in which morality cannot endure.

Having grown up within the liberal Jewish tradition, my opinions on morality are thus influenced by that tradition. This does not mean, however, that I am stating a Jewish point of view on this difficult question, for no one has such a full measure of authority. The intention is to clarify the roots of my convictions.

The Jewish religion places emphasis on theology and great emphasis on the law. Within the Christian religion, most conflicts,

254

heresies, and even religious wars have been concerned with divinity and with God's relation to His church and to the believers. There are disagreements within the Jewish community, but these are almost exclusively concerned with the law, its interpretation, and its degree of rigor.

Judaic law never requires that which the average human being cannot fulfill. Most religions agree that the vast majority of humans are sinners. Civil law in Christian societies also asks only that which the majority can accomplish. However, the Christian church asks for obedience to commandments that require a degree of selflessness not attainable by the common human being, but only by saints.

On this basis, I would say that the commandments taught by the Christian church tend more towards idealism, while Jewish commandments tend more towards realism. Both perspectives are necessary for the well-being of a moral community. Idealism promotes improvement, realism avoids the disaster that would make improvement impossible. Their extremes—romanticism and formalism—have little to contribute to a society.

For many years United States policy has been based on maintaining peace by deterring war. Since the mid-1960s, deterrence has been based exclusively on the threat of retaliation. Former U.S. Secretary of Defense, Robert Strange MacNamara, described this policy as *Mutually Assured Destruction*. For a Christian society whose tenets hold that one should "turn the other cheek," this policy was morally bankrupt from the beginning.

In the past, I did not see a way to escape the moral dilemma. The practical expedient was to stay ahead of the Soviets in the arms race, and thus avoid ever having to seriously consider exercising our policy. But this was not the way that history developed. From superiority we went to equivalence, only to find that equivalence could not be verified or even defined. Finally we were faced with the probability that in the quantity and perhaps even in the quality of arms, the Russians were superior.

Still, the balance of terror was maintained as policy, although there was little balance and undeniable terror. The hope was that as long as each side could inflict unacceptable damage upon the

other, there would be peace, no matter how great that unacceptable damage might happen to be.

Having our security depend on the retaliatory destruction we
were prepared to inflict on our opponent has had peculiar psychological consequences. Instead of the obvious statement, "Nuclear
war should be avoided," a belief gained wide acceptance—"Nuclear war is impossible because it will lead to extermination of
mankind." Such claims gained widespread credence. In succession, people were told that in a nuclear war, the human race would
be destroyed by radioactive fallout or by destruction of the protective ozone layer (which excludes an excess of ultraviolet radiation). Each of these dangers turned out to be highly inflated,
though this fact is not known to the general public.

More recently, exaggerated statements have been made
about a "nuclear winter" in which sunshine would be excluded by
the smoke from burning cities. This latest nightmare is full of
uncertainties. In the worst case, crops would be affected so that if
food had not been stored, hunger could become a real problem.
However, even in the worst case, the probable temperature
changes are unlikely directly to affect people.

The tragedy of a nuclear war would be dreadful—much
worse than what was suffered in the First or Second World War.
The hatred engendered might even be worse than the physical
destruction. But the human race would certainly survive. The
contrary statement is part of a romantic approach, and romanticism has never contributed to solving a real moral problem.

A few years ago a major change occurred in the technical
situation. The official name of this effort is the Strategic Defense
Initiative (SDI). Through ingenious inventions and diligent work
(more diligent on the Russian side), it became probable that an
effective defense against a nuclear attack could be constructed.
This would not be a defense using conventional means, nor would
it be an impenetrable shield. But it would be one which would
decrease the fury of the attack and would do so by means that are
easier and less expensive to provide than the attack itself.

The so-called Star Wars between space-based battle stations
bears no resemblance to what can and should be done. These
words describe a parody of what is needed and what is probably

feasible. Space stations are expensive to deploy and relatively easy to destroy. The opposite must hold for a real defense. Defense must be less expensive than the countermeasures that could overcome it or the attack which could destroy it.

The development of defensive weapons places the moral question regarding armaments in a new perspective. In their famous Letter, the Catholic bishops clearly and correctly stated that weapons are justified when they defend the innocent. That Letter is an extreme example of what I would call the simplified romantic approach. Having agreed that defense is justified, the Catholic bishops proceed to condemn all types of nuclear weapons, no matter how they are employed. This is not a cogent argument, but a crude appeal to widespread public opinion.

What should be opposed are methods of mass destruction: fire-bombing, nuclear rocket attack against cities, and biological warfare. On the other hand, the destruction of weapons attacking the innocent should be attempted by every possible means.

This will be difficult enough in any case. It may be done using lasers, rockets, small nuclear weapons, or other devices. And such defense work should be conducted jointly by all societies whose moral values are held so strongly that they consider them human rights. Aggression is wrong whether carried out by bow and arrow or by the hydrogen bomb. Defense is right whether it employs a stream of particles or utilizes the concentrated energy locked in the atomic nucleus.

This understanding, commonly acknowledged, would bring us a step closer to solving the dreadful moral problem of our age. We should not imagine that we have solved it, even if we succeed (as I hope we shall) in developing and deploying a viable defense. Other questions will remain: What do we call aggression? What justifies defense?

Creating desperately needed defense will release the tension in a situation that otherwise may approach the breaking point. In the long run, defensive weapons will not suffice. We must find a practical solution to the problem of how to decrease, and perhaps eventually abolish, the causes of war.

The problem of establishing, rather than simply maintaining peace has its own paradoxes, and it may even appear insoluble.

But the only way not to solve a problem—whether it be the limited problem of defense or the huge problem of a stable peace—is not to try.

There is a saying in Hungary, my country of origin, which freely translated, suggests, "Man plans, God decides." But if Man fails to try, how can God decide?

15

Final Solution—Universal?

Eliezer Berkovits

As students in Germany, we read Oswald Spengler's *Untergang des Abendlandes* (*The Decline of the West*). We considered it to be a clever and playful exercise, but not to be taken seriously. That which appeared almost sixty years ago as mere fantasy is today a serious possibility confronting the entire human race. Weapons of mass destruction threaten not only the West but all of humanity.

For the Jew who identifies with the course of Jewish history, however, the threatening *Untergang* does not come as a surprise. From the time that Christianity, by the sword of Constantine the Great, became the state religion of the Roman Empire, to the modern day, the Jewish experience has been one of oppression, persecution, and massacre. There were, of course, also periods of less suffering and of less injustice, but there hardly ever has been a period when Jews were not harassed and tormented in some part of the Western world. In addition, Jew hatred and anti-Jewish discrimination has prevailed even in times and places where there was no overt violence. Inhumanity and barbarism have been inflicted upon the Jewish people to the present day.

The experience of the Jewish people has been unique. No other nation on earth has endured so many centuries of persecution, imposed on it solely for daring to exist. A moral sickness, responsible for Jewish suffering, lies at the very heart of mankind. The martyrdom of the Jewish people is paralleled by man's inhumanity to man practiced in the rest of the world. From the perspective of the Jew who has lived in the Western world throughout its entire "civilized" era, his critical eye observes a picture of slavery, feudalism, colonialism, and totalitarianism. Proclaimed humanitarian ideals remained powerless in any confrontation with what was understood to be the "national interest." Especially in international relationships, the "national interest" has been the determining factor in national behavior. The moral code was left for individuals.

Upon what, in our present situation, can we rely? Universal brotherhood did not prevent two world wars in this century. Universal brotherhood which is expected to be effective because "the future of all mankind is at stake" is not to be trusted. It does not even deserve its name.

There was no universal brotherhood in the universe of the concentration camp, gas chamber, and crematorium. Does the Holocaust then delineate the moral bankruptcy of Western civilization or only reveal it? It was the legitimate child of Western culture. The historian, Arnold Toynbee, wrote insightfully:

A Western nation, which for good and evil, had played so central a part in Western history since the first emergence of a nascent Western civilization of a post-Hellenic interregnum, could hardly have committed these flagrant crimes if the same criminality had not been festering fully below the surface of life in the Western world's non-German provinces. The twentieth-century German psyche was like one of those convex mirrors in which a gazer learns to read a character printed on his own countenance through seeing the salient features exaggerated in a revealing caricature.

If the twentieth-century Germany was a monster, then, by the same token, twentieth-century civilization was a Frankenstein, guilty of having been the author of this monster's being.[1]

The behavior of most of the Western nations towards the catastrophe of the Jewish people proved that Toynbee was cor-

rect in his evaluation of the moral significance of European criminality during Nazi rule. Large sections of the population, even in
the countries languishing under the Nazi yoke, cooperated with
their oppressors in the elimination of the Jews. The indifference of
Western governments, including the silence of the deputy of
St. Peter in the Vatican, served as welcome encouragement to the
perpetrators of the most inhuman crime in world history. The
Holocaust was the testing ground, especially of the Western
world. It was history's challenge to make a stand on behalf of
those ideals of pious love and of enlightened humanitarianism to
which ample lip service had been paid. It was the opportunity to
regenerate the sick moral fiber of the human race. Nothing of the
kind happened. The exception of the "righteous Gentiles," insignificant in proportion to the catastrophe, only underlines the
vastness of the moral tragedy of human failure.

Is it, indeed, a mere coincidence that after the Final Solution,
intended for the Jewish people, mankind has maneuvered itself to
the brink of a possible Final Solution for all life on earth? The
present threat is not due to the almost limitless power that intellectual ingenuity was able to place in the hands of man, but rather
to the continuing process of moral decadence that set in with the
Holocaust. The universal expectation of continued progress has
been shown to be nothing more than a self-delusion. If the Jewish
experience at Christian hands through the centuries has proved
the Christian dogma of redemption by faith to be a mere *fata
morgana* (fantasm), then in this Holocaust age one of the most
tragic mistakes of our times is unraveling. Man deluded himself
into thinking that breathtaking scientific advances were identical
with human progress. More and more we shall have to acknowledge that scientific technological leaps forward were paralleled by
a process of depersonalization of man and decay of spiritual value
systems. The German sociologist Max Weber foresaw the direction into which mankind has been moving:

No one knows whether at the end of this tremendous development
there will be completely new prophets or the rebirth of new ideas and
ideals—or if neither of these—a mechanistic ossification embellished
with a desperate self-importance. Then the truth of about the "last

men" of this cultural development would be: specialists without spirit, hedonists without heart, these nothings imagine themselves to have climbed to a never-before achieved stage of humanity.[2]

We now know that the new prophets have not appeared; nor is there any hope for "new ideas and ideals." On the other hand, there are ample signs of "mechanistic ossification" strutting about with "a desperate self-importance." One cannot but note and suffer "the specialists without spirit and the hedonists without heart" who imagine themselves "to have climbed a never-before achieved stage of humanity."

Another secularist "prophecy of the future," which we already have achieved, reads as follows:

It could be that the process of functional specialization has gone so far that, particularly from the point of view of an emergent world society, we are entering a time when morals and values in the old sense have become irrelevant. At such a stage, the only criterion for choice would be based on technical appropriateness. The problem is that there can be rational programs for madness—the careful organization of the Holocaust is a monstrous case in point. . . .[3]

What can we trust within man's performance in history to prevent ultimate catastrophe? There seems to be nothing left other than the mutual fear of the consequences of a mega-war powers that can constrain the policies of both great and regional. Unfortunately, in situations where the "national interest" demands sacrificial heroism in the service of "the Cause," nations are not afraid of fear. There is ample potential in the human race to provide the needed Hitlers and Stalins, and their kin. Considering man critically, there can be little doubt that the midnight hour of history approaches.

Does not faith in God nullify this dark prognosis? But did faith in God prevent the Holocaust that was wrought upon the Jewish people? Without entering into the depth of theological problematics of faith after the Holocaust, this much can be said: Before the Holocaust, the genuine faith of the believing Jew would have ruled out the possibility of such a catastrophe. In the last postcard that I received from my father in Hungary, he quoted in the original Hebrew: "Behold, the Keeper of Israel neither slumbers nor sleeps" (Psalms 121:4). Did He slumber; was He asleep?

In this critical phase of world history, God seems to be even more silent than He was at Auschwitz and Birkenau. The abyss of God's silence seems to open up before us in its universal depth. And yet, it is no longer the fate of His people that is at stake, but that of all mankind. His earthly creation is in jeopardy. If He had any plans with His creation, it has reached the brink of a future of disintegration. Can He remain silent forever?

Jewish tradition through the ages has been familiar with the prophetic anticipation of an ultimate war that will take place *baharit hayamim*, at the End of the Days.[4] In this conflict God will take a hand. Thus, the apocalyptic End of Days coincides with the prophetic vision of universal messianic redemption. This twofold prophecy is related to the actual world-historic experience of the Jewish people. Our prognosis, as outlined above, has been based only on one facet of the Jewish experience, that of martyrdom. Given the moral sickness and perversions of world culture that have surrounded the Jew, the option of martyrdom has been natural. However, there is also the facet of the Jew's unnatural survival in the midst of darkness. On the basis of the laws of history by which nations live and perish, Jewish survival—in spite of unparalleled martyrdom—is inexplicable. The suffering has been normal, altogether "of this world." The abnormal survival is not "of this world." Survival points to another metahistorical dimension. It is timelessness jolting into the dimensions of time. It conveys a taste of eternity.

The Jewish people exist in this twofold dimension: in time and above time; in history and above history. While such an existence is not normal—as indeed the Jews are not a normal people—it does derive naturally from Israel's covenant with God. It gives meaning to both—the martyrdom and the survival. It explains their inseparable interrelatedness. A Dutch theologian appropriately described the Jew as God's partner. It is through us that He pursues one of His goals with man. After Jacob, with his wives and children, leaves Laban and before he encounters that mysterious "man" who wrestles with him in the darkness of the night, the Bible says: "And Jacob was left—alone" (Genesis 32:25). Interpreting another verse in the Bible, one of the rabbis explained: "None is like unto God and, yet, who is like unto Him? Israel of the Ages! Of the Holy One, blessed be He, it is said, 'God is exalted—alone'" (Isaiah 2:11). Jacob too was "left—alone."[5] God has been alone in time. Israel has been chosen by Him to share His lot of loneliness. It is His loneliness in the world that is the cause of His partners' martyrdom in history, and that gives meaning and dignity to martyrdom. We endure it together with Him; thus, while we are "alone," we are redeemed from loneliness. But just as we share in His plight in time, so are we also sustained above by His eternity. Thus martyrdom is forever accompanied by survival.

Survival because of its metamystical quality, means more, however, than not having perished in the catastrophe. It is the rise from ruin to a new vitality and creativeness.

After the destruction of the First Temple in Jerusalem, the synagogue arose. The divine service was passed from the priestly cast and became the responsibility of the people themselves. It meant a new phase in the history of Judaism. Soon after the destruction of the Second Temple the major contents of the Oral Torah were systematized in the Mishnah, creating a unifying and guiding structure for the Jewish people to continue in its course with faith and hope. When Jewry in the Holy Land disintegrated, a vital center of Jewish life developed in Babylon. It created the Talmud, a unique intellectual, religious, and ethical masterpiece, which became the lifeline of the Jewish people through the centuries that followed. After Babylon, a unique center of Jewish creativity arose in Spain—a Jewry of high cultural standards, outstanding in its achievements in talmudic law, biblical scholarship, philosophy, poetry, and science. And so it went on, practically to our own days: Ruin in time; renewal timelessly. Indeed, "The keeper of Israel neither slumbers, nor does He sleep."

It is unlikely that any generation of Jews has ever experienced Jewish life in the two dimensions with such intensity as ours has. One can hardly imagine two events more dichotomous than the Holocaust and the rise of the State of Israel. Ultimate disaster followed by the opening of the gates towards ultimate redemption.

The Holocaust was the darkest hour of aloneness in which God and His partner had to share. It happened both within the space-time continuum of the Western world and as the direct outcome from it. As such, it had its own logic. The rise of the State of Israel reached us from the dimension of reality beyond all time-bound logic. For many centuries Jews believed that one day they would return to the land of their fathers. In the context of world history, this was utterly illogical. Not only did this faith lack a basis in human experience; it was forever contradicted by it. And yet, Jews knew that their day of return would come. For long centuries they continued to pray for the redemption to come *bimherah b'yamenu*, soon in our days. They could act thusly without being defeated by a sense of futility, because their everpresent renewing survival placed them within the metahistorical dimension of timelessness. In survival, the approach of the Final Promise becomes reality.

When the day of return came, it was indeed in the tradition of Jewish timelessness. In the dimension of time-bound normalcy, however, it is inexplicable. That after almost two millennia of home-lessness, in conditions of unparalleled oppressions and persecution, there still existed a Jewish people, and that this people still had sufficient vitality to return and to reestablish itself in its ancient homeland, is one of the great miracles that penetrated into the space-time continuum of national as well as international history. Its most eloquent significance lies in the fact that this event occurred soon after the Holocaust: after the darkest ruin, the brightest hope. Immediately after the catastrophe the Jewish people found itself in a benign shock that did not allow them to realize the full extent of the tragedy. However, as the days and years passed and the vastness of the destruction and suffering gradually sank into our consciousness, it might have been natural to be overwhelmed by despair. Jewish existence might have appeared meaningless; the future dark and hopeless. The only thing that could save the Jewish people from the grasp of despair was, indeed, the realization of that "irrational" hope of the ages to return home. In the words of the prophet: "at the time of darkness light began to shine" (Isaiah 58:10).

Survival is the opportunity and challenge for renewal. Only now, as radical as the ruin was, the process of renewal must be equally as radical. More than anything else it must lead to a new spiritual and moral phase in the history of Judaism. The *Galut* (Diaspora) is not only the political exile of the Jewish people; but even more significantly it is the spiritual exile of Judaism. Originally, Judaism was intended as the way of life of a people in its own homeland and in control of the economic, social, political, and spiritual structure of its national existence. In exile, wide areas of Jewish teaching are inapplicable. In the *Galut*, although Judaism gives spiritual guidance and sustenance to the Jewish people, it exists in its inauthentic habitat. As Judah HaLevi put it: Only in *"Eretz Yisrael"* (Land of Israel) can the deed be complete. It is fully within the meaningfulness of Jewish metahistory that after the ruination of the *Galut* the hand of Providence should point the way to the redemption of Judaism from its exile.

We, still at the very beginning of this new phase of Jewish history, are hardly able to grasp its revolutionary significance. And yet, by the power of a faith, never faulted in our timelessness, we know that the promise is on its way to fulfillment. But given the condition of man today, his power of global self-destruction, we cannot doubt that the promise of ultimate redemption can only be realized within a global context. Does this mean that man may relax or that the final catastrophe will never happen because of divine intervention? We dare not prophesy. Man *is* on a course towards universal Holocaust. It may very well be that the greater the power in the hand of man, the greater his responsibility in its use. The greater man's responsibility, the more intense God's self-limiting nonintervention. The Jew's experience in time does not allow him to look to the future with easy optimism. But his experience in metaphysical timelessness saves him from barren pessimism. Indeed, God is not always silent.

NOTES

1. Arnold J. Toynbee, War and Civilization, from *A Study of History* selected by Albert U. Fowler (New York: Oxford University Press, 1950), p. 383.

2. Michael Harrington, *The Politics at God's Funeral: The Spiritual Crisis of Western Civilization* (New York: Holt, Rinehart & Winston), 1983.

3. Ibid.

4. *Ezekiel* 38 and the relevant midrashic and talmudic references.

5. Genesis *Rabbah* 77:1.

Appendix of Rabbinic Scholars and Terminology

Abrabanel, Don Isaac Ben Judah (1437–1508). Born in Lisbon. Rabbi, statesman, philosopher, and biblical exegete. Court treasurer of King Alfonso V. Writer of commentaries on the Bible, Passover Haggadah, Avot, and Messianic writings.

Ahai Gaon (680–752). Also called Aha. Born in Shabha, scholar of Pumbedita yeshiva in the genoic period and author of *She'iltot* (questions), which is the first written work (set as a commentary on the Pentatuch) after the closing of the Talmud. Left Babylonia (c. 750) and settled in Eretz Israel. Ahai Gaon's method was to connect the decisions of the Oral Law with the Written Law.

Aher, Elisha Ben Avuyah (second century C.E.). One of the four men who penetrated the secret *pardes* (garden) of mystic knowledge. His reaction was to "hack down the roots." Considered a heretic, thus called Aher (the other). Proficient in Torah, Greek poetry, and philosophy. Never rejected by his student, Rabbi Meir, who claimed he was able to extract the seed from Aher's teaching while rejecting the chaff.

Akiva, Ben Joseph (c. 50–135 C.E.). Born in Judea, Eretz Israel. Outstanding tanna, scholar, patriot, and martyr. Influenced halakhah. Credited with systematizing *midrashai halakhot* and *aggadot*. Encouraged the Bar Kokhba revolt against Rome in 132 C.E., seeing Bar Kokhba as the Messiah. Tortured to death by the Romans.

Amora. A rabbi of the talmudic period.

Babad, Joseph Ben Moses (1800–1875). Rabbi at Bohorodezany, Zabariz, Sniatyn, and Tarnopol, Poland. Best known for *Minhat Hinnukh* based on *Sefer ha-Hinnukh* (the Book of Education), which was ascribed to Aaron ha-Levi of Barcelona. He quotes halakhic commentators and analyzes the revelant laws. Covers all principles, laws, and customs concerning the commandments, from talmudic times to the *aharonim* (later authorities).

Ben Azai, Simeon (early second century C.E.). Died pondering the mysteries of the secret *pardes* (garden) of mystic knowledge. Member of Rabbi Akiva's Academy. Engaged in scholastic work in Tiberias. His opinions are quoted in the Mishnah, the Song of Songs, and Ecclesiastes. Very pious and diligent scholar. Died quite young.

Ben Pedat, Eleazar (died 279 C.E.). Third-century amora. Born in Babylonia and moved to Eretz Israel. Great communal leader with extensive knowledge. Often quoted in the Talmud and also known for his expertise in Aggadah. Major legal authority in both Eretz Israel and Babylonia.

Ben Zakkai, Jochanan (first century C.E.). Leading sage at the end of the Second Temple and in the years following its destruction. Received instruction from Hillel. Learned in Bible and Mishnah. Resided in the Lower Galilee and later in Jerusalem. Devoted himself to the mysteries of the creation of the world and the divine chariot of Ezekiel's prophecy, as well as traditional and legal studies. Escaped from Jerusalem to Jabneh, where he resurrected Jewish learning by convincing the Romans to allow him to establish a school there. From this school the rabbinic tradition continued after the destruction of the Second Temple.

Ben Zoma, Simeon (early second century C.E.). Tanna, contemporary of Akiva. Studied under Joshua Ben Hananiah and was considered an outstanding scholar. Mishnah states that he was the last of the biblical expositors and another had who entered the garden of knowledge (*pardes*). Ben Zoma became insane and died not long after. Never ordained as a rabbi but is referred to as such in the Talmud.

Berlin, Naphtali Zevi Judah (1817–1893). Born in Lithuania and known as ha-Neziv. Leading rabbi of his generation. Head of

Volozhin yeshiva for forty years. Taught the whole of the Babylonian Talmud, wrote commentaries on *Sifre*, and *Emek ha-Neziv* on the *She'iltot* of Rabbi Ahai of Shabha. Also commentary on Torah, *Ha'amek Davar* (1879–1880).

Gelili, Yose Ha (early second century C.E.). Born in the Galilee. Tanna. His halakhot are scattered throughout the Talmud, but mainly in the order of *Kodshim*. Died before the Bar Kokhba War (132–135 C.E.).

Geonim were heads of the academies of Sura and Pumbedita in Babylonia (7th–mid-11th century).

Gershuni, Judah Grodner. Contemporary American, born in Lithuania. Student of Rabbi Boruch Baer Lebovits of Knesset Beit Yitzchak of Kaminetz. Author of *Mishpat Hamilukhah* on Maimonides' *Laws of Kings*. Student of Rabbi Kook. Religious Zionist and legal thinker. Writes on contemporary legal and ethical issues of modern Israel.

Gersonides (Levi Ben Gershom) (1288–1344). Astronomer, mathematician, philosopher, and biblical commentator known as RaLBaG. Born in Bangols sur-Cèze, France. Wrote commentaries on Aristotle, Averroes, and biblical commentaries on Job, Song of Songs, Ecclesiastes, Ruth. His major work, *Sefer Milhamot Adonai* (*The Book of the War of Lords*), is written in technical precise Hebrew and contains an almost complete system of philosophy and theology.

Goren, Shlomo (1917—). Born in Poland. Brigadier General, former first chaplain of the Israel Defense Forces and paratrooper. Chief Rabbi of Tel Aviv and Jaffa and Chief Rabbi of Israel (1969–1979). Voluminous writer in all areas of Jewish and legal issues, including a three-volume halakhic work, *Mashiv Milkhamah*, on the ethics of war.

Halevi, Judah (1075–1141). Born in Tudela, on the border of Christian Spain. Later he settled in Toledo, the capital of Castile, where he became court physician to Alfonso VI. Persecutions against Jews in 1108 forced him to leave Toledo and settle in Cordoba. Wrote *The Book of Argument in Defense of the Despised Faith* (*The Book of the Kuzari*) before departing for the Holy Land. *The Kuzari* is a dialogue between a Jewish scholar and the king of the Khazars, who converted to Judaism in the eighth century. *The Kuzari* emphasizes a profound love for the Jewish people, their land, and their religion—all of which have a "divine influence" impervious to philosophical analysis. Halevi died in Alexandria.

Hanina Bar Hana (early third century). Palestinian scholar of the generation that moved from the tannaim of the Mishnah to the amoraim of the Gemara. A major student of Judah HaNasi (redactor of the Mishnah). Hanina eventually succeeded him as head of his yeshiva.

Hoffmann, David Zvi (1843–1921). Born in Verbo, Slovakia. Biblical and talmudic scholar. Also studied at the universities of Vienna, Berlin, and Tuebingen. Chairman of the court of Adas Yisroel congregation in Berlin. As a rabbi and professor, he became rector of the Modern Orthodox Rabbinical College, The Hildesheimer Seminary in Berlin, and supreme halakhic authority of German Orthodox Jewry. Interpreted the Talmud by critical method.

Huna, Rav (c. 216–c. 296). Born in Diakora. Leader of the second generation Babylonian amoraim and head of the Sura Academy, which he presided over for more than forty years. Mentioned in both Talmuds for his saintliness.

Ibn Ezra, Abraham (1189–1164). Born in Tudela, Spain. Poet, biblical commentator, philosopher, astronomer, and physician. Lived as a wandering scholar. Major works are his commentaries on all the books of the Bible, where he emphasized a strict philological and grammatical approach. His philosophic theories are primarily derived from the Neoplatonists.

Ilai, Judah Bar (mid-second century C.E.). Born in Usha in Galilee. Pupil of Eliezar Ben Hyrcanus, who studied under Akiva, and was ordained by Judah Ben Bava at the time of the Hadrianic persecutions. Opened the convention of scholars in Usha, where the Sanhedrin was reestablished. Many series of mishnayot and halakhot, as well as Mishnah and whole chapters in the Tosefta are from his Mishnah compilations.

Israeli, Shaul (contemporary). Former Rabbi of the Kfar HaRoeh settlement and later dean of Merkaz HaRav Kook Yeshiva. Former member of the Supreme Rabbinic Court of Israel. Writer on many contemporary legal issues from a religious Zionist perspective. Editor of legal journals including *Birkai.*

Isserles, Moses Ben Israel (1525 or 1530–1572). Acronym "Rema." Born in Poland. Rabbi and codifier, one of the great halakhic authorities. Also a kabbalist, philosopher, astronomer, and well versed in history. Founded a yeshiva and was member of the Cracow Bet Din (1550). His works include the *Darkhei Moshe* on the *Tur.* In the *Mapah* (Tablecloth) he presents the Ashkenazic (European) practices in his glosses to Joseph Karo's *Shulhan Arukh* (The Set Table).

Johanan Ben Nappaha (180–279 C.E.). Born in Sepphoris. Palestinian amora whose teachings are a major part of the Jerusalem Talmud. He mastered the Merkabah mysticism and became a very popular teacher in Sepphoris in the yeshiva of Rabbi Bana'ah. Johanan later opened his own academy in Tiberias.

Josephus Flavius (38–100? C.E.). Born in Jerusalem. Jewish historian and one of the chief representatives of Jewish hellenistic literature. Appointed commander of Galilee at the outbreak of the Jewish War (66 C.E.). Most famous work was *The Jewish War,* written under the patronage of the Emperor Vespasian, in which he was against the Bar Kokhba revolt. Josephus was favored by the Roman rulers and hated by his fellow Jews, who regarded him as a traitor and self-serving when he defected to the Romans.

Karo, Rabbi Joseph Ben Ephraim (1488–1575). Born in Spain. A profound mystic, Karo wrote the analytic *Beit Yosef,* a commentary on the authoritative legal code, *Tur.* Later he composed the *Shulhan Arukh* (The Set Table), the most influential code in modern Jewish life. The *Shulhan Arukh* aims at giving a simple statement of the law as it affects Jewish daily life. It is also a reflection of Karo's background and the law of the Sephardic Jews of Spanish and Portuguese descent who resided in Greece, Turkey, and the Land of Israel.

Kook, Rabbi Abraham Isaac (1865–1935). Born in Grieve, Latvia. Religious Zionist, prolific writer, and charismatic personality. Served as rabbi in Lithuanian towns. Later Chief Rabbi of Jaffa, Eretz Israel (1904–1919). Elected to the Chief Rabbinate of Jerusalem (1919) and soon after became the first Chief Rabbi of Eretz

Israel, serving in this post until his death. Writings included the multi-volume *Orot ha-Kodesh*. Famed for his love of Israel and great universalism, Rabbi Kook's thought integrated law, aggadah, mysticism, Hasidism, philosophy, and theology into a rare poetic and penetrating mix.

Loew Ben Bezalel, Judah (1525–1609). Known as the Maharal. Born in Prague. Famed Renaissance Jew. Traditional thinker whose compelling kabbalist philosophic works illuminated Judaism. Evident in the Maharal's unity scheme is his incorporation of dialectical reasoning, with an acute sensitivity to rabbinic and biblical texts. Wrote classic commentaries on Rashi, *aggadot*, Talmud, and Passover Haggadah. Concerned with such topics as Redemption, Diaspora, and Holiness.

Luzzatto, Samuel David (1800–1865). Born in Italy. Scholar, philosopher, biblical commentator and translator, known as SHaDaL. Wrote Hebrew commentary on the Pentateuch and other parts of the Bible. He was well versed in secular sources and interested primarily in the ethical import of biblical teachings.

Maimonides (Rabbi Moses Ben Maimon—RaMBaM) (1135–1204). Born in Cordoba, Spain, from which he fled in 1148 due to the persecutions. Wandered from place to place. Settled in Fez in 1160 and was appointed physician to al-Fadil in 1185. He gained a reputation as one of the greatest masters of halakhah. He wrote a commentary on the Mishnah and the first code of Jewish law entitled *Mishneh Torah* or *Yad Hahazakah*, which synthesizes brilliantly all of Judaic teachings in a lucid style. His greatest philosophic work is his *Guide of the Perplexed*. The inscription on his grave reads, "From Moses to Moses, none arose like Moses."

Malbim, Meir Liebush (1809–1879). Born in Volhyania, Hungary. Rabbi and writer of massive commentaries on the Bible emphasizing the absolute necessity of each word and its correct placement in the text. Staunch defender of tradition in the wake of liberal forces, including the Reform movement. His commentaries include philosophy, philology, and ethical discussion.

Meir, Dan Plocki (1886–1928). Born in Poland. Former president of the Union of Orthodox Rabbis in Poland. Known for his penetrating analytical works, including *Hemdat Yisrael* on the *Book of Commandment* of Maimonides.

Meiri, Rabbi Menachem Ben Solomon (1249–1316). Born in Perpignan, France. Provençal scholar and commentator on the Talmud. Literary activity covered halakhic rulings, talmudic expositions, biblical exegesis, customs, ethics, and philosophy. Primary work is the *Beit ha-Behirah* on the Talmud, in which he summarizes the subject matter in the Talmud, giving both meaning and law derived from it.

Menahem Mendel of Kotsk (1787–1859). Born in Bilgoaj, near Lublin. One of the most outstanding and original leaders in the hasidic movement. Interested in teaching only true scholars, emphasizing the search for truth. Similar to Søren Kierkegaard (1813–1855) in his melancholic, uncompromising search for the absolute truth.

Midrash. From the Hebrew verb meaning to expound, interpret, and deduce. Primarily lessons to explain the precepts and ethical ideas of the Bible.

Mishnah. First post-biblical compilation of short epodictic, mainly legal teachings. Arranged topically into six orders by Judah Hanasi in c. 200 C.E.

Mizrahi, Elijah (1450–1526). Foremost Turkish rabbinical authority of Constantinople. Author of many responsa in which he rendered strong opinions. Wrote a long classic analytic commentary on Rashi.

Nahmanides (Rabbi Moses Ben Nahman—RaMBaN) (1194–1270). Born in Gerona, Catalonia, he became a leading Jewish religious authority in Spain. Philosopher, kabbalist, poet, and physician, he probably served as Chief Rabbi of Catalonia until his emigration to Eretz Israel in 1264. Wrote on the Talmud and halakhah. His commentaries on the Torah are classic and include a fine sense of narrative and character development as well as profound mystical shadings.

Nathan (Ha-Bavli—"the Babylonian") (mid-second century C.E.). Tanna, born in Babylonia. Exilarch who had studied under Rabbi Yose ha-Gelili and others in Eretz Israel. Fled to Babylonia during the Hadrianic persecutions. Took part in the convention of Usha and later became chief of the court. Said to be the author of *Avot de-Rabbi Nathan* and the forty-nine heremeneutical rules of Rabbi Nathan. Considered one of the most outstanding scholars of his day.

Onqelos (Onkelos, also known as Aquilas) (second century C.E.). Converted to Judaism at the time of Hadrian (whose nephew he may have been) after the destruction of Jerusalem. Contemporary of Rabban Gamaliel of Jabneh and a colleague and pupil of Rabbi Eliezar Ben Hyrcanus and Rabbi Joshua Ben Hananiah. Translated the Pentateuch into Hebrew/Aramaic. His translation is now known as the *Targum Onkelos*.

Philo Judaeus (20 B.C.E.–50 C.E.). Jewish philosopher born in Alexandria. Wrote an exposition of the Pentateuch as a legal code from the original Greek. Left Alexandria in 39–40 for Rome with others to plead with Emperor Gaius not to demand divine honors from the Jews.

Rashi (Rabbi Shlomo Ben Yizhak) (1140–1105). Born in France. Studied at the German and French academies and was active in many spheres. Wrote numerous works on halakhic rulings. His greatest achievements are his commentaries on the Bible and his monumental work on the Babylonian Talmud, where he introduced exegetical methods. His school was influential for hundreds of years after his death.

Resh Lakish (Rabbi Simeon Ben Lakish) (third century C.E.). Palestinian amora. Born in Tiberias and active there in communal and religious spheres. His halakhic argumentation was grounded in keen logical deduction and on a knowledge of the tradition. Emphasized the mitzvah of studying Torah. Resh Lakish lived during a volatile and difficult political situation in which the Jewish population was subject to the military anarchy of the period. Many of his homilies refer to this period.

Samuel, Mar; or Samuel Yarhina'ahi (end of second century to mid-third century). Born in Nehardea where he headed an important third-century school. Outstanding authority of his day in civil law and author of the principle that in civil matters for Jews "the law of the state is the law."

Schmelkes, Rabbi Isaac Judah (1826–1906). Born in Galicia. Head of the court in Lemberg and author of six volumes of responsa, *Beit Yizhak*, on the *Shulkhan Arukh*.

Schorr, Rabbi Yitzchak Isaac (1875–1952). Author of *Tevu'ot Shor* and head of the famed Slobodka Yeshiva, where his lectures on the Talmud and ethics were highly esteemed. Son-in-law of the famed Der Alter (the old man—Zevi Hirsh Finkel) of Slobodka.

Sforno, Rabbi Obadiah Ben Jacob (1470–1550). Born in Cesena, Italy. Biblical commentator and physician. Learned in philosophy, mathematics, philology, and medicine. Settled in Bologna and established a school that he conducted until his death. His reputation rests upon his insightful commentaries on the Pentateuch, Song of Songs, and Ecclesiastes.

Shapiro, Abraham Dov Ber Kahane (Schapira) (1870–1943). Last Rabbi of Kovno. Well known for his sermons, and honorary president of the Union of Orthodox Rabbis of Lithuania. Involved with continued negotiations on behalf of the Jews in response to the *Altestenrat* (Jewish Council of Kovno Ghetto). Also author of responsa and analytical articles on the Talmud. Died a martyr.

Simeon Bar Yohai (mid-second century). Tanna who survived the Bar Kokhba revolt to revive the study of Torah, according to the tradition of his martyred teacher Rabbi Akiva. Much of his teachings are in the Mishnah. Continued strong opposition to Roman rule and culture. Central figure in Jewish Kabbalah, which names him as the author of the *Zohar*.

Sofer, Moses (Hatam Sofer) (1762–1839). Born in Frankfort. Halakhic authority and leader of Orthodox Jewry. Appointed Rabbi of Pressburg in 1806. Founded famous yeshiva, the largest since the Babylonian yeshivot, and made it the center of Orthodox Jewry's fight against the Reform movement. Wielded great influence through his voluminous writings published after his death. His works included seven important volumes of responsa (*Hatam Sofer*), twelve volumes of sermons on the Talmud, as well as commentary on the Torah, letters, and poems.

Soloveichik, Rabbi Hayyim Brisker (1853–1918). Born in Volozhin. Talmudist and prominent figure in Orthodox Jewry. Initiated a new trend in talmudic study where he could subdivide the subject under discussion into its categories and parts. He created a suitable terminology with which to describe the various concepts, showing the differences in the Talmud itself, and the authoritative interpretations derived from them. Succeeded his father as Rabbi of Brisk (1892). His major work was his novella on Maimonides' *Mishneh Torah*.

Talmud. Gemara is the record of the long discussion of the rabbis on the Mishnah; together the Mishnah and Gemara comprise the Talmud. The Talmud is found in two editions, the *Yerushalmi* (Jerusalem or Palestinian Talmud edited c. 350 C.E.) and the more authoritative *Bavli* (Babylonian Talmud), achieved closure between 500 and 550 C.E. The Talmud is the primary and fundamental work of rabbinic Judaism.

Tanna. A rabbi of the mishnaic period.

Tosafot. The collection of comments on the Talmud arranged according to the order of its tractates. The concept of the *Tosafot* was originally bound up with the method of study characteristic of the schools of Germany and France in the 12th–14th centuries that continued the dialectical questioning and answering of the Talmud. The masters of the *Tosafot* were from the school of Rashi.

Uziel, Rabbi Ben Zion Meir (Ouziel) (1880–1953). Religious Zionist and Sephardic leader, known for his special sensitivity to issues involving the estranged Jew. Author of Responsa *Piskei Uziel*. Founded a yeshiva for young Sephardic men. Later Chief Rabbi of Tel Aviv- Jaffa, and former Chief Sephardic Rabbi of Eretz Israel from 1939 to 1955.

Waldenberg, Eliezer (1917–?). Born in Israel. Former chief chaplin of Shaarei Zedek Hospital. Later served as chief of Jerusalem's rabbinic court. Major rabbinic decisor, he was the author of eighteen volumes of responsa on all areas of Jewish law, with a special concentration on medical ethics.

Yanai, Rabbah (the Great) (early third century). Palestinian amora known as a great authority in halakhah and aggadah. Counseled realism in legal decisions and upheld the eternal validity of the law.

Zevin, Shlomo Joseph (1890–1978). Created a new modern rabbinic style of legal research, which he first contributed as a journalist for religious newspapers. Became chief editor and guiding spirit of the *Encyclopaedia Talmudit*, which synthesizes all halakhic material on a given topic. Wrote one of the first descriptions of Jewish attitudes toward war in *LaOr Ha-Halakhah*.

Ziemba, Menahem Zemba (1883–1943). Born in Poland. Active in Orthodox religious politics but at the same time was considered a great traditional scholar. Last rabbi to remain in the Warsaw Ghetto. Gave rabbinic sanction for the uprising of the Warsaw Ghetto and refused safe passage from the Church. Author of a number of works on legal subjects. Died a martyr.

CONTRIBUTORS

Louis René Beres is Professor of Political Science at Purdue University, West Lafayette, Indiana.

Eliezer Berkovits is former Chairman of the Department of Jewish Philosophy at the Hebrew Theological College, Skokie, Illinois.

J. David Bleich is Professor of Law at Benjamin Cardozo School of Law and Professor of Talmud at Rabbi Isaac Elchanan Theological Seminary, Yeshiva University, New York City.

Elliot N. Dorff is Provost of the University of Judaism, Los Angeles.

David Ellenson is Professor of Jewish Religious Thought at Hebrew Union College-Jewish Institute of Religion, Los Angeles.

Maurice Friedman is Professor of Religious Studies, Philosophy, and Comparative Literature at San Diego State University, California.

Irving Greenberg is President, National Center for Learning and Leadership (CLAL), New York City.

Lord Immanuel Jakobovits is Chief Rabbi of the British Empire.

281

Reuven Kimelman is Professor of Talmud at Brandeis University, Waltham, Massachusetts.

Daniel Landes holds the University Chair in Jewish Ethics and Values at Yeshiva of Los Angeles, an affiliate of the Rabbi Isaac Elchanan Theological Seminary of Yeshiva University, and is Director of National Educational Projects for the Simon Wiesenthal Center in Los Angeles.

Jon D. Levenson is the Albert A. List Professor of Jewish Studies, the Divinity School, Harvard University, Cambridge, Massachusetts.

David Novak is Bronfman Professor of Judaic Studies, University of Virginia at Charlottesville.

Pinchas Peli was Chairman of Hebrew Studies and senior lecturer of Jewish Thought at Ben Gurion University, Be'er Sheva, Israel.

Edward Teller, father of the the H-bomb, is at the Hoover Institution on War, Revolution, and Peace, Stanford University, Palo Alto, California.

Walter Wurzburger is Professor of Philosophy at Yeshiva University, New York City.

Index

About the Editor

Rabbi Daniel Landes is a founding faculty member of the Simon Wiesenthal Center in Los Angeles, California, where he is Director of National Educational Projects. His articles have been published in several magazines, including *Tikkun*, and he is the co-author of *Genocide: Critical Issues of the Holocaust*.